W9-AEI-865

A LIGHT TO THE GENTILES

A LIGHT
to the GENTILES

The Life Story of the Venerable
FRANCIS LIBERMANN

by ADRIAN L. VAN KAAM, C.S.SP., PH.D.

Milwaukee • THE BRUCE PUBLISHING COMPANY

NIHIL OBSTAT:

NICOLAUS FERRARO
S.C. Rituum Assessor
Rome, Feb. 6, 1959

IMPRIMI POTEST:

VERNON F. GALLAGHER, C.S.SP., PH.D.
Provincial Superior

NIHIL OBSTAT:

RT. REV. JOSEPH A. NELSON, D.D.
Censor deputatus

IMPRIMATUR:

✠ FRANCIS CARDINAL SPELLMAN
Archbishop of New York
October 30, 1958

The *nihil obstat* and *imprimatur* are official declarations that a book or pamphlet is free of doctrinal or moral error. No implication is contained therein that those who granted the *nihil obstat* and *imprimatur* agree with the contents, opinions, or statements expressed.

Reprinted by arrangement with Duquesne University Press.

Library of Congress Catalog Card Number: 62–19998

PREFACE

The Venerable Father Francis Libermann died more than a hundred years ago. During that century, a sizable number of books and articles have been published about his life, but the complex facets of his personality have never been adequately described and interpreted in those earlier studies. In fact, it may take many more years before we can arrive at a definitive picture of the personality, historical mission, and significance of this great convert from Judaism.

The varied sweep of his career and the many-sided historical development of his spiritual sons' activity appear somewhat chaotic at first glance. Yet the human mind rejects chaos and seeks after a meaningful synthesis. Men of faith in particular refuse to look at the various aspects of God's plan as disjointed phenomena. They regard them as elements in a purposeful harmony. Our work stemmed, therefore, from a desire to visualize the latent pattern involved here.

Until now, no attempt has ever been made at presenting a synthesis which would demonstrate the coherent and telling relationship between the multiple factors in Father Libermann's life story and the manifold activities in which the Spiritans subsequently engaged. This biographical study is a modest initial step toward that end. It endeavors to trace a line of influence between the different phenomena in his personal record and the development of certain *modi agendi* in the Congregation which he so wisely guided. Inasmuch as this is a first attempt, however, it will necessarily be somewhat tentative.

Rabbi Lazarus wanted his son Francis to become a shining light in Israel. God had other ideas. Just as Israel itself had pierced the surrounding darkness of the pagan world in Old Testament times, Francis was destined to shine, not within the household of Judaism, but across broad stretches of the outer world, a veritable light shining unto the revelation of the Gentiles. He became the pioneer and fountainhead of the doctrine of simplicity and childlike surrender to God which in our times has become the commonly traveled path to holiness.

In another sense too he shone like a light unto the Gentiles. An entire continent lying at the very gate of Europe still lived in the darkness of idolatry and despair. He became its apostle. Providence called him to inspire legions of missionaries who would bear the torch of faith to a race which contemporaries callously called the unhappy "children of Cham." Because of him and his followers, great sections of Africa are dark no longer.

Originally, the book was written in Dutch and published in Holland. This English adaptation of it is more concise than the original text and we have seriously tried to render it more consonant with the mentality of the English-speaking world.

I wish to express my thanks to Father Vernon F. Gallagher, C.S.Sp., Ph.D., Superior of the United States Province and former president of Duquesne University, for revising the style and adapting the text for English readers. I am indebted also to Father Walter J. van de Putte, C.S.Sp., Ph.D., for making a literal translation of the Dutch text, to Father Engelbertus J. van Croonenburg, C.S.Sp., S.T.D., Father Henry J. Koren, C.S.Sp., S.T.D., and Father John P. Gallagher, C.S.Sp., M.A., for the many stimulating discussions that enabled me to improve certain passages in the biography, to the "Revisor" of the Sacred Congregation of Rites who, while suggesting a few minor changes, called this biography a "smoothly written and solid piece of work." Finally, Father Koren's complementary research in a number of historical areas has been particularly helpful in the preparation of this new version.

I can only hope that all these men may have been amply rewarded by their deeper insight into the inspiring life of a man who was a hundred years ahead of his time.

ADRIAN L. VAN KAAM, C.S.SP.

CONTENTS

CHAPTER ONE

IN THE GHETTO

Lazarus Libermann felt a deep sense of contentment. His position in the Jewish community of the old Alsatian town of Saverne had grown in importance these past few years. The elders had recognized his mastery of the Torah and the Talmud; they had sent serious-minded and hardworking students to his modest home to be instructed in the mysteries of the Law. Even now they were planning a number of rabbinical schools over which, six years hence, he was to be placed as general supervisor. And now, on this fine spring morning, the twelfth of April, 1802, Leah had presented him with their fifth son. True enough, little Jacob, or Jaegel as they were already calling him, did not have his older brothers' strength, but Lazarus consoled himself with the thought that feeble bodies often house strong minds. This one would be a scholar. This one would open his soul to the flood of ancient wisdom which his father stood ready to pour into it. Yahweh had indeed caused his cup of joy to overflow.

Rabbi Libermann was not far wrong. Jaegel's little body never knew the bloom of health, but his glowing spirit blazed forth almost immediately. It was quick and perceptive and deeply, painfully sensitive. It vibrated with a quivering awareness that would ultimately prove its greatest blessing and its heaviest burden. Even in his infancy, the boy sensed that terrible isolation in which Jewish families lived. Their way of life, their provincialism, their religion, their very appearance put the seal of separation upon his people. In Alsace particularly, feeling between Jew and Gentile ran high. Centuries of persecution had driven the Jews of Europe into borrowing and lending, buying and selling. Injustice and sharp practice on both sides led to noisy litigation, name-calling, and appeals to the King. Hatred, contempt, and revenge grew apace in this malignant atmosphere. The Jews drew closer together. Cut off from surrounding society, they accentuated their difference and their isolation.

Jaegel, by nature sensitive, shy, and fearful, felt all this very deeply. Though still too young to fully understand the language of his elders, he allowed the menacing force of their gestures and the somber tone of their voices to plunge him into dark depression. He saw bitterness in the eyes of passersby. He grew to feel that Jews were not like other people. Others were gay and lighthearted. They dressed in their best finery on Sunday mornings and went in crowds to a large stone building from whose rooftop sprang a massive tower. The building with the tower was marvelous indeed, but his father had spoken about it with such aversion that it now became for him a dark and threatening symbol of the hated otherworld that lay outside his home, that terrifying world where one felt small and miserable as if he were always losing his way.

Jaegel never knew the springtime of life. Pure air and sunlight, warm earth and singing birds, kindly strangers and smiling neighbors failed to cast the rosy glow of their influence over his early years. Outside the shelter of his home there spread a world of anxiety from which his best defense was hurried flight. On one occasion he met a funeral procession returning from the cemetery with a man in white marching at its head. All the dark, unintelligible words he had heard at home began to crowd in upon him. With heart pounding wildly, he turned and fled like a frightened hare into a store and, shoving customers aside, pushed his way under the counter and remained cowering there for some time. On another occasion, when he was walking along with his father, he met a priest dressed in cassock and surplice returning from a sick-call. Though the old Rabbi was his tower of strength at home and in the synagogue, Jaegel's confidence now drained away. He darted to the side, leaped over a wall, and flew across the fields.

Even among his own, Jaegel often fell victim to waves of loneliness. Too frail of body to join in the games of his contemporaries, he wistfully stood apart and listened to their shouts of joy. Sometimes his brothers, although they loved him dearly, teased him about his inability to take part in their fun. It was then that a nervous twitch began to play around his mouth and, try as he would, there was no controlling it. Gradually, he came to lean more and more on his oldest brother Samson who was strong and self-reliant. In fact, the little fellow almost worshiped Samson as a sort of higher being, a hero who symbolized all that was right and admirable.

So frail and sensitive a child should have had the benefit of a mother's tender understanding and loving guidance. Unfortunately, Leah had to limit her role almost entirely to household activities. Jewish tradition made the father alone responsible for the education of his children and Lazarus, always hoping that his sons would become rabbis, kept their mother away from them as much as possible. Even the limited comfort and consolation she could provide was soon snatched away. When Jaegel was only eleven years old, Leah died and Lazarus became the uncontested educator of his family.

The atmosphere at home now approached the point of suffocation. Music and beauty, laughter and good-humored banter were rigorously shut out. Nothing ever was read but the Law and commentaries on the Law. Rabbi Lazarus regarded every other branch of knowledge as suspect and harmful. Although the boys had to use German in their daily contacts with people, they were forbidden to learn how to write and read it. The Libermann children never experienced that joy which comes of turning the pages of a glowing picture book or listening with radiant face and sparkling eyes as someone began a tale of wonder with "Once upon a time, long, long ago . . ." According to Rabbi Lazarus, once upon a time, long, long ago, there was the Law and nothing but the Law, with its thousands of prescriptions and subtle interpretations. It colored his every word and action. Because of it he grew merciless in the face of legal offenses. On one occasion, for instance, when a coreligionist confessed that he had killed a flea on the Sabbath because it bit him so painfully, Lazarus delivered himself of a severe reprimand and imposed a penance of thirty days' fast on bread and water.

Despite his unbending character, however, Jaegel's father was capable of boundless generosity and love. Even with limited domestic facilities, he kept a room in readiness day and night for the poor and needy who might seek shelter under his roof. He accepted free of charge the Jewish students who came to stay with him and receive their education at his hands. He instructed and guided them with the same careful solicitude that he bestowed on his own children. But above all he lavished on Jaegel the greatest measure of his strange affection. Convinced that the boy had a bright future as a rabbi, Lazarus watched over his development with an anxious eye. Goaded by ambition for his son, he drove the lad ceaselessly and overloaded him with rabbinical lore.

At the age of five, Jaegel learned the Hebrew alphabet. After that he turned to spelling and reading, and then to the Hebrew Pentateuch which was explained to him verse by verse and word by word. This completed, the young scholar was set to a biblical commentary by Rabbi Jaecke. Since the boy proved to be studious and endowed with extraordinary talent, his father soon gave him permission to take up the Mishnah, a collection of regulations and decrees, and to proceed from there, at the amazingly early age of ten, to the complicated study of the Talmud. For eight long years, Jaegel labored from morning till night over the stubborn texts, listening to his father's explanations and searching through the commentaries of ancient and contemporary authors. Through all these feverish pursuits, the young student never relaxed, but Lazarus was much too excited to feel concern. It became increasingly evident that Jaegel was called by God to be a light in the synagogue and the prospect of rabbinical eminence more than offset any danger of mental or physical exhaustion.

While Lazarus dreamed happy dreams of his son's deft mastery of Talmudic subtleties the boy's inmost soul must have smoldered with discontent and unrest. The old man's unbridled eagerness seemed to take away his very breath. It left no room for self-expression. One can imagine moments during these years when he would feel as if he were so near suffocating that the emotional disturbance would mount to a climax of revulsion and revolt. But suddenly he would put down these feelings of disloyalty in a panic of anxiety. He loved his father and his father was bending every effort in his behalf, that much was certain. Yet, somehow, a barrier was rising between them. He had gradually grown closer to Leah while she lived. Her tenderness, her way of leaving him free to grow according to his nature, her sympathy with his desire to explore the world about him, all left an indelible mark on him. Now that she was dead, the memory of her love etched itself so deeply in his being that he began to conduct himself with extraordinary gentleness.

This delicacy of soul was to put its stamp on his entire life. He recognized it as a source of that mysterious suffering which God uses to purify the human soul and unite it more closely to Himself. Years later he would analyze the phenomenon as follows:

> Lethargic personalities, whose sensitivity appears to be little greater than that of the brute, do not really suffer in this world. Nothing hurts them, nothing bothers them as long as they have enough to eat. Should we envy them? No more than we would an animal. . . . It is quite certain that sensitivity is a gift of God. Admittedly, it gives rise to suffering and spiritual affliction, but God loves us and that is why He allows us to pass through the crucible of pain.[1]
>
> Try to benefit by every experience; let everything that happens contribute to your progress. The more sensitive we are, the more we must suffer in this world. Nonetheless, if we remain faithful we shall advance with giant steps along the path of perfection.[2]

As the years went on, young Libermann's inarticulate rebellion against his father's oppressive educational methods grew apace. It assumed various forms: sporadic resentment against the old rabbi personally, occasional uneasiness with the accepted patterns of tradition, and outright opposition to whatever stifled his own individuality. Subsequently, through a process of gradual supernaturalization, God would transmute these flashes of revolt into a quiet but firm resistance against that empty formalism which cramps human personalities and hinders the operation of grace in the souls of men. Throughout his life, anxiety plagued him whenever he felt obliged to act in opposition to his environment or his associates. Each time he made an important decision, each time he resisted the demands of those among whom he lived, he suffered agonies of apprehension, for the one thing he feared more than

---

[1] Adolph Cabon, C.S.Sp., ed., *Notes et Documents relatifs à la vie et l'oeuvre du Vénérable F.-M.-P.-Libermann* (Paris: 1929 ff.), 8, 206. 13 vols. with 2 appendixes (hereafter quoted as N. D.) and 1 vol. of "compléments" (quoted as N. D. Compl.).

[2] N. D. 9, 113.

anything else was to repeat his father's mistake of refashioning men according to a preconceived pattern.

"We must," he urged, "concede to everyone the freedom to follow his own ideas and to do good in his own way. When we permit everyone to act according to his own convictions, his character, his mentality, and his emotional make-up, you may count on it that substantially good results will be achieved. . . . My most effective means in guiding others is to ignore and tolerate their faults when I foresee that I shall not be able to correct them. For this reason I occasionally bear with the most unseemly and crude behavior. I find it utterly important that people preserve their own temperaments. I merely help them improve themselves according to their own nature. . . . Let me advise you, therefore, to leave everyone free to follow his own way of acting. God made him the way he is."[3]

It was during his childhood and adolescence also that Jaegel formed religious concepts and views which were never to lose their vividness. Chief among these was his boundless respect for a transcendent God in whose presence every creature melts into nothingness. Worship and adoration were constantly preached to him by the Psalms, the prescriptions of the Law, and the directives of the Talmud. Consequently, an awareness of God as the Infinite All and man as nothing in comparison with Him always remained the guiding beacon of Libermann's life. After his baptism and his admission to the seminary, he naturally gravitated to those masters of the French school of spirituality whose doctrine had as its core the all-importance of God and the comparative insignificance of man. In his guidance of souls that were far advanced in their union with God, this fundamental principle prompted him to warn them against an undue familiarity that might militate against proper respect for divine majesty. On his very deathbed he summarized his whole life and doctrine in the parting statement: "God is everything; man is nothing."

His early studies left another deep impression on him: a keen realization of God's abiding presence and His all-pervading influence in the development of history. Scripture contains a holy and imperishable record of that divine providence which watches over

[3] N. D. 8, 111 ff.

the affairs of men. They presented it so graphically that the interlocking designs of Jahweh formed a well-defined background against which Jaegel's life and thought unfolded. During the full course of his adventurous maturity he moved in a lucid atmosphere of unshakable faith in God's solicitude for His creatures. It characterized him and became the natural element in which he lived and moved and had his being.

As he immersed himself in Talmudic studies, he developed an impatience with purely abstract and farfetched speculations. He grew increasingly opposed to the rational isolationism and divorce from reality which often result from the more theoretical academic disciplines. In later years, grace was to purify and ennoble this tendency and make of him a trusted guide who would form and direct people toward participation in reality and life. In preparing young men for the apostolate, he repeatedly warned them against the narrow limitations of their syllogisms, urging them to allow their emotions, their intuitions, and the grace of God above all, to season their endless reasonings and temper their intellectual smugness.

CHAPTER TWO

SAMSON'S BETRAYAL

It is hard for a Jew to become a Christian. Centuries of persecution, antipathy, and distrust have steeled him against Christianity. Moreover, the Jewish family of the nineteenth century stood like a solitary fortress in which its members were united defensively against the world around them, alone, withdrawn, and never fully assimilated by society at large. They compensated for this isolation by developing strong emotional ties that bound them together in their island of loneliness, the family. Thus, when a Jew left the Synagogue for the Church, he was equivalently tearing himself away from security, confidence, and love. He was a solitary figure going off to an enemy country, leaping blindly into the unknown, heartlessly renouncing his birthright and his loved ones. To those left behind in the Jewish home, such a one had died. They communicated their grief and desolation to their fellow Jews by wearing the somber garments of mourning for a long time after the defection.

Like the rest of the world, however, the Jews of Alsace soon felt the impact of eighteenth century rationalism and deism. Voltairian concepts of liberty and the Encyclopedists' ensuing propaganda were fast invading the farthest corners of Europe. The dream of utter freedom, endless progress, and scientific triumphs, all embodied in Voltaire's libertarianism, Rousseau's romantic humanism, and Leibnitz's rationalism, conspired against both revelation and tradition, the accepted foundations of religion. Liberty and progress now became the battle cry throughout Europe.

The new doctrines exercised a particularly magnetic attraction over Jewish intellectuals. They were carried away by fresh enthusiasms and set about striking off the shackles of Talmudic thought and practice. In Germany they organized themselves into a group of advanced thinkers and, aroused by the inspiration of Mendelssohn, they demanded a more liberal education for their children. When they were cast out by their coreligionists, great numbers of them joined local Protestant sects.

Jaegel's brother Samson had a fellow student who was deeply fascinated by these new ideas. He was David Drach, a well-known biblical scholar whose knowledge of Hebrew, Syriac, Aramaic, and Arabic had gained for him the admiration of the Jewish community in Alsace. Despite this local renown, he went off to Paris to study literature and the arts. While collating the Hebrew and the Septuagint versions of the Bible, he delved into Patristic writings and eventually saw a valid relationship between the Messianic prophecies of the Old Testament and the story of Christ in the New. Contacts with Catholics, visits to churches, and the grace of God eventually led him to the baptismal font.

Before long, the spirit of the age invaded the Libermann household itself. Samson, the eldest son, conceived a strong aversion to rabbinical learning and insisted on going off to Strassburg to study medicine. Once there, his sudden emancipation from the stifling atmosphere at home cast him headlong into the prevailing current of liberalism. He devoured contemporary literature so eagerly and threw off tradition so radically that in very short order he found himself without any religion whatsoever. Life was now open and free, great with prospects and promises. Nonetheless, there were times when this fugitive from the past experienced a feeling of unspeakable emptiness and wretchedness. When homesickness overwhelmed him he sought refuge in a nearby synagogue and tried desperately to pray, but only tears of hopelessness welled up from the great void in his soul.

After graduation from medical school, he married an earnest and intelligent Jewish girl who shared his repugnance for the minute prescriptions of Talmudic legalism. With her he held endless discussions about God and religion. Through Protestant neighbors they made their first acquaintance with the Gospel. The warmth, humanity, and sublimity of true Christian charity left them breathless. They resolved that their soon-to-be-expected child would be baptized, but when they confided this decision to Mr. Hoffner, president of the Protestant Confession of Augsburg, he coldly turned them away by observing they need not be in such a hurry.

Just at that time, a tremendous Catholic renaissance was taking place in Alsace. New and old religious societies had awakened to the threat of liberalism and dedicated themselves with renewed fervor to counteracting it by schools, seminaries, missions, and cultural agencies of various types. The progressive Jewish group to which Samson belonged soon came to feel that their best hope of participating in contemporary civilization lay in establishing intimate contact with this enterprising Christian movement. Dr. Libermann, attorney Mayer, and businessman Dreyfuss — all young Jews who felt strongly about the situation — addressed an appeal to the Catholic hierarchy. In their memorandum they expressed great admiration for the Church's interest in backward peoples throughout the world and observed that they were mystified by its apparent lack of concern for the Jews living in Europe itself.

The memorandum eventually found its way into the hands of the bishop of Strassburg and he invited the signatories to an interview. Since youthful enthusiasm on their part had made the proposal resemble something of a Catholic intellectual conspiracy against the Jewish community, Bishop Tharsis could not give their plan much encouragement. He did, however, put Samson and his wife in touch with the vicar-general of the diocese, a priest whose name, by strange coincidence, was Liebermann also. Father Liebermann was a brilliant apologist, a recognized author, and a thoroughly cultured man. Through pleasant discussion and a program of careful reading, he guided the two young wanderers through their journey toward the Light. The quest ended in their baptism on March 15, 1824.[1]

The stunned old rabbi back in Saverne did not hear the news until much later that year. In a daze of utter misery he dressed himself in the habiliments of a mourner while the Jews of Strassburg read Samson out of the synagogue and proclaimed him a faithless traitor to his kind. With every means at their disposal they tried to undermine the new doctor and boycott his medical practice until at last the poor young couple had to withdraw to the neighboring town Illkirch, where Samson eventually became the burgomaster.

[1] N. D. 1, 40. This is the date given by Dr. Libermann himself. A footnote indicates that he may have been mistaken by six months. Cf. also N. D. 1, 96.

CHAPTER THREE

THE REBELLION OF YOUTH

After Samson left home to study medicine, Jaegel's loneliness increased appreciably. During their boyhood Samson had always been his protector and friend. Now that he was gone, it felt as though one more sustaining prop had been rudely pulled away. To make matters worse, the old rabbi bore down even harder on the younger son who remained behind. He set up a new objective for Jaegel, a goal of renewed zeal and higher achievement which would counteract Samson's disappointing defection from the rabbinical profession, and he drove ever harder to realize his ambitions for this last great hope of his life.

In the burning tension of these months, small shadows began to drift across Jaegel's limited horizon. He was appalled at the merciless severity of the rabbis. In his meditations on the Scriptures, he was plagued with little gadfly doubts. He longed to ask his father if a text here or there did not seem to indicate that the Messias had already come. Withal, however, his insecurity seems to have melted before his father's massive certainty. By the end of the summer of 1824 he was ready to leave for Metz. There, at the age of twenty-two and with these long years of strict paternal tutelage behind him, he would really be a shining light in the Hebrew school. Rabbis visiting Metz would soon discover the insight, the scholarship, and the piety of this dedicated student and then they would procure for him a place of honor from which he could dispel by his brilliant leadership the shame of Samson's renunciation. Lazarus might then lay down his head and look on death with equanimity.

Jaegel's poverty made it necessary for him to travel on foot. At every step he experienced an ever greater sense of elation in the knowledge that he was free at last from the oppressive atmosphere of home and family. As this new emotion struggled for a place in his soul alongside the natural sadness of first separation, he watched with anxious concern. Was it decent for a son to be so relieved at the prospect of cutting parental ties? He quickened his pace and tried to shake off frivolous thoughts. However, by the time he reached Metz, his heart was beating wildly with excitement and happy expectation.

One of the rabbis at Metz had been a pupil of Jaegel's father. The old man had taken him in as one of the family and shared with him his meager resources as well as his abundant learning. Surely the gracious hospitality received at Saverne would now prompt this former pupil to extend a hearty welcome to the son of his former preceptor. Beaming with warm anticipation, Jaegel rapped on the rabbi's door. It opened and the now famous scholar peered at the tired young man before him. The few curt words he deigned to utter caused Libermann to tremble from head to toe. It was as if something had snapped in his frame. Crestfallen and humiliated, he turned away never to return. Once more he felt the old uncertainty he had experienced in the past when certain rabbis at home shocked him by their coldness.

Fortunately, he found a suitable room and plunged directly into his studies. Soon he found that his fellow students, less cloistered than he, gave evidence of diverse interests and broad culture. Their lively debates on current events and contemporary literature amazed him and at the same time left him miserably conscious of his own limited development. In his hunger for the new and the strange, he reached out feverishly for all the alluring books whose titles kept cropping up in the animated conversations that went on round him. The great Rousseau and the master satirist Voltaire tantalized him particularly, but they lay behind the locked doors of the French language. Soon he was driving himself toward the mastery of French and Latin.

Some of the students with whom he came in contact tried to break his attachment to Judaism by enticing him to join them in their frivolous and licentious escapades. In this they were completely unsuccessful. Their sarcastic and critical remarks about his faith had much more effect. Memories of former doubts, harrowing experiences with rabbis, echoes of Voltaire, and insidious lines out of Rousseau gradually weaned him away from the old doctrines and made him more receptive to the rationalistic ideas of his associates. He began to transfer his disillusionment from modern religious leaders to the Hebrew giants of old and set down his thoughts with almost blasphemous candor:

> When Moses was still alive, he did not receive the respect that we now give him. I think the same about the prophets. We find Jeremias twenty times in prison, and rightly so, for he was actually a traitor who had been bought by Nabuchodonosor. All these personages were probably forceful orators who were later made out to be prophets when their speeches were collected in due order.[1]

In the process, he was unconsciously identifying the prophets and patriarchs with the old man of Saverne whose severity had made a nightmare of his youth. The thoughts propounded by his fellow students became deadly weapons with which he would henceforth defend himself against that sternness and oppression which had robbed him of so much. The prophets (and his father) need no longer disturb his rest. Now he would be free, free from the iron rule they had laid on him. Far from being supernatural heroes, they were ordinary men with ordinary faults and weaknesses. The so-called miracles attributed to them were folktales fabricated over the centuries.

> The patriarchs, he wrote, had nothing that made them worthy to receive special favors from God; neither their faith, which was a gift of God, nor their virtue, which was quite ordinary. Therefore they did not deserve the wonders which, it is claimed, were performed on their behalf. Even granting that they exercised the highest virtues, ought we to admit that these virtues were rewarded with a progeny that gave itself over to vice? Even God's justice does not permit us to agree that Adam's mistake was avenged on all his descendants. Moreover, it is impossible to explain how God could prefer the Jewish people and reject all other nations. And who can understand the unbelief of the Jews if they had been blessed with so many wonders?[2]

After a sleepless night of such agonizing analysis, Jacob would put away his big bible for several days. Then, when he opened it again, he was all the more irritated by accounts of miracles which

[1] N. D. 1, 54. [2] N. D. 1, 53.

he could no longer accept. Of that period he later wrote: "I read the Bible, but with distrust. I had a distaste for the miracles it related. I no longer believed them to be true."[3] The Book that had made his boyhood miserable would no longer be his guide now that he was a man. From here on, he would think his own thoughts and determine his own conduct. It was enough to accept God as a higher being and then try to be human toward one's fellows. Thus he broke the chains that bound him to oppressive authority by taking refuge in a sentimental sort of rationalism.

Just at this point in his career, he learned the horrifying news of his brother's conversion to Catholicism. He reacted with indignant fury at what he regarded as a cowardly act of treachery against their father. After all, a modern Jew might reject the Talmud and question Scripture, but it was quite another thing to dishonor by open defection an old man who had never spared himself to provide for his children's welfare, who spent hours instructing them night after night, who had dreamed of their great rabbinical future. It was an ugly, ungrateful act and he graphically set forth its meanness in a burning letter that he whipped off to Samson.

The poor doctor was sure that the outburst meant the end of their close relationship. In his reply, he begged for understanding and sympathy. He even went so far as to suggest that Jacob read Bossuet's *Discourse on Universal History,* a work that had exerted such profound influence over him and his wife. When the letter came, Jacob read and re-read it. Little by little he grew calmer. It now became clear to him that Samson had not maliciously set out to offend his father. On the contrary, his motives, whatever they might be, seemed sincere and honest.

With a good deal more kindliness now, Jacob sat down and penned another letter to his brother. It contained this surprising statement: "I do not know the principles of philosophy and could easily be mistaken. Therefore, it seems to me that I had better speak out to an educated man who is able to bring me back to the truth. You, my beloved eldest brother, must come before everyone else in this respect."[4] He went on to tell Samson everything he himself had undergone. With undisguised satisfaction, he confessed to having become a free-thinker. As such, he admitted, even if he should eventually

[3] N. D. 1, 62. [4] N. D. 1, 52.

become a zealous promoter of the synagogue, he could not logically reject his brother.

Somewhat inconsistently, however, he refused to read Bossuet's *Discourse*. Its author believed in Scripture and he had put the Book away forever. He had now come to realize with shame and sorrow that faith in the Bible had inhibited his development. He feared nothing more than a return to the source from which only rigid and joyless existence could flow. Henceforth he would live a naturally good life, enlightened by the clear wisdom that wells up from the depths of every human being and prompted by the spirit that speaks from within. "I have come to the conclusion," he wrote, "that God merely asks that we acknowledge Him and that we live an honest, human life. It follows that there is little importance in whether I be a Jew or a Christian; if I worship God, it does not matter whether I consider Him in one or three Persons. But I can assure you that I would not be better as a Christian than as a Jew. For that reason also, I cannot find fault with you for changing your religion."[5]

The doctor replied immediately. He took issue with Jacob's attack on biblical wonders and pointed out that the miracles done in Israel's behalf might be explained as signs whereby the promised Messias might be manifested to the world. While this introduced a new concept into Jacob's rigid line of thought, and while it impressed him momentarily, the favorable disposition soon melted away in the face of that terrible antipathy which his early training had so firmly planted in him. It would take two more years of restless seeking before the light of grace would penetrate his soul.

Meanwhile, his relationship with Titescher, his teacher of Latin, became more and more friendly. Titescher's affection for him further stimulated this lonely young Jew's passionate zeal for classical literature. The recurrent nervous twitch that played around Jacob's mouth and his shockingly awkward movements made the older man wonder if the lad was not afflicted with epilepsy. Then too, he noticed the inner conflict that was going on in his pupil and sympathetically tried to ease the tension. Jacob deeply appreciated his consideration and kindness, but it made the disappointment all the more bitter when Titescher had to leave him and take up a teaching position at Luneville.

---

[5] N. D. 1, 54.

Without a good instructor, it would be ever so much more difficult to master the intricacies of classical rhetoric. The situation called for redoubled efforts. That is why he wrote: "I am continuing my work with greater stubbornness than ever. If the road is somewhat longer and the journey more burdensome because I am alone, I shall take my zeal for my guide."[6] His earnest striving after an up-to-date plan of life made him neglect the study of Hebrew. Without funds to achieve his literary goals, he bought Cicero and Virgil on credit. Then he turned to his brother David and repeatedly urged him to repay an old debt. Finally, David surrendered the needed money and Jacob continued his clandestine reading program with books that were now his.

One day, a fellow student asked his help in interpreting a Hebrew text. It turned out to be a book of the Gospels and Jacob took it in his hands with evident prejudice. Though he had to admit that the attractive personality of Christ impressed him favorably, the miraculous episodes irritated him beyond measure. Here they were again, those tales of wonder that took him back to the patriarchs and the prophets. "I was deeply moved by the reading," he said, "but I felt a repugnance for the miracles which Jesus performed."[7]

Reading Rousseau was much more pleasant. Beyond all else, the fourth book of *Émile* went straight to his heart. In it, the confession of faith which the author attributes to a rationalist priest came so close to expressing Jacob's position that he read it over and over again. He saw himself mirrored in this country priest who had been forced into the clerical state by an overambitious father: "I learned what they wanted me to learn, I said what they wanted me to say, I assumed the obligations which they wanted me to assume, and I was ordained a priest . . . because, in spite of my classes and studies, I lived a regular, simple life. I preserved in my mind all the clarity of the first light. The world's teachings had not obscured this, and my poverty preserved me from the temptations that are inspired by the sophisms of immorality."[8]

Jacob smiled as he read this. He too had preserved the first light.

---

[6] *Ibid.*

[7] N. D. 1, 63.

[8] Jean Jacques Rousseau, *Émile* (Paris: n.d.), 3 vols., 2, 120 (hereafter quoted as *Émile*).

Despite his rabbinical studies, it had guided him through life. Then too, his poverty, like that of the country priest, had kept him morally pure.

When Rousseau's hero went on to speak of Jesus and the Gospel, Jacob grew uneasy. Somehow, he had a feeling that his recently acquired certitude might be shaken by his strangely provocative passage and in this his instincts were correct. One line struck home like an arrow: "If the life and death of Socrates are those of a wise man, the life and death of Jesus are those of a God."[9] Jacob immediately felt a vague restlessness, like one who knows he has been wounded but will not be conscious of the extent of the injury and fierceness of the pain until the initial shock has worn off. Inexorably, the country pastor went on: "Jewish authors could never have invented that tone and that ethical sublimity. The Gospel has such great, striking, and totally inimitable marks of truth, that anyone who could invent such things would be more admirable than the Hero Himself."[10] From his intimate knowledge of Hebrew lore, Jacob was forced to agree. Indeed, no Jew could ever have invented such a thing. It was all so disturbing that he abruptly put the book aside. But it was too late. The idea sank its barbs into his heart and refused to be dislodged. It was easier to close the book than to close his mind. Before long he remarked in astonishment that he had become another man.

His brother Felix had gone off to Leipzig to learn bookbinding and had fallen in love with the boss's daughter. She was a Protestant girl who seems to have been pleasant enough, but Dr. Samson prevented their marriage by persuading Felix to return to France. He even offered the temporary hospitality of his home at Illkirch to the lovelorn youngster. In the Catholic atmosphere of Samson's family and later in his frequent contacts with Dr. Drach at Paris, Felix soon developed a respect and affection for the Church. He was baptized on Holy Saturday, 1826. Not long thereafter another brother, Samuel by name, likewise became a Catholic through Dr. Drach's assistance.

Jacob was badly shaken. Could it also happen to him? A flood of repugnance blotted out the thought. On the other hand, why was

---

[9] *Émile* 2, 180.
[10] *Ibid.*

he hesitating about committing himself irrevocably to the life of a rabbi? Lazarus Libman, a fellow rabbinical student and an intimate friend of Jacob's, broke in on these tortured meditations and quite frankly admitted that he felt just the way Jacob did. Both finally decided to give up their careers in the synagogue and then Lazarus urged Jacob to talk things over with Dr. Drach in Paris. Despite what looked like a penchant for proselytizing, Drach, they agreed, was an honest man whose sincerity and scholarship were beyond question.

Before long, a somewhat timorous communication went off to Dr. Drach in Paris. It reached him just as he was preparing an open letter to his former coreligionists.[11] In it, he was planning to deal with interpretations of the Old Testament prophecies and had already gathered a wealth of striking data. His letters to Jacob drew heavily on this fund of erudition and before long he felt convinced that the light had already conquered his pupil's heart.

---

[11] *Deuxième lettre d'un rabbin converti aux Israélites, ses frères, sur les motifs de sa conversion,* 334 pp. (Paris, 1827). A first letter (88 pages) was published in 1825, and a third (364 pp.) followed in 1833. In 1831, Dr. Drach replied to biblical questions raised by Francis Libermann by publishing two dissertations entitled *L'inscription hébraique du titre de la sainte Croix restituée et l'heure du crucifiement de N. S. J. C. déterminée,* Rome, 44 pp. The dissertations are in the form of letters addressed to Libermann.

CHAPTER FOUR

JOURNEY TO LIGHT

Samson and Felix did their best to induce their brother to go to Paris. Jacob himself looked favorably on the idea, if for no other reason than to find another vocation in life now that he had abandoned the rabbinate. He had grown keenly aware of his speech defect, his awkwardness, his appearance, and his Jewish accent. Such handicaps would be less noticeable in a large cosmopolitan city where strange people were the order of the day. As a sort of by-product, he might even bring some order to his interior life by immersing himself in new environs and engaging in conversations with Dr. Drach. But would his father agree? He made up his mind to go home to Saverne and find out.

The shock of their first meeting was great indeed. Rabbi Libermann looked old and tired. Deep dark lines furrowed his face and his eyes were dull and expressionless. People had not spared him. They tortured him about his other sons and now they were saying horrible things about his Jaegel. He motioned the boy to a chair and then sat down heavily in another. For a long while he stared silently at this young son who was to have been his consolation and his pride. At last his hollow voice crackled through the silence. Could he ask some questions about the Talmud?

The blood rushed to Jacob's face. When it drained away he sat there pale and motionless. After all, the Talmud is something that requires daily memorizing and constant discussion. No one who has neglected it for even a short time can deceive a master of rabbinical lore. Clearly, the tragedy of his life was about to be stripped naked for all to see. He swallowed hard and strained to catch his father's words as they competed with the pounding in his ears. Then came the question, slowly and carefully phrased, with centuries of learning behind its mocking simplicity. A long bleak moment ensued. Then suddenly his mind was flooded with light. Texts that had been read only superficially now stood out in shining clarity. Jacob listened to himself as to a stranger while his answer took the form of a sure and fluent commentary. Never in his life had he experienced such readiness of speech.

The bent old figure before him straightened visibly. A look of indescribable pride shone through the tear-filled eyes. At last, Rabbi Lazarus leaned forward and caught Jacob's hands in his own. "I thought so," he whispered. "They were calumniating you when they told me you were studying Latin and neglecting Hebrew." In a burst of excitement, he rummaged through his desk and brought out the letters of warning that people had sent him. Then he hurried off to open a bottle of his best wine so that he and this loyal child of his heart might fittingly celebrate their mutual vindication.

Jacob stared after him in an agony of self-reproach. He had come unscathed from the awful ordeal and the feeling of relief was undeniable, but the contrast between his father's faith and his own unbelief burned like acid in his heart. The horrible prospect of deceiving an elder merged with the happy thought that God might have specially enlightened him in order to make the Paris trip possible. When he could no longer bear the old Rabbi's beaming gaze, he blurted out his request for permission to go to the capital and without hesitation Lazarus not only granted it but gave him a letter of introduction to Deutz, the chief rabbi of Paris. The old man sent him away with a prayer and a blessing, peering happily from the doorway as the pride of his life disappeared down the street. Then he closed the door with a sigh of joyous satisfaction and thanked Yahweh for giving him a boy like that.

On the way, Jacob stopped at Illkirch. Samson opened the door for him and froze momentarily when he saw before him this tense, sharp-featured youngster, whose face reflected every play of emotion. After so many years of separation, that face appeared somewhat strange, even though it soon took on the old familiar glow of admiration while the physician's practiced eye appraised his little Jaegel. During the early moments of that glad reunion, Jacob could not help contrasting his own insecurity with the calm self-assurance of his elder brother, now a trim and well-balanced man of thirty. He had never met Samson's wife before. She turned out to be a dark young woman, more expansive than her husband, somewhat quick and emotional but filled nonetheless with an inner certainty that he envied greatly. Pauline, their little daughter, took to her uncle immediately and loudly re-echoed her parents' delight over their unexpected visitor.

In the warmth of this family circle, Jacob found once more the intimate hominess he had missed for so long. With polite curiosity he observed all the little tokens of Catholic life and practice — the Sign of the Cross before and after meals, Pauline's evening prayer lisped at bedtime from the safety of her mother's lap, the holy-water font at the bedroom door. In such an atmosphere, it was inevitable that the conversation should sooner or later veer toward the story of Samson's conversion. One night, when the doctor came home from making his rounds, Pauline was put to bed and the three of them sat around the hearth reminiscing. Before long, Samson was engrossed in the telling of his spiritual Odyssey. It began with a description of his aimless and feverish questing and moved swiftly to its climax. Now and again, Isabel would interrupt the recital to contribute from her own store of memory a word of explanation or a lively little narrative. Jacob listened breathlessly. At length, he told them of his own difficulties and posed a number of questions that led inevitably to further discussion.

In the days that followed, these friendly talks served only to confuse him all the more. He envied their inner happiness and spiritual peace and at odd moments during a conversation he would even find himself agreeing with their reasoning. On one such occasion his sister-in-law remarked quietly: "You will be a priest some day." It was an outrageous thing to say, but in the calmness of the moment, it did not disturb him. Then again, storms of perplexity would overwhelm him. At such times he would recall his orthodox old father in Saverne or his liberal free-thinking associates in Metz and contrast their views with those of his brother and sister-in-law. Who was right? He must continue on to Paris and find out.

As Jacob was saying good-bye, Samson gave him a letter of introduction to Dr. Drach and asked him to convey the family's best wishes to their brother Felix. Thus he was setting out for the metropolis under the perplexing duty of meeting a former rabbi now turned Catholic, visiting another brother who had abandoned the synagogue, and paying his respects to his father's friend Mr. Deutz, the chief rabbi of Paris. All of these conflicting tasks, coming as they did so soon after the fatiguing experiences of Metz, Saverne, and Illkirch, left him mentally and physically exhausted when he finally reached the cold gray streets of the capital. His first instinct was to flee from it all by going back home, for he realized full well that it was here he must come to a basic decision. The emotional strain could not continue indefinitely. The inner conflict would have to stop. Why not give up this painful search for the truth and be an unbeliever like the gay students at Metz? It would be so much easier.

Yet something in him set itself inexorably against a life that was estranged from God. Peace did not lie that way. Unheeded by the turbulent stream of humanity that swirled about him in the streets of Paris, he made his way to the home of Felix, the bookbinder, and diffidently entered the little shop. Felix, although older by three years, seemed to have preserved all his boyish enthusiasm and lightheartedness. Less inclined to the heavy seriousness so characteristic of Samson, he talked volubly about his business, his family, and his friends. As he rattled on, a thousand perverse thoughts raced through Jacob's brain. Should he go to Rabbi Deutz or to Dr. Drach? He had promised his father that he would visit Deutz, but Drach seemed to have done so much for Samson and Felix and even Samuel who was now in America. Nonetheless, it had ended by all of them deserting their father. Would he follow the same path? And if he did, how could he support himself? The frightful migraine headache that had bothered him for the past week now reached a crescendo of agony. It abated only the next day while Felix was telling the story of his conversion. Once again the now familiar elements of peace, happiness, doubt, and envy merged in a confused pattern, just as they did when Samson had recounted his experiences.

Not long after, Jacob went to see Dr. Drach. He did not know why; he just went. As the renowned scholar entered the room where his visitor was waiting, he quickly and quietly put the nervous young man at ease. Before long, the soft melodious voice was asking about Rabbi Libermann, about the years in Metz, and about the brothers who were now so widely dispersed. Jacob could not help thinking, "This man must have been a great leader in the synagogue." Before he knew it, he was unburdening himself of the doubts, anxieties, and questions that plagued him.

"You will be able to think about all this calmly at Stanislas College," said Dr. Drach reassuringly. "I have reserved a room for you there and you will find a number of books to read. Then we will talk things over quietly. When can you come?" Jacob was thunderstruck. A room for him in a Catholic seminary! That was carrying things too far. And what about his father's plans? And Rabbi Deutz? He mumbled something about thinking it over and rose to go. Drach smiled understandingly. "The room will always be ready for you," he said. "Come when you feel up to it."

A few days later, Mr. Deutz received him cordially. He carefully read the letter of introduction and then proceeded to advise Jacob about studies that he might pursue in Paris. After promising a full measure of his help, he sent his guest away with a book that had recently appeared. "Read it through," he counseled, "and we shall talk about it more at length when you return."

Back on the street, Jacob felt warmly grateful to this kind old man. If the rabbis in Metz had not been so cold and disinterested, he thought, things might have been different. Now it was too late. Unbelief poisoned his soul and neither Rabbi Deutz's kindness nor his father's all-consuming ambition could revive his faith. He carried the book home and dropped it carelessly on Felix's table. He had obeyed his father and made the prescribed visit. In a short time he would return the book and murmur something noncommittal. That would be the end. He and Rabbi Deutz would be like ships that pass in the night.

Strangely enough, he could not dispose of Dr. Drach quite so neatly. Why had such a learned man succumbed to the lure of Catholicism? Why not pay a visit to Stanislas College and find out? That much would not entangle him. It would be just one more adventure among so many.

The college itself was an old institution. Six years before it had added a seminary division and Dr. Drach taught Hebrew to the clerical students in attendance. The rector gave Jacob a warm welcome and saw that he was shown the library, the refectory, the garden, and the little room that had been set aside for him. In that tiny cell, the tortured young man sat hour after hour without reading the volumes Dr. Drach had recommended. Now and again a bell sounded in the distance. Otherwise, the silence was so sepulchral that it covered him with a pall of gloomy depression. *The History of Christian Doctrine* and *The History of Religion* lay before him. Their solemn leaden phrases, he knew, would have nothing of the fire of *Émile*. Rousseau captivated you on every page, even when you disagreed with him. These old tomes — he rose impatiently and paced the floor like a prisoner in the little bare room. Through the skylight he could see a small patch of bleak November gray. Outside, dark silent figures glided by — strange men of another nation, another religion. The distance between him and the old Saverne homestead stretched almost to infinity. Life seemed meaningless, existence miserable. Why could he not be like other people, happy in the midst of his family, confidently secure in his own religion? His meditations became so oppressive that he was afraid he was going to faint. Suddenly, he fell to the floor and cried out to the God of Abraham, Isaac, and Jacob. Echoes from the psalms formed themselves on his dry lips. Crushed in defeat, he prayed as he had never prayed before. Like a drowning man clinging to a piece of driftwood, he raised his head and adjured Yahweh to lead him into the light.

All at once, with a burst of glory it was there. "I saw the truth," he wrote later. "Faith flooded my mind and heart."[1] Now there was no more reasoning, no more debating. His mind had been prepared and cultivated for this long ago. The heart alone was waiting. Now that his prayer had opened heaven, divine grace swept through his soul. His journey to the light was ended.

Filled with a new wisdom, Jacob eagerly sat down to his books once more. The sober lines now seemed radiantly transfigured. "When I began to read Lhomond," he stated afterward, "I readily accepted everything he said about the life and death of Jesus Christ. Even the mystery of the Holy Eucharist, somewhat imprudently offered for my consideration, did not repel me at all. From then on, I wanted nothing so much as to be plunged into the waters of Baptism. This blessing was not far off. My preparation for it began immediately and I received it on Christmas Eve."[2]

[1] N. D. 1, 65. [2] N. D. 1, 66.

CHAPTER FIVE

OVERTURE

In 1826, the Vigil of Christmas came on a Sunday. That evening, in a delirium of happiness, Jacob knelt before the high altar of the college chapel, with Dr. Drach on one side and Felix on the other. Baron Francis de Malet and the Countess Aglaé Marie d'Heuzé, his godparents, were nearby. Behind them he heard the shuffle of feet and the passing of books as the seminarians prepared to intone their chant. Just then, the memory of his father intruded itself upon his consciousness and an overpowering agony seemed to rack his frame. The torture would have been unbearable had not a brief recollection of his mother served to calm him like the presence of a consoling angel. Though she had been taken from him thirteen years before when he was eleven years old, he somehow felt that she was very close to him in this solemn hour.

At that moment, Father Augé came out of the sacristy, Jacob stepped forward, and the ceremony began. As the priest said the words of exorcism, commanding the evil spirit to depart from this catechumen, a tremor passed through Jacob's body. It was an experience he never forgot. Years later, when he talked about it with others, a similar thrill would shoot through him, so violent, in fact, that it affected bystanders like a magnetic shock.

As the lustral waters coursed over his brow and his name became Francis-Mary-Paul, the new convert was lost in ecstasy. "When the holy water flowed over my head," he reported, "it seemed to me that I was in another world, in the center of an immense ball of fire. I no longer lived my natural existence; I neither saw nor heard what was happening around me. Things went on inside me that I cannot describe, and this lasted through much of the ceremony."[1]

"I shall never cease to be amazed at the change that came over me. . . . I actually became a new man. All uncertainty and anxiety vanished immediately. I felt a courage and supreme strength for keeping the Christian law; I felt a quiet affection for everything that belonged to my new religion."[2]

With such a dramatic display of divine power operating in his soul, Jacob — now Francis — realized better than most of us that life takes on full meaning only when one gives free rein to the workings of this heavenly force in the depths of his being. Every master of the spiritual life speaks of grace as the source of supernatural activity and development. But every author is not equally emphatic on the point. This humble Jew, after his baptism, became an important ascetical writer, one of the greatest of modern times, largely because he took up again and again the motif of grace. In the thousands and thousands of lines that he wrote and the hundreds of conferences that he gave it was never passed over in silence. It became his favorite theme, his inevitable starting point.

The day after he was baptized, Francis made his First Holy Communion. Now not he, but Christ lived in him (Gal. 2:20). He discovered Him who is Love Itself and the sword of the spirit cut to pieces once and for all the veil of his childhood through which God had appeared so stern and menacing. Like one of the figures on Thabor, it was good for him to be there.

A timid desire now made itself felt. It began to draw him irresistibly. Could he ever hope to be a priest? He mentioned the idea to Dr. Drach, but his mentor surprised him by asking for time to think it over. After all, there were difficulties in the way. Francis was poor and the years of study would be long and costly. Father Augé, however, was more encouraging. He had conceived a deep affection for the shy new convert and now moved to secure a scholarship for him. The Countess and a group of kind ladies would be able to provide whatever else he might need.

It was Felix who brought the good news. Francis joyfully put on the black cassock that had made him flee in terror as a child, began at once to study philosophy and, along with the other seminarians,

---

[1] N. D. 1, 90.
[2] N. D. 1, 66.

followed classes at the Sorbonne. Unfortunately, philosophy courses in those days were dry and uninspiring. The arid abstractions had little reference to reality and life. Francis found little in them to compare with the stimulating authors he had read so passionately while he was in Metz. The remote philosophizing seemed to be foreign to his very nature.

As a matter of fact, his penchant lay rather in psychological analysis. This was the talent that would subsequently enable him to probe deeply and accurately into the souls who came to him with their difficulties. Through it he discovered realities in men that were not known in those days, and because no technical vocabulary had as yet been developed, he occasionally had to express himself by giving new meanings to old terms. Years after, a seminarian wrote: "He knew a soul through and through in an instant. It was as if he had known you before. You couldn't help wondering if it wasn't a sort of inspiration. Thanks be to God, I have had very good spiritual directors in my life, men of great reputation, but I must admit that no one knew me so well from the beginning of the first interview as Father Libermann did. He went right to the basis of my character and to the source of my trouble. Then he immediately pointed out what I should do and how I should do it, showing me meanwhile the crosscurrents of influence that I had hardly been aware of. I found him lucid and precise and possessed of a sure insight when he analyzed the question of my vocation. No one ever gave me such a clear picture of my present condition nor has anyone ever sketched the future better and given me more perfect assurance than he did. It was for this very reason that our spiritual directors often sent us to Libermann . . . and [they] maintained emphatically that they had gained a much clearer idea of the spiritual life through their conversations with him."[3]

In those days, however, such gifts did not attract much attention at Stanislas. Pastoral theology, applied asceticism, psychology and educational methodology — so familiar to students in a modern seminary — were as yet unheard-of curricular components. Had such courses been available, along with studies in the natural sciences, Francis' extraordinary talents would have had a chance to manifest themselves academically. As it was, he turned in only an average

[3] N. D. 1, 310.

record despite his zealous application. The brilliance of his mind passed unnoticed before a group of teachers whose main criterion was facility in the stereotyped argumentation of the day.

While Francis studied with love and devotion, he no longer gave way to the wild and fiery eagerness with which he had plunged into literature and science during his stay in Metz. Then it was food and drink to the craving soul in quest of certitude. Now he had found peace. He had found the meaning of life in the depths of his regenerated humanity. Academic pursuits were now subordinated to the radiant reality of grace.

Naturally, his fellow students discussed him. They were intrigued by the phenomenon of a rabbi's son who had prepared himself for the synagogue and then had become not only a Catholic but a seminarian. One of them watched him more closely than the rest and always managed to be unkind. Something about this young man reminded Francis of the policeman in Saverne who used to eye the little Jews suspiciously while they played in the narrow street beside the synagogue. Did he not think, this inquisitor asked, that he had acted a bit hastily in coming into the Church? What was his precise reason for becoming a Catholic? And then this inclination toward the priesthood — would it not have been wiser to test it for a while before entering the seminary? Francis was caught off guard. He replied as best he could but the smug rebuttals of his adversary demolished every reason he could adduce. The self-constituted defender of the Faith went away satisfied, to return in a few days with a flood of arguments that completely overwhelmed the timid little Jew.

The experience left Francis feeling insecure. He began to imagine that a great number of the seminarians shared his critic's views. He seemed to read it in their eyes and the recognition of it brought back his old loneliness. At that moment his father's sorrowing features intruded themselves on his imagination. Had he already been informed? Would he ever forgive him? Francis gripped his head in his hands. It always gave him physical pain to think of his father. He knew that he was and would remain a Jew. That in itself was a barrier. Then there was the nervous impediment in his speech and the awkwardness of his bodily movements. The strain had begun to tell. He did not want to complain. He would bear it all for Jesus and hide his grief behind a smile.

Soon after, he was hurrying down the seminary corridor, thinking, as he often did these days, of his poor old father back in Saverne. Without warning, a throbbing pain started to pound in his head and a wave of weakness came over him. He clung desperately to a window frame to keep from falling. A horrible flood of anxiety engulfed him and every cell in his body seemed to tingle. After an eternity of apprehension, the seizure left him as quickly as it had come. He was breathing hard when he reached his room and threw himself on the bed. As the hot tears rolled down his cheeks, he softly prayed, "Thy will be done."

In the days that followed, he continued to feel weak. There were times when he had to stop on the way to class and lean against the wall or grip a doorjamb. If he studied particularly hard, he was sure to wake up with an unbearable headache the next day. A questioning letter to Dr. Samson brought the comforting but not very helpful assurance that one need not be too concerned about these crises; they merely indicated that he was exhausted and in need of rest.

All this while, he lived in the midst of high-spirited, healthy young men. Some obviously pitied him; others were openly disdainful. Whatever their attitude, he strove to bear the humiliation cheerfully, stifling every tendency toward preoccupation with himself and endeavoring to remain unperturbed in the most embarrassing situations, confident in the knowledge that he was doing God's will. Surprisingly enough, it now became easier to meet people. Then, as the years went by, he became so adept at this God-centered indifference that the nervously afflicted sought him out for guidance and help. In fact, fifteen years later, we find him writing to one of his many clients: "You must forget about those nervous spells; ignore them, don't keep track of them. The thing that did me more harm than anything else was the anxiety, the restlessness, the precautions. In moments of stress we have to shake off such jittery feelings and forget ourselves, refusing to be gripped by anxieties. We must deal firmly with such emotions and be supremely indifferent about our ability to bear our affliction well or badly. Once we achieve this, we might as well not have the illness. That is what I have done ever since I gave myself to the Lord. I followed this procedure in a spirit of faith and with a desire to please God, never even thinking that this might be a way of restoring my health because the idea never crossed my mind. As a matter of fact, it had a great deal to do with my cure."[4]

Apparently, the remedy was really effective, because his fellow students at the Sorbonne soon began to perceive a new serenity in his face. Unruffled peace seemed to radiate from him. Subsequently, a priest from Martinique recalled it vividly: "He was already stamped with that fine character of mildness and modesty that was to stay with him throughout life, and even after all these years I have not forgotten his engaging smile. I must admit rather shamefacedly that in those days I was inclined toward tensions and excesses. Yet, all I had to do to regain my composure was to exchange a few words with this young Jewish convert."[5]

On the Vigil of Pentecost, June 9, 1827, Francis received tonsure and was thereby officially enrolled in the clerical state. His happiness, however, was clouded by a problem of conscience. Archbishop de Quélen had just decided that the seminary should thenceforth devote itself to preparing home missionaries for France and Libermann did not feel called for this type of priestly work. He liked Stanislas, he had a scholarship there, and the authorities were willing to advance him to orders despite his nervous condition. Dr. Drach and the rector felt that he should stay and take the chance on developing a vocation for missionary activity, but his customary docility did not seem to be in evidence now. He clung stubbornly to his conviction that he must in all honesty go elsewhere. "My conscience," he told Dr. Drach, "does not allow me to continue my studies here, for even though I am determined to go on for the priesthood, I am not at all sure that God wants me to be a missionary."[6]

In the face of such resoluteness Dr. Drach decided that there was nothing left but to visit the Archbishop and tell him the whole story. The interview went surprisingly well. After they had analyzed the situation, the old prelate slowly raised his head, looked steadily at Dr. Drach, and said, "We will put him in St. Sulpice Seminary and give him a full scholarship." Thus it was that Francis came to be accepted at St. Sulpice, the most renowned seminary in France, where the famous scholars on its staff gave their seminarians a deeply spiritual training. He was indeed fortunate to have such a splendid opportunity.

---

[4] N. D. 7, 237 f. [5] N. D. 1, 75. [6] N. D. 1, 76.

CHAPTER SIX

SPRING

Francis and Dr. Drach sat tensely in the seminary parlor. Nothing broke the silence of that stuffy, high-ceilinged room but the incisive ticking of a clock on the mantelpiece. Somehow the older man's reassuring smile failed to cast even an illusion of warmth over the occasion. Francis had torn up his roots once again and the old waves of insecurity were surging back and forth across his soul. Abbé Augé's parting blessing had served only to conjure up the vision of his brokenhearted father once again. It rose up before his mind's eye as the clock ticked on inexorably. Then the door opened and Father Garnier appeared.

He was a coldly dignified man, this seminary rector who had already spent forty years in the Society of St. Sulpice. His was an important and influential institution — a center of piety and learning — and he meant to keep it so. Undesirable candidates could expect little encouragement from him. That much was evident in the quizzical tilt of his old gray head and the appraising sweep of his cautious glance.

Jacob withered under the questioning stare. It took him back to his father's parlor and the doorstep of the rabbi of Metz. He wished with all his soul that the interview were over, but by this time Dr. Drach was talking volubly. There were some painfully unnecessary remarks about the weather, but the temperature of the musty, high-ceilinged room did not rise one degree. Undaunted, Dr. Drach proceeded to discuss the offer of a scholarship, a point which the rector conceded with visible but impotent regret. With devastating honesty, Dr. Drach concluded his little speech with the solicitous observation that Francis had been troubled with headaches these past few weeks and that his general health was not too good.

"That too?" said Father Garnier, as if to himself.

"Don't you think," Drach persisted, "that early rising will be just a bit too hard on him?"

Francis silently pleaded with his friend to be quiet. But it was too late. The rector stood up and said in a slow, even voice, "If he feels that we rise too early here, he had better not enter the seminary."

Dr. Drach desperately swung around to save the situation. He remembered Father Garnier's reputation as a Hebrew scholar and felt that here at least they might find a common ground for discussion. Accordingly, he launched into an embarrassing panegyric that traced in enthusiastic detail all of Francis' accomplishments in Hebraic language and literature. At length he paused for the reaction. It came, swift and icy. "Our classes," Garnier observed, "are taught in Latin, not in Hebrew." After that there was no sound for a long time except the ever present ticking of that merciless clock. After a long while, the rector dredged up all his dissatisfaction in a long sigh and whispered, *"Enfin, nous verrons."* (All right, we'll see.) On the way out the door, he cast a sidelong glance at his new recruit and said, "Come with me."

Francis followed the rigid figure down those dark mysterious corridors with a leaden heart and spinning brain. Conflicting thoughts climbed over each other to engage his attention. Here he was again, new, strange, uncertain. But if it was God's will, how could it be uncertain in the long run? What must the rector think of him? But why should he care what people thought or said if God was pleased with him? Father Garnier's observations back in the parlor still rankled, yet the disturbance was only on the surface of his emotions. Deep down, the unshakable peace of Christ still flooded his soul. It was an interesting phenomenon, this superficial sort of turmoil that failed to ruffle him substantially. Francis paused to observe it as he had done so many times since his baptism. In this desperate hour, his hypersensitive nature was particularly raw and yet the serenity of grace suffused his soul and left it basically unaffected. This play of nature and grace intrigued him. He must study it further.

Just then, Father Garnier stopped at a door, ushered him in, and stiffly bade him good night. There it was, another new home. But he must get used to it. In a few short hours he would be thrust among the students. At that prospect, he groaned interiorly, for he knew the ways of students with a Jewish lad who has come to live with them. It was going to take all his strength to weather the storm.

Oddly enough, things went rather well. The rector, who at first seemed to float about with the majestic rigor of an iceberg, thawed out remarkably and even gave evidence of a fatherly heart under the cloak of his frigid dignity. He now gave Francis permission to sleep longer in the morning and evinced genuine concern for his health. Francis availed himself of the dispensation for a while, but as soon as he felt stronger, he rose at the appointed time. Shortly thereafter, he felt able to advance the schedule by an hour so that he might serve the early Mass. These quiet moments before dawn, when he was alone with the Host and the priest in a warm circle of candlelight, were full of special graces. Sometimes he grew so keenly absorbed in prayer at the altar that he lost all track of time and space. It was as if someone else were praying within him. Tears poured from his eyes and an excruciating happiness filled his whole being.

Studies at St. Sulpice were of a high order. Its renowned staff numbered men whose scholarship was respected throughout Europe. Francis listened as the students spoke admiringly of Father Mollevaut, one of the greatest Hellenists of his time, and of Father Pinault, a product of the *École Normale Supérieure,* whose manual on physics had attracted widespread attention and would have been adopted as the official textbook for all state colleges if he had agreed to delete the dedication to Mary, the Mother of God. Father Fallon, Libermann's own confessor, was a rigorously scientific historian, and the rector himself enjoyed no mean reputation as an orientalist.

More admirable than the erudition of these men, however, was the quiet humility that they displayed in all circumstances. Theirs was obviously a profoundly spiritual life. Even while they drove home the lessons of secular learning, they cautioned the seminarians against that distorted sense of values which places exaggerated importance on erudition an as end in itself. Theirs was the motto of St. Sulpice: "Be learned without parading your learning and, above all, be holy." Their ancient Rule spoke again and again of the surpassing value of sanctity in relation to all earthly things.

Francis readily absorbed this attitude. It always remained with him. Down through the years, he put the spiritual life before all else, but at the same time he demanded a strict scientific training for his seminarians, dedicated teaching in his professors, careful scholarship in the textbooks he inspired, while all the while insisting that the members of his Congregation be holy men.

His own course in theology cannot be termed brilliant. In fact, he had been merely an average student in philosophy, though this might be attributed to lack of ease with the Latin which he had studied so recently and briefly. Poor health might also account in part for the unimpressive record. The main reason, however, seems to lie in the fact that his characteristic talent found little scope in the highly systematized philosophy and theology of his day. Francis was a man of creative intuition whose habit of careful observation made him eminently practical. He found it tedious to engage in the art of juggling abstractions — a practice that was all too often the academic fashion of his age. Moreover, postrevolutionary theology in France lacked the security and clarity that it enjoys in more peaceful times when, after the battle of wits is over and the controversial masters have won the day, new concepts are integrated within the imperishable framework of revelation and tradition.

Despite his difficulties, Francis doggedly pursued his studies. By the end of his course, his notes were set down in impeccable Latin and his final examinations brought him abreast of the most able students in his class. The shame of those earlier years caused him to write to a discouraged seminarian: "As far as proficiency in studies is concerned, I was just like you in the first years of my seminary career. But what can one do about it? He just has to live through the humiliating experience. Bear up under it courageously and do the best you can every time you are quizzed. In any event, do not neglect your work."[1]

He sought earnestly for an effective method of study. The blind memorizing of those years in Saverne had convinced him of the need for thinking things out independently. "Try to understand con-

[1] F.-M.-P. Libermann, C.S.Sp., *Lettres spirituelles,* 2nd ed., Paris, n.d., 4 vols., 3, 7 (hereafter quoted as L. S.).

cepts," he counseled years afterward, "without slavishly holding to the author's exact words. Rephrase the material in your own language."[2] It was a procedure he had faithfully adhered to and, coupled with constant application, it paid dividends. Francis' eventual mastery of theology shines through the short spiritual essays he sent to seminarians, the conferences he gave as novice master for the Eudists, and the Commentary he wrote on St. John's Gospel. The difficulty of relating the mysteries of revelation to the most delicate psychological phenomena held no terrors for his ready pen. When he began the Commentary, he had been away from the books for ten years and frankly admitted that fact at the outset. However, he went on to observe: "I believe it would not take me long to revive that knowledge, for my mind has been occupied continually with such things, particularly the dogmas, even though I was not formally studying them."[3]

That was his usual approach. He would analyze a proposition thoroughly. Then, after he had fully grasped it, he would quietly assimilate it. Finally, he would meditate on it at great length. In the early days at St. Sulpice, when he was rising later than the other seminarians, he missed the customary instructions on mental prayer. Instead, he was given the book and told to study it for himself. It was a queer volume, strangely reminiscent of a stagecoach schedule. It marked the point of departure, indicated the changes to be made en route, and treated the mind, the emotions, and the imagination as if they were teams of horses to be harnessed and unharnessed at specific times. Francis shook his head in amazement. Why such complications? Prayer seemed so easy and simple for him. It welled up naturally from the depths of his soul. He had already been raised far above this laborious textbook method of prayer through the purification of suffering and through the great care he took to preserve his peace of mind and let grace unfold its workings unhampered by positive efforts on his part. He was already possessed of that wonderful freedom from men and things which alone opens the way for the divine adventure we call mystical experience.

---

[2] L. S. 3, 8.

[3] F.-M.-P. Libermann, C.S.Sp., *Commentaire du S. Évangile selon S. Jean,* Ngazobil, 1872, VI (hereafter quoted as Comm.).

The seed of his new life germinated quickly. It was pushing upward from a soil that had been well watered with his tears. Only one strong and intimate attachment remained to be broken before he was cut free of every natural bond, and it found its terminus in the bent and bearded figure from whose burning eyes the lamplight still seemed to cast ominous reflections. Had the old rabbi heard the news? Would he forgive another wayward son? Perhaps if he knew the move had been made after much consideration and mature conviction, some vein of understanding might be touched. Francis sat down to compose a letter.

The reply came one day when the seminarians were gathered for the noon recreation. One of their number was distributing the mail. Francis hoped very much there might be some for him. News from Samson was overdue. His musing was interrupted by an outstretched hand that reached a letter to him through the crowd. Even before he took it, he saw the old palsied script on the envelope and recognized at once his father's writing. The flush of joy turned to deathly pallor on his cheek. His fingers trembled and a searing pain raced through his head as he tore open this fearful letter. The seminarians stood aghast as he turned ashen gray, moaned audibly, and swayed as if to fall.

A merciful mist now rose before his eyes and he could no longer see the cruel phrases: "you are damned forever . . . cast out like a leper . . . as one dead . . . Yahweh's wrath be upon you . . ." or even the soft, cajoling words of sorrowing love: "Come back . . . you are my last hope . . . return to your house . . . to the arms of your old father before he dies . . ." The seminarians watched as convulsions attacked his frame. They heard him groan: "But I am a Christian, I am a Christian," and then saw him shuffle off to his room like a man bereft of reason.

Once there, he pressed his throbbing head between his hands. Felix and Dr. Drach rushed over to visit him, but their words of consolation never went beyond the surface of his benumbed and weary consciousness. All he could say was: "May the name of the Lord be blessed in all things." From the abyss of pain he was already surrendering to the will of God.

Nor was that heroic *fiat* pronounced in vain. An irresistible force suddenly overpowered him and he stood in mystical rapture before the divine Ruler of his soul. The days that followed brought the same high elation. "God drew me to Himself," he later wrote, "without asking my consent and with a force which up to now I have never observed in anyone else. Our Lord gave me the grace to resist my father who wanted to tear me away from the faith. Instead, I renounced him rather than my faith. Once that step was taken, the good Master came unexpectedly to tear me away from myself. He held my faculties captive for almost five years. During all that time, the thought never occurred to me to cultivate any special virtue. My entire concern centered on being united with Him. And that was very easy."[4]

Shortly thereafter, he wrote a long and affectionate letter to the old rabbi. He assured him of his love, his gratitude, and even his happiness in the new religion. Secretly he hoped that Lazarus would read and think over what he said and then, who knows, the light might dawn again in the Libermann family. Now the long wait for a reply set in. After many weeks, David wrote to say that their father was slipping fast. Nothing more was heard until two years later when a letter came from Esther. Father was dead. Shame and grief and bitterness had struck him down before his time. For Francis, the last sweet tie with earth was severed.

As the elements of personal tragedy played themselves out on the natural level, Francis still moved serenely in the supernatural sphere. His heart and emotions were immersed in a sea of affective prayer and on occasion he rose to heights of mystic contemplation. It was the memory of these experiences that helped him subsequently when he set out to describe man's relationship to God. This, along with his psychological insight and his penetrating observation, enabled him to paint affective prayer in all its forms and manifestations. It made him an inspiring reporter of interior phenomena, a ready analyst of causes and effects, who clearly traces the soul's passage from affective prayer to contemplation.

The second year at St. Sulpice (1828) passed uneventfully. He had begun to feel at home. There were friends on the faculty and in the student body. Courses seemed less formidable and his health had much improved. The headaches and fits of dizziness had diminished in frequency and intensity now that he knew complete emo-

[4] N. D. 8, 203 f.

tional peace and recognized that God is not in the whirlwind. "The Holy Spirit," he maintained, "cannot reach our ear when we are all wrought up inside. When we are buffeted about by our own faculties, tossed left and right by our emotions, we cannot be led by the Spirit of God." "Gently put the brakes on the imagination and the feelings that are too strong. In the beginning, it might even help to slow up a bit on your external activity so as to lend a peaceful and ready ear to the grace of the Holy Spirit who is in you."[5]

Throughout his life, Francis was preoccupied with this preservation of peace of mind. Considering the lack of balance in his physical constitution, this emphasis on interior serenity must have been hard to maintain. Nonetheless, he mastered the secret and thereby became the guide and inspiration for a world that languishes in a web of neuroses.

His life, though peaceful, was far from secluded. Felix came to see him every visiting day; there were letters to and from his old friend in Metz, Lazarus Libman, soon to become the husband of his sister Esther; and above all he engaged in a voluminous correspondence with Samson in which every detail of family news received careful and loving attention. Contacts with the other seminarians grew more intimate and rewarding. For the most part, they were an outstanding lot, and his conversations on prayer inspired some of them mightily.

It was customary at St. Sulpice for each new arrival to be assigned a *bon ange,* an older student who would introduce the newcomer into the mysteries of seminary life, point out his faults, and guide him generally through the early stages of his assimilation into the community. Francis had had one, and now he was in turn appointed to exercise a measure of solicitude over a jolly, bumptious, and somewhat scatterbrained recruit named Viot. Because there was no lack of good will in this youngster, Francis had considerable success with him, enough at least to make him redouble his efforts at careful guidance.

Near the end of his first vacation, Viot wrote to his "big brother" an enthusiastic appraisal of the weeks just past. In his reply, Francis said he was happy to hear how pleasant the holidays had been, but he immediately went on to express some anxiety over the possi-

[5] L. S. 1, 74.

bility that Viot might have become embroiled in too much worldliness. "You tell me," he wrote, "about your visits, your excursions, and your picnics, but you don't tell me about your companions in all this or how you behaved on these outings. You merely say in passing that they have prevented you from keeping your rule. It worries me. I know your exceptionally lively temperament and can't help thinking that you have spent your time in pleasure seeking. I am afraid much of your recreation went by without being offered up to God."[6] He then proceeded to apologize for his frankness and to soften the criticism by admitting that he too had lost ground even though he stayed within the seminary walls the whole summer.

This simple contact with Viot was the first evidence of that spiritual power which Francis was to wield throughout his life. The first spiritual letters confined themselves to broad principles and their application, but as time went on, they developed into that minute analysis of individual souls which was to characterize his method of direction years hence.

After Viot there were others. Little by little the word went around St. Sulpice: "Have you heard the little Jew talk about God?" More and more seminarians came to listen to him and to ask him questions. While he moderated the abundance of his light and tempered it for the less gifted of his hearers, he urged them on with friendly persistence to advance as far as grace would lead them. It was the uncertain beginning of an apostolate that he had never sought, an apostolate of guidance that unfolded spontaneously wherever he went. The terrifying responsibility weighed heavily upon him at first and prompted him to seek laboriously for a properly balanced approach. Once it was achieved, Francis excelled in easy adjustment and understanding moderation when dealing with the foibles of human nature. Once more he demonstrated his wonderful gift for making theological truths come alive and his exquisite psychological tact in applying these truths to the need of an individual soul.

All the while he was steadily advancing toward his goal. On December 20, Archbishop de Quélen conferred Minor Orders on him. The next steps would be subdiaconate, diaconate, and priesthood. Francis was indeed a happy young man.

---

[6] N. D. 1, 132 f.

CHAPTER SEVEN

MYSTERIOUS TORMENT

The winter of 1829 was cold and severe. Cutting winds blew up mercilessly from the Seine and howled around the ancient buildings of St. Sulpice. Professors and students shivered as they hurried along the drafty corridors. Francis suffered intensely from the cold, but his inner happiness held the discomfort at bay in the outer reaches of his consciousness.

Then suddenly the nervous seizures came. At first he paid no attention to them. When a fainting spell threatened, he simply stopped where he was, waited for it to pass, and went on as if nothing happened. As the weeks rolled by, however, these crises refused to be ignored. The headaches returned, now more insistent and paralyzing than ever. Study became impossible. "I believe," he wrote, "that the mental strain wore me out. I was continually occupied with theology all day long. Even now, every time I do a little work, there is a pressure in my head as if my skull were clamped in a steel band."[1]

At last he realized he would have to give up. Every class, every assignment was a torment. He spent more time merely resting in his little room. When spring came, waves of discouragement surged over him. What would happen now? If he could not study, how could he be ordained? If this business persisted, would they not dismiss him?

His old friend Abbe Augé came to visit him. Francis described his headaches, his weak spells, and his secret fear that he would never reach the subdiaconate. Augé tried to laugh away his fears. He offered to take Francis back with him to Stanislas and give him

[1] N. D. 1, 150.

an easy job till he recovered. The offer was touching in its kindness, but it brought no lasting reassurance.

By April, however, there seemed to be no alternative. Francis went back to Stanislas, hoping to regain his health and fully resolved to work henceforth without driving himself so hard. He had begun to see that one really went counter to the will of God when he sought to attain by violence results that exceeded the potential which Providence had established for him. During the years of trial that were about to begin, he gradually attained an interior synthesis that led him to accord academic pursuits their proper place in the scheme of things. Always keeping his zeal for study, he never advocated exceeding the divinely prescribed limits which manifest the will of God through an individual's aptitude, health, and special vocation in life. That is why he recommended constant moderation of the mind's impetuosity. When his friend Viot urged Francis to bring back a Greek dictionary from the bookbinder as soon as possible, the following warning was issued: "There now. You seem to be impatient. Why? . . . It's because you are strongly attached to the study of Greek! 'But,' you will object, 'God's honor requires me to study that language.' True; there is no doubt about that. But the glory of God does not demand that you apply yourself to it with such vehemence. One must never give in to impatience when he's promoting the honor of God."[2]

Thanks to Abbé Augé's tender solicitude, Francis relaxed again. He even improved enough to join his fellow seminarians the next summer. Then the new term began and he settled down to prepare himself for the subdiaconate. It was to be conferred during the pre-Christmas Ember Days and the hour was fast approaching. The nearer it came the more uneasy he grew. His sensitivity and irritability increased alarmingly. He found it ever harder to control himself. If only he could run away from it all and hide in some inaccessible dark corner. The headaches came pounding back and he longed for sleep — hours and hours of it. He felt as if he were dragging himself through a heavy fog that dulled the loudest sounds and made everything seem vaguely unreal.

Through every phase of this growing terror, he held on desperately to the figure of Christ. Like Jesus, he must be amiable toward

[2] L. S. 1, 1.

others. Like Jesus, he must show concern for others even in the midst of his own suffering. Jarrier, another seminarian, was sick in the infirmary. He must go and visit the poor fellow.

Jarrier was delighted. They had just settled down for a quiet chat when Francis went ashen white. A wild shock ripped through his body, coursed down his limbs, and then concentrated on his head. A screaming whistle competed with the buzzing roar in his ears and every object in the room took on extravagant proportions. With a horrible cry he lurched forward, swayed, and fell to the floor with a sickening thud.

The haunting sound of his seizure echoed down the silent corridors and brought the seminarians running. They stopped in the doorway, horrified at the sight of the little Jew lying there, his face contorted, his eyes rolling wildly, and his head beating mercilessly on the wooden floor as waves of convulsions jerked his rigid frame again and again. Bloody foam stained his lips and cheeks. His labored, stertorous breathing rattled hollowly. Gradually, the convulsions abated until a last deep sigh brought silence and release. They lifted him onto a bed where he lay for a long time in a deep coma. When he awoke, he was still unsteady. There was an annoying mist before his eyes. He wondered how he came to be lying in the infirmary, but the mystery held only remote interest for him. He was tired — so very, very tired. He would close his eyes and think about it some other time. Then he drifted off again and he slept for several hours. When they finally awakened him, he looked around in bewilderment and fell back into another deep sleep. At last he awoke of his own accord and the throbbing in his head was insupportable. He felt as if he had been beaten with clubs. To make matters worse, a black depression bore down on his soul.

Despite it all, his heart was close to Christ. "It is well, O Lord," he prayed, "that Thou hast permitted me to be subject to all this. I am in the midst of torment, but I will not yield to despair." When Doctor Lombard slipped into the room, he was astonished to see a serene and smiling face looking up from the pillow. As he left, he shook his head in mystified amazement. Your true epileptic portrays gloom, depression, and extreme sensitivity after an attack, but this curious patient radiated such quiet peace and assurance that it made one doubt about the diagnosis. When the rector inquired anxiously about Francis' condition, the old doctor could only say: "He is either an angel or a saint."

But the demons of anxiety were not long in coming. As soon as the doctor had left, strange thoughts plagued the weary mind of the young man he had treated. Could all this be the result of his father's curse? No! That was unthinkable for a true Christian. Yet the bitter feeling of guilt persisted. He relived again that last cruel scene in Saverne. He was not guilty. It was his duty to act as he did; reason told him that. But the heart has reasons that reason does not understand. Self-reproach rose up from the inmost recesses of his being. He felt the need to pay for what he had done, to suffer in atonement for his offense. Could this affliction be his just punishment? Again he rejected the idea. The good Lord had simply permitted it out of love for him. His ways are not our ways. The battle surged back and forth until sleep claimed him once more.

Meanwhile, word ran through the house: Francis, the little Jew, had the falling sickness! It was possible and even probable that he would have other seizures. Francis knew it too. He knew that the victim of *grand mal* cannot be advanced to orders. Were his dreams of the priesthood shattered forever then? If so, what could he do, a renegade from his own people, further cut off from them and from society by his loathsome disease? Only heroic faith saved him from utter despair. It was this deep, abiding faith that would some day call him to be the courageous champion of all wretched souls who live in isolation, completely abandoned by their fellowmen. It would lead him to write and say and do many things to give new hope and confidence to the abandoned souls of the earth. This grievous ordeal would make him a comforting example for those who know from personal experience the agony of nervous derangements. It would constitute him an inspiring patron for all who have dedicated their lives to these ailments. The picture of the peaceful smile on his tired and pain-furrowed face might well become a fitting reminder on the walls of waiting rooms, clinics, and wards where such patients are treated.

When Francis recovered sufficiently, he followed classes as usual. Everyone tactfully spoke as if nothing had happened, but he knew that the threat of dismissal hung like the sword of Damocles over his head. There were moments of wild sweet hope when he felt that there would be no more seizures, although fatigue came on much more rapidly now and the books had to be put aside more frequently. The doctor kept prescribing rest, "as much as possible."

After a few weeks it clutched at him again. He was very deliberately climbing the stairs with an armload of books. As he reached the top, that now-familiar aura descended upon him. Instinctively he cast himself forward into the corridor to avoid falling backward down the stairway, and the bloodcurdling cry rang down the halls. Students came running again and found him writhing horribly as before.

Now the seizures quickened their tempo. Though their intensity varied, their frequency increased. In this early period of his illness, there was no great premonition of an impending attack. Without much warning, the flash, the cry, the fall, and the convulsions would come in swift succession. He might be walking along the corridor, kneeling in chapel, or strolling with friends during the recreation period. Later on, the menacing aura extended over two or three days before he was to be stricken. That awful black depression would enshroud him and he had to hold on to God with all his might to avoid being overcome by despair. At such times, he took refuge in the chapel, kneeling there before his Eucharistic Lord and counteracting the natural anxiety of the moment by peaceful abandonment to the love of God.

Dr. Drach kept telling him not to make any rash decisions but to wait for a clear manifestation of the divine will. Felix came more frequently now, though his inability to help made the visits sheer torture for him. Samson and Isabel wrote encouraging letters and did their best to distract Francis by detailed accounts of the children's activities. The seminarians, with all too obvious charity, went out of their way to ignore his condition, overplaying their part to such an extent that he began to wonder if they were not repelled by him.

Because more and more rest was prescribed, Francis was increasingly excused from class. This left him free to help with the seminary's works of charity. He looked forward in particular to the weekly distribution of alms to the poor of Paris. One bitter cold day, their number was unusually large. They huddled together shivering in the long white corridor — old men in threadbare clothes, bent women in patched skirts and frayed shawls, young mothers with emaciated faces holding sick babies and trailing tearful youngsters from their apron strings. They stood there, waiting for the dole, their faces lined with wretchedness and pain. Francis silently wondered how much of their suffering was caused by man's inhumanity to man. His boundless compassion made him wish with all his heart that he could make every one of them happy. He knew what it was to suffer, to be abandoned, and he sympathized deeply with these forgotten and neglected wretches.

Slowly, this procession of Parisian misery shuffled toward the table from which Francis and another seminarian were distributing provisions. There were so many of them today and the supply seemed so limited that the ones in the rear began to press forward anxiously, stretching out their hands and clamoring for attention.

"Francis," the other seminarian called, "tell them we won't give anything to anyone that's pushing and shoving." Libermann looked around at him in amazement. "Surely we can't punish these poor people," he gasped. "They are suffering enough already." His companion saw the horror-stricken look on the sensitive Jewish features and bowed his head in shame.

These poor people of Paris soon came to know him. They sensed intuitively that his gentle politeness, even to the worst outcasts, betrayed a heart that was genuinely devoted to them. The neglected and the downtrodden have a sure instinct for such sympathy. They are quick to discover Christlike charity and they found it in this pale, smiling cleric.

With the coming of spring, the dampness and chill retreated from the white-washed corridors of St. Sulpice and warm sunlight projected changing patterns over floors and benches as it played on the ancient walls of the seminary. The open casements admitted clouds of perfume from flowers that rioted in the cloistered court below. With it all, Francis' heart stood open too, and a fresh new hope quickened it. The rector had made no move as yet to dismiss him. Did Father Garnier think there still was some chance for a cure? Perhaps.

A few miles out of Paris, on a picturesque hill near the village of Issy, stood a Sulpician house called "The Solitude." It served as a novitiate for candidates who wished to join the society and as a house of philosophy for the seminarians. Once a week the theologians went there from the capital for a day's outing. Francis loved the place. That hilltop house with its limitless view was a welcome change from the crowded cobblestone streets of Paris. He found it refreshing to stroll through the rustling wheat fields, past the glowing flower beds, and around well-tailored shrubbery that echoed with the song of birds.

On the morning of July 28, he set out with a band of high-spirited seminarians to visit this idyllic spot. A clear blue sky spread over them as they walked along chatting and laughing like school-boys. Suddenly, in the distance, a muffled roar resounded across the rolling fields. Soon the clangor of church bells rang out above artillery thunder and then human voices added to the din. Clearly, the long-suffering mobs had gone berserk and some sort of upheaval had Paris in its grip. The little knot of seminarians broke into a run. They reached the Solitude breathless and alarmed.

Only much later did they learn that the proletarian revolt had been victorious. King Charles X fled to England and France was thrashing about in the throes of forming a new government. Unrest pervaded the land. It pervaded even the cloistered calm of the seminary. Students took sides and argued heatedly. Peace and recollection nearly disappeared, and Francis saw the dangers of such controversy. He set down his ideas on a seminarian's place in the scheme of things when he wrote to Viot: "Always keep calm. Preserve an inner quiet and peace of mind. Don't allow yourself to be upset by things going on in the world. Don't even look for news about it. Let others argue and do things while you keep on improving yourself. You have only one job: to make yourself pleasing to God and to do His holy will. Everything else is silly. People get steamed up on the pretext that the welfare of religion is involved in current events. My dear fellow, that is mistaken zeal. I'm sure God disapproves of it."[3] Later on he would be a masterful diplomat, visiting the Parisian ministries and wielding considerable influence. Right now, as a seminarian, he meant to be a man of prayer and recollection.

On June 20, 1831, the seminary celebrated with customary solemnity its very own feast of Christ's Priesthood. The altar was resplendent with festive ornaments. Priests and acolytes moved with

[3] L. S. 1, 18.

solemn deliberateness through the majestic ritual. The seminarians in white surplices lined the time-burnished choir stalls and sang their liquid plain chant with more than usual reverence. Francis stood among them, his mood of exaltation heightened by a feeling of conscious union with the Eternal Priest.

Suddenly his whole being thrilled to a sweet rapture that overwhelmed and penetrated every fiber of it. A mighty stillness surrounded him and he saw with crystal clarity the figure of Christ the High Priest passing along the stalls. To each of the seminarians he lovingly distributed His gifts, but when He came to Francis, He passed by. After everyone had taken his share, the figure of Christ returned and placed in his hands the very treasure of His graces. Somehow Francis immediately understood that he was called to distribute the treasures of the Lord to all the priests he would thereafter encounter. Then the vision disappeared.

With characteristic modesty, he hid the experience from everyone but Father Fallon, his confessor. Humbly, he interpreted it as a sign that he was forever barred from the priesthood but that he could console himself in remotely contributing to the work of the clergy. Father Fallon disagreed. His opinion seems to have been verified in unexpected fashion by the words of Pius XII, who stated among other things more than a hundred years later: "This century of active consecration to the work of the priesthood has amply justified the confidence which our Predecessor, Pope Pius IX, placed in the sons of Venerable Francis Libermann. Today we can count thousands of priests who have received their spiritual formation from their hands."[4]

During that whole summer, Francis had no serious attacks at all. Those that did occur were mild and he had ample warning beforehand in the form of mental fatigue, physical exhaustion, and violent throbbing headaches. These preliminary symptoms gave him time to slip into his room and close the door. There he would kneel before his crucifix, calmly awaiting the now familiar episode. Convinced that God arranges everything in love, he accepted it all as a gift from God's hands. In the light of that truth he was able to look with affection on his illness and from his busy pen there now flowed

[4] *Bulletin Général* (de la Congrégation du St. Esprit), Paris, 1857 ff., Vol. 43, p. 58 (hereafter quoted as B. G.).

a paradoxical expression: "My beloved malady." "I am a Christian," he wrote. "Our Lord Jesus Christ died for me. I am overwhelmed with His gifts and graces, but I have only a little share in His sufferings and His cross."[5]

That summer he was finishing his third and last year of theology (only three years were required at that time). Something had to be done. For the moment, they sent him with one of the faculty to a seashore resort, hoping that the salt air and the bathing would cure the professor's stomach ailment and help the student's epilepsy. Things did not work out that way. When the school year reopened, Francis showed no improvement. In one of his letters at that time he frankly faced the situation: "You ask me if I am to stay at the seminary. I don't know. I'm still here, but I don't know if the rector will keep me here. Up to now he has done so out of pity, but sooner or later he'll have to ship me off, for what can he do with me here? I'm of no earthly use to him. All I can do is eat, drink, sleep, and be a burden to everybody."[6]

They had to send him away. He knew that. The inevitable decision could not be put off much longer. But what then? He simply placed his trust in God. Samson and Isabel worried about him a good deal. When their letters betrayed their anxiety, he hastened to allay their fears: "I am still in the seminary and will stay here until my superiors decide that the moment has arrived for my dismissal. If I am unable to be a priest, they can't keep me forever. Please don't grieve for me or worry about my future. Our Father in heaven knows very well what He has in store for me. My body, my soul, my whole being belong to Him."[7]

Winter was moving in. The cold gray days were getting shorter. At noon, on the seventh of November, a seminarian knocked at his door. "Father Carbon wants to see you." Father Carbon was the assistant rector. This was it! Francis felt his breath catch, but he quickly regained his poise and resolutely walked down to the office. Father Carbon cleared his throat and stared at the papers on his desk. Gently, and with careful deliberation, he broke the news. The archdiocesan councilors had been discussing his case for a long time. The seizures, you know, had begun in 1828 and here it was

---

[5] L. S. 1, 17. [6] L. S. 1, 28. [7] N. D. 1, 154.

the end of 1831. Despite all the rest and medical attention, there seemed to be no improvement. Then too, he was holding a scholarship that someone else might use with more profit.

Francis swallowed hard. He understood that all too well. St. Sulpice and the archbishop had been most kind, he said, and he knew the situation could not go on. In fact, he was most grateful that they had tolerated him as long as they did.

"Have you any idea what you will do?" Father Carbon inquired.

"No, Father. Until God clears things up for me, I haven't the slightest idea. All I'm sure of is that I can't return to the world. I don't belong there and couldn't go back to it of my own accord. If the authorities send me back, I'll have to go. Then God will take care of me and let me know His holy will."

Francis returned to his room and closed the door. Father Carbon's words still rang in his ear. They hurt but did not shock him. He had known all along that it was inevitable. By this time, his suffering had trained him in the art of gentle surrender, an inner readiness to accept everything from God's hand. What next? Would he leave this holy quiet and return to the turmoil of the city, there to seek a pathway in which to walk and grow old and die? He did not know. His faith was ready for anything now.

News of the decision leaked out. It went the rounds quickly and silently by means of that marvelously efficient system of communication which only seminarians know. Faculty and students watched unobtrusively for some reaction, but the only thing they saw was an imperturbable peace which, under the circumstances, truly amazed them. How could such a man be turned out of doors to make his way alone? Some other solution just had to be found. In the end, they told him to go out to the Solitude. The bursar there needed someone to help him with the little odd jobs around the house. Father Carbon himself came to bring the good news and, through a haze of tears, Francis thanked him heartily.

CHAPTER EIGHT

AN ELITE

Libermann went to work as soon as he settled down in the house on the hill. There was plenty to do. Landscaping and gardening were his first assignment. Then he began to run errands, first for Father Mollevaut, the novice master, and later for the whole household. He did the shopping, went in for the mail, took things to be repaired, and did a host of chores with a willing smile. As a matter of fact, he was constantly on the go between Issy and Paris. Sometimes he missed the midday meal, and when he did, he simply stopped in the kitchen and picked up a piece of stale bread. His care and astuteness in carrying out business transactions in town gained him quite a reputation and the delighted seminarians began to joke with him good-humoredly about the special ability of his race in commercial affairs. Behind it all, Providence knew that this sort of training would later stand him in good stead when he was called upon to organize and consolidate important works in the Church.

But the epilepsy held on. "He never spoke about it," reports a friend, "except to help someone else who was suffering too. Once he told me, 'I suffer an awful lot; it feels like something were torturing me and tearing my insides apart. It's frightfully painful.' And while he was saying this, the lines on his face showed clearly that he was enduring unbearable distress."[1] Moreover, the illness often left his speech impaired and confused. Some of the more callous seminarians referred to the condition as a kind of insanity.

Worse still, his hypersensitivity inclined him to react on the natural plane with fiery impatience and even with violence. It was

[1] N. D. 1, 299.

grace alone that gave him the power to master both his emotions and his affliction. As another contemporary observed: "When you saw the terrific emotion that shot right through him and the continual calmness, poise, and earnestness that characterized him, you easily realized how much violence it took to give himself entirely to God."[2] Another analysis bears out the same point: "It always seemed to me and to everyone else who knew him that he was naturally sincere, openhearted, and highly considerate, but that he was also temperamentally sensitive and quick-tempered. Time and again you could see him fighting to control his natural tendencies. Sometimes his explosive character made him react too quickly to a situation and he showed it momentarily, but a second later shame and self-mastery took command."[3]

At all times, the undercurrent of his soul was suffering — the suffering of loneliness, of failure, of nervous affliction that held out no hope. Discouragement sometimes overwhelmed him. Depression overpowered him and gave him no peace. It pursued him on the road to Issy and on the boulevards of Paris. Most of all, when he crossed the Seine, it plagued him mercilessly. Those dark flowing waters possessed a strange attraction for him. Their siren call floated up from under the majestic arches of the bridge: "Come, lose yourself in our embrace. Be done with this unbearable life for once and for all." At such times, his muscles would grow taut as the temptation swept over him to scale the balustrade and let himself fall into the merciful river, ending this inhuman existence and ceasing at last to be a burden to himself and others.

In these black moments, the flame of faith seemed to die. He wanted to believe, he did believe, but it was all he could do to force his leaden feet ahead and hurry across the mesmerizing span. Once on the other side, he breathed normally again. The crisis had passed. But he subsequently confessed that he never crossed one of those bridges without feeling the diabolic urge to cast himself over the parapet into the waters below. It was an inward terror that reared its ugly head unexpectedly even in the confines of his room, gripping his soul so cruelly that he dared not keep a knife or other sharp object within reach.

---

[2] N. D. 1, 303.
[3] N. D. 1, 307.

To make matters worse, the inner consolations that sustained him in the years immediately following his baptism now began to diminish. That wonderful spiritual joy was disappearing. In the memory of previous happiness, his present experiences seemed all the more bitter. He had arrived at the stage of purification, of interior aridity, during which God slowly slips the last support from under every great mystic and strengthens him for the final flight.

Cholera swept over Paris in March, 1832. It lasted seven months and exacted a toll of twenty thousand deaths. More than anything else, the city needed courageous men who were willing to risk infection in caring for the sick and burying the dead. All the seminarians at St. Sulpice volunteered and the rector sent their names to the Department of Public Health. Thirty of them were accepted, the rest were sent home and the seminary was temporarily converted into an emergency hospital.

At long last, when the epidemic subsided, this once peaceful house of studies found that politics and illness had shattered its quiet routine. The forced dispersal of students during the plague had brought them more closely in touch with public affairs. Political changes and social rumblings caused violent reactions in the minds of some of them. They developed a passionate interest in France's mission among nations, and their zeal for the things of the spirit slackened alarmingly. A number had to be dismissed. For the rest, a program of reform, of renewed fervor, was clearly indicated.

Libermann, a humble domestic at Issy, was gradually drawn into the movement of restoration. People still came to discuss their spiritual life with him. Formerly he had spoken in generalities. Now he addressed himself specifically to the individual problem at hand and offered precise suggestions for its resolution. In May of that year, he had already urged Samson to think things out through meditation. Next came de Conny, a seminarian who asked Francis to make a thorough analysis of his state of soul. This resulted in a detailed description of de Conny's faults and an indication of the results that could flow from them. The amazed seminarian wrote later: "He realized what was going on within me and what the outcome might be, and he knew this better than I would ever have discovered."[4]

When they asked him at the seminary what he thought was the

[4] N. D. 1, 401.

best way to bring about a renewal of fervor, he inspired everyone present by his ensuing conversation. Even before he had left St. Sulpice, a small coterie of students had gathered around him to discuss ascetical matters, the priesthood, and the apostolate. Results had been so gratifying that Francis spoke to his former collaborators about doing something similar at Issy. After preliminary discussions, they decided to organize a new group. It was to be modeled on the Confraternity of the Sacred Heart for which Francis had already written a special rule.

Before he set about these activities at Issy, however, he experienced some misgivings about his worthiness and went to discuss the matter with his confessor, Father Mollevaut. Surprisingly enough, Mollevaut urged him to go ahead prudently with his organization. As things developed, the other priests on the staff were sharply divided in their opinion regarding Libermann's activities. Some favored what was going on, others vehemently opposed it. One of these opponents, Father Pinault, condemned it roundly. He was a particularly competent man whose spirit of deep faith and whose well-balanced judgment were universally respected.

One day, Francis accompanied Father Pinault on the way back from Paris. Conversation came around to the seminary and the need for a renewal of its spirit. Once it appeared that God's moment had arrived, Libermann launched into a lively discussion of his aims and ideas. As the story unfolded, the priest began to see that God was with this frail Jewish seminarian. By the end of the trip he had been completely won over. The experience changed him for life. Much later, they spoke of him as one who was a great admirer of Libermann and who, twelve years after the event, "seemed to have changed completely into a totally different man in whose words and deeds one could easily recognize his model. Everyone used to say that Libermann was living in him and still speaking through his lips."[5]

After Francis had explained to Father Pinault his plan to unite the more fervent seminarians into an unobtrusive nucleus of idealism and ardor, it was presented to the Superior General of the Sulpicians and to the rector of the seminary. They accepted it with silent reserve. It might do some good, they felt, but there would be concomitant difficulties. At all events, he was authorized to proceed.

[5] N. D. 1, 310.

Calling into play his great talent for organization and his keen sense of diplomacy, he carefully undertook the project.

It was in the prosecution of this work that Francis gradually learned how to conduct successful conversations on spiritual affairs. Later he would make ample use of that knowledge in the apostolic and ascetic doctrine that was so widely disseminated through his letters, instructions, and conferences. As a matter of fact, subsequent developments in Catholic Action cells and Legion of Mary praesidia were to use his technique with dramatic success.

Despite his precautions, the difficulties foreseen by the Superior General and Father Garnier began to arise. Less prudent members of these little bands found it hard to control their youthful zeal and here and there some noticeably violent efforts were made toward sanctity. Sometimes results were more amusing than edifying and the ensuing criticism indirectly affected the whole group. Moreover, nonmembers demanded of these neophytes a perfection they had only begun to aim at. Each petty fault was branded as a scandal on the part of those youngsters who loved to speak about holiness so much that their words flew ahead of their deeds.

Soon the opposition swung its guns from the activity itself to the young convert who had instigated it. While they admired his considerate charity and his religious conviction, they felt that such conduct in a seminarian was contrary to the traditional way of doing things. They feared he would bring on serious division in the student body. Mr. Gardereau, who later became a Benedictine, felt it his duty in conscience to openly combat the new movement. He and his sympathizers fought Libermann vigorously.

The type of life espoused by critics of this type is one that has been determined long before by fixed norms and simple rules of conduct in which a good deal of general experience has been crystallized. Such rules are followed unquestioningly and are imposed on others by well-meaning but not always intelligent minds that often lack the gift of careful observation and the knack of adjustment to particular situations. They lack perception and are powerless to assess intuitively the value of those exceptional developments that sometimes manifest themselves even within a closed community. They take as their unfailing guidepost the motto, "It has always been done that way," and this stultifying blind attachment to tradition replaces a reflective, open mind.

Limitations of this nature can remain hidden for a long time. Those who rule in such fashion may appear to be successful administrators, but their success will vanish on the day when a talented person like a saint, an artist, or a richly endowed intellect invades their peaceful domain. Gifted personalities do not always fit into the categories prescribed by rules and regulations. They often walk spontaneously outside the beaten track on pathways of their own, and they upset the comfortable mediocrity of those who hide their weakness in the apparent strength of antiquated formalism, and they annoy people whose scheme of things has no place for someone or something that was not foreseen by neat white patterns laid down in the sweet long ago. That is what made Libermann say at a later date: "These days, the education of seminarians must be totally different from the methods in vogue before the Revolution of 1793. Experience shows that the old approach is now no longer applicable."[6]

We do not by any means wish to imply that inner circles in a seminary are commendable or even tolerable under ordinary circumstances. They are all the more dangerous when one of the seminarians themselves has organized and led these groups, for everyone is agreed that a student in training does not usually possess the ability, the mature wisdom, and the special grace that spiritual guidance requires. Indeed, some time after Libermann's departure from the seminary, his own groups had to be disbanded, because his successors lacked these qualifications and therefore disrupted the good order of the house. It is easy to understand, therefore, the reaction of those well-meaning antagonists who objected to Francis' program while he was there, but it is equally easy to marvel at the unusual perspicacity of the rector and his staff. Despite student opposition, and contrary to accepted procedure, the governing body of the seminary voted against a small minority of their own number to give Libermann permission to carry on his work.

Francis continued the way he had begun. Out of his great respect for the science of theology, he submitted his little essays on the

[6] N. D. 12, 525.

spiritual life to the judgment of experts in the field. Then he proceeded with his task, binding more and more hearts to Christ and leaving many unforgettably impressed. "His piety was devoid of all artificiality and tension. It was vital, practical, and never exaggerated, always based on sound theology, of which he had a thorough mastery, and on the example of Our Lord and His Saints."[7]

Among the opposing seminarians, a certain Mr. Maigna now took up the cudgels. He used every occasion to make Francis appear ridiculous and he did his best to arouse as many seminarians as possible against him. One day, Libermann was looking for a place at table in the refectory. The chair next to Maigna was vacant and he took it. Maigna contorted his face in mock despair and the other seminarians snickered knowingly. They were all aware of the antipathy which existed in that quarter and they watched eagerly for the scene to develop. Maigna did not fail them. He turned on Libermann and snarled, "If you only knew how I despise you!" The cruelty of it was more than the seminarians had hoped for. They held their breath for the rejoinder while Francis mustered up a smile. "If you only knew how much I like you," he answered.

No bully can maintain his self-assurance in the face of so much poise. Maigna began to ask himself where this young invalid got his imperturbability. The question gave him no peace. After dinner he resolved to see Francis and find out. He conveyed this information to one of his friends and everyone standing around burst out laughing. When he came back beaming, he announced: "Now I know what it is. 'The peace of God that surpasseth all understanding.' I want that peace. From now on I'm going to search for it."

All his friends had another good laugh. They thought he was making fun of Francis again. But somehow it did not look that way any more. There was a new ardor in his eyes and he kept saying over and over again: "The peace of God that surpasseth all understanding." After a while they agreed that Maigna was "getting queer." The fact of the matter was Maigna had at last found the road to interior life. He began to moderate his excessive enthusiasm for the natural sciences and, instead of drawing geometrical figures on the palm of his hand during visits to the Blessed Sacrament, he now did his best to pray. Thereafter, he listened attentively when Francis

[7] N. D. 1, 305.

spoke and in almost every subsequent recreation period he brought an additional hearer. When the old concierge took sick, it was Maigna who stayed up whole nights with him. Soon afterward he himself grew ill and when he died at home they learned through the papers left behind in his room that he had practiced severe mortifications.

Maigna's earlier preoccupation with science was not exceptional. There were a number of students in the seminary who were so much carried away by academic zeal that they grossly neglected their spiritual development. It was all part of the feverish eagerness for invention and discovery that captivated Europe in the early nineteenth century. One can readily understand how the best and quickest minds in the house were inflamed by the new knowledge and the fanatical faith in progress which animated contemporary thought. Yet faith in human achievement seemed to throttle faith in other values. Francis did his best through conversation and correspondence to preserve both zeal for studies and zeal for holiness. Both were important. Both were priestly. It is not the cleric's vocation to reject modern advances. He must assimilate and Christianize these new discoveries and developments, and before he can do that he must achieve a knowledge of modern science on the one hand, and on the other, grow in personal sanctity and such mastery of theology that all earthly things are put in their proper place in the scale of values.

For this reason we find him repeatedly urging the students to apply themselves to their studies, but not so as to divorce themselves from God. "We must study," he said. "We must study all the subjects in our curriculum, but we must put our trust in God alone. We shouldn't allow our hearts to become tied up in the sciences. God wants us to study. He wants us to study with every ounce of energy and attention. But we've got to study in view of God and solely for love of Him."[8] Later on, he composed an examination of conscience for his friend de Conny, in which he explicitly pointed out the dangers of intellectual laziness. Among possible faults, he listed "mental sloth in putting one's hand to the task, lack of application, discouragement in the face of academic difficulties."[9] His own great penetrating mind, his sure insight and sound

[8] N. D. 1, 279.
[9] N. D. 1, 401.

judgment had been developed through proper application, for he practiced what he preached, studying with a quiet concentration that allowed free play of the faculties and with a purity of intention that never threatened perfect union with God.

Another sign of his growing maturity at this time was his recognition of the fact that decorum in dress and conduct were essential for a representative of the Church. He repeatedly urged the seminarians to watch their appearance, to avoid slovenliness of dress, and to observe the rules of decency and etiquette at all times.

Now once again, summer was climbing the hill of Issy. A spotless expanse of sky was stretching over it and over the little village that lay at its foot. The tempo of seminary life picked up. It seemed happier, gayer, and Francis shared the general jubilation. He showed it in his reply to a seminarian who had sought guidance for the holidays. "How should you spend your vacation? Joyfully! Get a good deal of rest, relax with games, hiking, and amusements, but don't lose sight of the fact that God alone must possess all our love. Once that is assured, we can let ourselves go, relaxing and having fun unconcernedly and without the least bit of self-consciousness, for if we really love God we can do anything with a light heart. You know the words of St. Augustine very well: 'Love and then do what you please.' "[10]

This particular summer marked another decisive milestone in his life. A friend of Father Mollevaut, Father Louis, was energetically working toward a restoration of the religious Society of St. John Eudes, a clerical congregation that had for its purpose the conduct of home missions and the direction of seminaries. After the Revolution, most of its members were dead and the rest seemed hopelessly scattered. The few survivors who could be located were now old men and they showed little interest in the projected restoration because they had become involved in other ecclesiastical positions and responsibilities. The future of the Eudists could hardly be termed encouraging at this point.

One of their number, Father Blanchard, had saved his neck by fleeing to Spain during the Revolution. At the age of seventy, he had now succeeded in bringing together several of his dispersed confreres — five old men and Father Louis — and after the meeting

[10] L. S. 1, 110.

in which they chose Blanchard as Superior General, all the electors but Father Louis withdrew to the security of their current posts, leaving the General with only a paper army. When Father Blanchard died in 1830, the Society had only six younger members. Under the pressure of circumstances, forty-year-old Father Louis succeeded to the generalate. It was then that he turned to his old friend in the Sulpicians, Father Mollevaut. He had succeeded in opening a novitiate at Antrain, north of Rennes, and was looking for a competent novice master. He had already tried Father Lucas, whom people regarded as a saint because of his seeming recollection, but it turned out that much of Father Lucas' otherworldly appearance was accounted for by incurable absentmindedness. He proved to be quite incapable of arousing interest in his charges and failed to achieve the careful surveillance that a novitiate requires.

Father Mollevaut pondered the request for a long while before making his recommendation. He mentally reviewed the religious he knew and the priests whom he had encountered. Which one of them was equipped for the task of guiding the novices of a newly restored Congregation? Who was it that could understand their problems, analyze their state of mind, help in the solution of their difficulties, and direct them in the way that best suited their individual personalities? Through all this questioning the name and face of Francis Libermann kept reasserting themselves in his thoughts. There seemed to be no one else who would exercise as much personal magnetism and supernatural influence over young minds, no one who had such a profound insight into the mysterious workings of the human heart.

But Francis was not a priest. He was an epileptic seminarian who had just finished theology and could go no further. Father Mollevaut kept putting the idea aside until he no longer had an alternative. At first, Father Louis raised his eyebrows at the proposal, but as Mollevaut's glowing description continued, it began to look more plausible to this hard-pressed superior of the Eudists. In fact, he began to think of the benefits that might accrue to his society if Francis chose to join it. With growing enthusiasm, he concurred with his friend's nomination.

Francis himself, when the news broke, was astonished. With his thoroughgoing simplicity, however, he quickly aligned himself with the apparent will of God. Deep down inside he could not help thinking how strange it was that he should be chosen for the weighty task, but when one is living off the charity of another, it ill behooves him to question the judgment of his host. The proposal had its pleasant side, of course. Two aspects made it particularly attractive: the promise of quiet and solitude far from the bustling streets of Paris where his errands took him all too frequently, and the prospect of kindling a flame of spiritual fervor in the young novices that would be entrusted to his care.

Before his departure for Antrain, Libermann had a supremely happy experience. He had been praying every day for the conversion of his brothers and sisters. Samson and Felix, both Catholic already, joined him in these prayers. They concentrated particularly on David, because he had lost his Jewish faith and was planning to go off to America that very year. One can imagine their jubilation, then, when they heard that David had at last promised to be baptized, before sailing. Francis wrote the glad tidings to his little niece, Mary:

> Dear little girl, I have good news for you. I'm sure it will make you very happy. Remember how irreligious your Uncle David was? When he came to Illkirch he never wanted to go to church. We couldn't get him to pray to the Good Lord and he always wanted to eat meat on Friday.
>
> You didn't like him and the only reason why you didn't was because he did these things. Last vacation we spent eight days together at home. They tried everything to get him to say the rosary and all those nice little kids were constantly after him to say grace before meals. Nothing did any good. He kept on being bad and nobody could make him serve or pray to God. Dad and Mother and I felt very sorry about it. We prayed a lot for him and now the Good Lord has heard our prayer. He was converted before he left to join Uncle Alphonse in America.[11]

David was sailing off to the new world just when Francis started for Antrain. Both brothers were striking out into the great unknown.

---

[11] L. S. 1, 268 f.

CHAPTER NINE

DARKNESS

Libermann left for Rennes during the summer holidays of 1837 and a few seminarians went with him. Since he did not officially take on his new responsibilities until November, he used the intervening weeks to familiarize himself with the works of St. John Eudes so that he might give the novices a clear idea of their founder's spirit.

Before long, without being aware of it himself, Francis created a deep impression on his surroundings. Even the students in the Eudist college next door felt the influence of his personality. Nearly everybody liked him, for he was always ready to listen to their problems and give them the full attention which people in trouble need so badly. "He was so easy to approach, so soft-spoken, and so genuinely kind, that he put people at their ease at once and gained their confidence."[1]

Even though engrossed in a host of personal relations, he retained and increased that natural business acumen which had been so much in evidence when he was helping the bursar at Issy. His interests in the material welfare of the little Eudist community reached surprising lengths. For instance, we find him writing to Alsace and asking Samson for high-quality vegetable seeds. He wanted a good garden and a good table. At the same time, his letter writing developed into a correspondence of considerable magnitude. As many as twenty-five or thirty envelopes came in one mail, each of them containing involved questions and requests for guidance in the spiritual life. Uncomplainingly, he replied to every one

[1] N. D. 1, 352.

of them with a personal attention that brought deep satisfaction to the recipient.

His judgments about others were stamped with the same respectful charity that made him see some good in everyone. A faculty member from the seminary at Nantes once asked him about the Jansenists, a group of rigorists that plagued France in those days. As a result, Libermann found himself forced to speak about certain suspect priests. Then he quickly added: "But let's not offend against charity . . . , let's not condemn them in our hearts or be unkind in our thoughts about them."[2] "No matter how much I hate to do so, I have to tell you the names of those professors. . . . Please be prudent . . . lest charity suffer. Don't take my word for it and don't do anything simply because of my misgivings."[3] In all this, one senses the struggle of a man who wanted to do his duty but feared to harm anyone else in the process.

He was surprisingly well aware of what was going on. Charity never blinded him to the facts. Once he was put under obligation to state the case as he saw it, he did so uncompromisingly. Thus, when he was asked to evaluate an apparently Jansenistic secretary of the Bishop of Vannes, Libermann wrote with utter candor about the young man, listing all his faults in detail. Francis did not feel hampered by the thought, which could easily have entered a less God-centered soul, that he would perhaps be failing in charity. The energetic and incisive side of his character then came out when unhesitatingly he indicated the line of action ecclesiastical authorities ought to take for the welfare of the Church and the benefit of the individuals involved in the case.

Throughout the winter, he would sit at a table in the front of the little conference hall while the novices worked at their desks. His pen raced interminably over the paper in a constant effort to overtake the mounting pile of correspondence. Now and then a chair creaked as someone moved uneasily and soon a troubled novice or postulant would hesitantly come forward. This sort of thing happened scores of times. In each instance, Francis would look up from the sentence he had just begun and flash a welcoming smile that signaled his readiness to help. One of the novices, Mr. Mangot,

[2] N. D. 1, 538.
[3] N. D. 1, 541.

asked him if these constant interruptions and the pressure of his occupations did not militate against his union with God. "Not at all," Libermann replied. "They have just the opposite effect. I turn to God for help every time a new problem arises. As a result, the more I have to do, the more frequent are my contacts with God."[4]

During a passing conversation with one of his novices, Francis once remarked that it was a great pity so many spiritual advisers started off with cold theorizing. Without any of the love that should first enliven the soul, they seemed to proceed from the beginning with mechanical routines. No doctor would ever think of prescribing a course of therapy unless he had previously diagnosed the patient's condition, but these people seemed to dispense their ascetical formulary with high disdain for individual needs. Libermann's approach was anything but tailor-made. With marvelous empathy, he penetrated the very core of another's being and, in the light of the Holy Spirit, he saw that person's weaknesses. Then he moved with decisive kindness to adjust himself to the individual character and temperament involved so that proper remedies might be gently and respectfully applied. In fact, this respect for another's personality was the hallmark of his direction.

Throughout his life this amazing dualism persisted: first the keen sympathy, the fear of hurting, the dread of making a wrong approach; and then the strong, calm, realistic decision. Any time he was called to execute that decision himself, he carried it out with massive determination even though his emotional make-up rebelled ever so strongly against the dictates of his practical insight. His realism and his existential attitude found expression also in the rules he laid down for the novices to follow when they were teaching catechism to the children of Rennes. Since they are illustrative of the pedagogical principles that run through all his writings, it may be of value to pause and consider them here. Like his teaching on correct behavior and good manners, they embody both natural and supernatural considerations. At bottom, Francis was opposed to one-sided and rigid intellectualism. He never excluded the intuitive approach and one wonders if this might not be due, in part at least, to those years in Metz when his mind unlocked to the riches of western thought and authors like Rousseau opened wide

[4] N. D. 1, 521.

new vistas. He urged the novices not to be satisfied with imparting their doctrine scientifically. Rather, they should put those doctrines into daily practice in their own lives and strive to translate mere information into vital application. He wanted them to teach what they lived and felt so that their pupils would live and feel it too.

"It is not enough," he wrote, "to give them a nicely correct and well-planned lesson. You should also inflame your hearers with religious inspiration. [On the other hand] it doesn't suffice to adopt a tone of enthusiastic conviction. The lesson should also be accurate, meaty, well arranged, clearly formulated, and pointed to the capacity of the children's minds." Above all, there should be a personal interest in the little ones. "We should deal with them very gently and with unfailing kindness. We should make use of every available means to get their interest and attract their attention to the matter at hand."[5]

Later, we find him extending these principles to teaching in general. He warns especially against that curious sort of supernaturalism that expects divine inspiration to replace proper academic preparation. "[Professors] should prepare their classes with the utmost care and take advantage of whatever their wisdom suggests to make the student advance in the particular subject they teach. . . . They must avoid treating the students unkindly, or speaking harshly to them, or committing other mistakes that stem from excessive severity. They ought to be self-controlled and considerate, always demonstrating that, within the bounds of strictness and kindness, they are deeply interested in the students' progress."[6]

Libermann's was a pedagogy of love and respect for the human personality even when things went wrong. "One should rarely resort to punishment," he maintained. "Punishment is in order only when every other means has failed. At such times, the reprimand should be public if the fault was public, and private if the recalcitrance is not generally known. In this way, one will lead his pupils more through love than through fear. Under no circumstances should students be struck, or kicked, or subjected to any other bodily injury. Nor should there ever be question of scathing personal insults. If punishments must be meted out, let them be just."[7] In an

[5] N. D. 1, 552. [6] N. D. 1, 556 f. [7] N. D. 1, 557.

era of crotchety and often muscular schoolmasters, these were strangely temperate words indeed.

In the rules given above one will again detect that ever present concern for courtesy and politeness, for delicacy in dealing with others, for moderation and good order. It carried over into the regulations he set down for the novices to follow when they met to discuss their catechetical methods and achievements: "Speak only when your turn comes around. Of course, a passing comment on what has just been said is perfectly permissible, but even that should be made with polite reserve. Under no circumstances should you interrupt or attack anyone. When you make an observation, do it without bitterness, antagonism, or exaggerated self-esteem. Never ridicule another and do not cling stubbornly to your opinions. Say your piece quietly, charitably, simply, and modestly. When a group decision is arrived at, adjust yourself to it even if it is contrary to your own ideas."[8]

Francis was a gentleman in the best sense of the word and he refused to tolerate any form of asceticism that brushed aside even the minor prescriptions of etiquette and good form. He tartly observed that some people confuse carelessness with holy simplicity. "Such persons," he said, "rather enjoy being crude and vulgar and they gravitate toward others who are equally ill-mannered. They don't care what people think about them, but this indifference is based solely on their inclination toward rudeness. They are quite content as long as they are allowed to give free rein to their low and uncouth tendencies. All this stems either from bad habits acquired in childhood, or from their peculiar twist of mind, or from a lack of training."[9]

With his usual concern for avoiding extremes, however, Libermann cautioned his charges against the dangers of foppishness and dandyism. He inveighed against make-believe gentility that shrouds a lack of respect and considerateness with a semblance of deference, and covers insincerity with a veneer of culture. Once he told a priest: "If you cringe before the world, if you flatter it, or if you merely ape its manner, you may be sure that your priestly work will be sterile. Don't be afraid of the world. Approach it as one

---

[8] N. D. 1, 553.

[9] N. D. 1, 588.

who belongs wholly to God. Face it without fear. Do not stop to consider what people will say or think about you. The world's judgments have little effect on a true priest."[10]

Around this time also, Francis began to diagnose other manifestations of unhealthy spirituality. He encountered several overly conscientious people who feared to choose as their spiritual director anyone who inspired in them any sort of natural admiration and affection. "I am far from opposed to such a choice," he wrote. "In fact, I believe it may have been really the good Lord who brought about this natural attraction. Admittedly, you may have become aware of his desirability as a director only after you had observed his even disposition and his great kindness, but that is no reason for saying that your selection is based on insufficient and purely natural grounds."[11]

The same reassurance was given to those who tended to avoid the vice of pride by going to the opposite extreme and seeking humility in an almost pathological fear of excellence in any form. "There is nothing wrong," he maintained, "in admiring, loving, and striving after that which is excellent. God has implanted that tendency in our nature so that we would ordinate all things toward Him in whom every perfection resides."[12] Then the encouraging tone continues: "When someone comes to the door of your room, don't wonder nervously if he has permission to do so. That's none of your business. If anyone stops you in the corridor during a period of silence, answer him calmly and kindly, but do it quickly and in businesslike fashion. Above all, make sure that you don't yield to anxiety."[13] Those who feared that catechism teaching might disturb their recollection were urged to relax. "Put your trust in Our Lord and don't worry about doing anything but His holy will. That should encourage you, for He will help you. I am firmly convinced that you should not neglect your lesson-preparation. On the contrary, give due attention to your work. In general, we ought to set out to do everything as well as we can for the love and glory of God. If you rely too much on a spirit of 'holy indifference' in your work, you run the chance of giving in to laxity, laziness, and self-delusion."

[10] L. S. 1, 41.
[11] N. D. 1, 377.
[12] N. D. 1, 580.
[13] N. D. 1, 439.

"When you write something," he went on, "don't ignore style entirely. Here is what you should do: set down the ideas as they come and don't worry about beauty or effectiveness of expression at this point. Simply try to get on paper the way you see things. Afterwards, remain in the presence of God and re-read what you have written, correct stylistic errors that have crept in through carelessness, and then relax. But, my friend, beware of self-conscious rhetoric and do not indulge in turgid figures. Be yourself at all times and you will see how easy and forceful your style will become."[14]

His great common sense thus led him to reject that exaggerated romanticism which plagued so many of his contemporaries and cast the pall of its sickly sentimentality over many of the artistic productions of his age. His rules are widely applicable: express yourself simply and avoid undue attention to refinement; concentrate on the idea, on what you have felt inside you, and then proceed to give it form and substance without being preoccupied with the process. Under these conditions, if the person involved is an artist, what he produces will be artistic. If he is not an artist, he will at least give honest adequate expression to his inner experience without trying to scale heights that are ridiculously unattainable for him.

This urge to cultivate what was authentic, true, and sincere served him in good stead in guiding others. He ripped the mask from egocentricity and distinguished sharply between pseudovirtue and real holiness. In a little essay on humility, for instance, he outlines in vigorous strokes the self-love that sometimes prompts one to adopt retiring poses and then derive satisfaction from his apparent simplicity. "Such people say and do humble things and conduct themselves in humble ways. They think that makes them humble and they are even quite proud of their humility."[15]

Nor did he confuse timidity with humility. He was naturally timid himself. In fact, a shadow of the scared child of Saverne remained with him all his life. But that did not prevent him from wielding the blade of objective analysis. "Timidity stems from weakness of character. It is a far cry from the virtue of humility. It actually goes back to a fear of disapproval. . . . When anyone contradicts a timid person, he promptly agrees, not from humility but because he

[14] N. D. 1, 451. [15] N. D. 1, 585.

lacks courage. Some of them scarcely dare to speak for fear that they may say something unacceptable."[16] Obviously, there is a certain measure of autobiography in these lines. It is all the more amazing, then, that under the mighty inspiration of grace he was able to counteract the handicaps of temperament and early training to become so strong and forceful as the years went on.

In the novitiate at Antrain, things were beginning to go badly. The Congregation of the Eudists found the road to restoration exceedingly rough. Father Louis had hoped for a return to the traditional work in home missions and seminary teaching, but other institutes appeared to have moved in before him. Though he scoured the countryside, he could not seem to unearth anything that his men might do. Finances suffered and the morale of his group dropped alarmingly. Unlike Libermann, the Eudists found it impossible to proceed quietly about their business when the future was so indefinite, and general insecurity was not long in invading the novitiate.

Then conflicts arose over the internal administration of the house. Francis was naturally anxious to maintain an atmosphere of quiet and prayerful recollection in the novitiate. This was the seedtime. Without a process of ingestion, these men would have no store of holiness from which to share the riches of grace with others later on. But Father Louis had his own worries. Promotion of the Society and increased financial income — both so necessary for survival — required greater activity on the part of his men. He took on work for them in the neighborhood and absenteeism from the novitiate increased apace. Moreover, he recommended that the novices give conferences to each other.

Still another difficulty came to the fore. Francis, though not a priest himself, had to direct novices who had already received the priesthood or were very near it. This responsibility for ordained ministers of God weighed heavily upon him. With things so uncertain in the newly restored Congregation and with so much outside interference, he was often reluctant to make decisions. It was so easy to do lasting harm under these circumstances.

His apprehension was fully justified. One evening he gave a conference on the dangers that face a priest living in the world. Despite

[16] N. D. 1, 586 f.

his limited practical experience with such matters, he expressed himself rather strongly on the subject. Some of the novices disagreed with him and told him so later. He listened to their criticism humbly and attentively, fully aware of his limitations. He was not at all surprised that he had made a mistake. What really grieved him, however, was the thought that he might have hurt someone. At the beginning of the next conference, therefore, he said the prayer as usual and then, still on his knees and with tears in his eyes, he asked his audience to forgive him for any disedification he might have given by his previous remarks.

The strained relations with Father Louis would have made life painful enough, but now Libermann found his discomfort intensified by troublesome novices as well. Ironically, one of the most annoying was Mr. de Brandt, a former leader in his "bands of devotion" at Issy. Francis had been counting on de Brandt to exercise a profound influence for good on the novices around him. Instead, the lad seemed to grow more hateful and rebellious with each passing day. Worst of all, he struck up a close friendship with Mr. Dupeloux, a young novice to whose spiritual formation Libermann meant to devote special care. The problem grew into a persistent worry that tortured the novice master night and day. At last he wrote to Father Carron at St. Sulpice and asked for help.

"This cross," he confessed, "has weighed me down for the last three months. I held off speaking to you about it for fear that I might just be looking for human consolation. The problem involves that little devil Mr. de Brandt. For the last three months he's been in a dreadful state. Imagine the most dissipated, nasty, proud, and malicious seminarian you can think of and you'll have a picture of this poor fellow. His obstreperousness and ill-will are so bad that I've never encountered anything like it. I don't know where to turn. I can't make any impression on him. He's conceived a mortal hatred and profound contempt for me. He doesn't keep any of the rules and he's thoroughly recalcitrant. From dawn to dusk he seems to think about nothing but wickedness. During spiritual exercises he sleeps or laughs or disturbs everybody else by acting up. He often carries on in front of the Blessed Sacrament. Now he's developed a close friendship with Dupeloux — a most unfortunate thing, because he's ruining the boy. The relationship is strong and characteristic, but it is really diabolical and arises out of pure malice. . . . It's really terrifying the way de Brandt makes him share his hatred for me.

"Blessed be the Lord. I'm willing to take the beating. Admittedly, there are times when it's almost unbearable, but I bless the Holy Name. . . .

"Mr. de Brandt's mood is actually devilish. I had a little hope at first, but for some time now things have deteriorated and intensified. At first he kicked up only once in a while and at least there were short intervals of decency; now it's continuous. . . . I believe his nerves are affected and his physical condition is involved. In other words, I can't see any answer to his problem from now on."[17]

On top of all these cares, Libermann's sickness contributed its own share of violence. The gray mist of confusion and uncertainty around him closed in on his soul and robbed his prayer of all joy and satisfaction. Things had looked so hopeful at first. The epilepsy abated enough to lead him to believe that he might be ordained after all, and his apparent uselessness vanished in the tangible service he was rendering to the Eudists. But everything seemed to be taking a wrong turn again. He had dreamed optimistically of the peace and solitude he would find at the novitiate. Instead, insecurity and misunderstanding surrounded him everywhere. Worst of all, the air of tension and conflict that pervaded the house now took its toll on his health. It was ever thus. The horror of his old father's curse brought on the first seizure and thereafter any violent emotional strain had the same effect.

The novices began to notice how his illness was reasserting itself. It was painfully humiliating to see them glance at each other knowingly when he had to repeat a word several times before he could go on with the conference. Nervous facial contractions sometimes made it impossible for him to enunciate properly. On occasion he had to make as many as seven attempts before he got it out. He wondered what the novices thought, especially those who were disaffected. And suppose he should have an attack when they were around!

Quickly he made an act of faith and surrender to God's will. It would be all right if God wanted it so. His job was to be quiet and

[17] N. D. 1, 496 f.

peaceful. But suppose he were forever barred from the priesthood? Would life have no meaning for him? Would he be utterly useless? The dark wave of anxiety crept closer. Maybe his life had followed the wrong track. Was it not foolhardy for him to presume to direct priests and seminarians? Remember the biting criticisms and the harsh accusations some of them had leveled at him? And oddly enough in retrospect, those accusing and critical voices sounded so much like the voice of his father back in Saverne. They were right. He was wretched and sinful, rash and presumptuous. Remorse ate its way deeper and deeper.

In the midst of this inner tumult, it cost him tremendous effort to keep his supernatural calm. He began to fear for those whom he was directing and echoes of the struggle appear in his letters: "I want to draw your attention to the fact that I am still in the throes of that terrible anxiety in which it has pleased God to cast me. . . ."

"Do not pay too much heed to my great sadness and affliction. It's all due to my sins. They are more numerous than the hairs of my head."

"It's about two months now since I've been living in worry and anxiety."[18]

This was his night of the soul. He almost felt rejected by God, but he meekly and humbly bowed before Him as his people had done for centuries before the God of Israel. Childhood memories of the kings and prophets, punished and submissive, came flooding back. "There's nothing left for us to do," he wrote, "but bless the Lord for everything that He has done, for everything that He's doing each day, and for everything He will do through His infinite mercy for His wretched servants. They are not worthy that He look down upon them. Instead, He should chastise them and cast them out of His sight. His hand is constantly raised; I know that all too well. I see clearly and am convinced that I have done great harm to all the souls that it has pleased the Lord to put in touch with me."[19] This Hebraic outburst, so redolent of the Old Testament, portrays the depth of Libermann's melancholy at that time. Faith alone saved him from despair.

---

[18] L. S. 1, 505.
[19] L. S. 2, 46.

On the feast of the Holy Heart of Mary, Francis gave a conference to the superior, the community, and the novices. In the midst of it, with the whole house assembled before him, he fell heavily to the floor and lay there quivering pitifully for three-quarters of an hour. When the convulsions subsided, they picked him up carefully and carried him off to bed. After a long time he awoke with a deep-drawn sigh. The novice Mangot was standing beside him. "How do you feel?" he whispered. A wonderfully serene smile spread over the tortured features. Then he heard Libermann saying feebly: "The Good Lord wanted you to know what a wretched fellow you have as your director." It was a hollow sound that seemed to float upward from a bottomless ocean of sorrow.

CHAPTER TEN

THE DECISION

Through the intervening years, Francis had kept close touch with two Creole seminarians at St. Sulpice. The friendship started when he was there as a student himself. One of them, Frederic Le Vavasseur, had come from the Island of Reunion (Bourbon); the other was Eugene Tisserant, the son of a Parisian pharmacist and a Haitian general's daughter. The retiring Jew and the fiery Creoles made a strange combination, but their friendship was destined to last for life. Through the changing circumstances of the days to come, these two men would be at Libermann's side, now his strongest support and again his heaviest cross.

Frederic Le Vavasseur was born in Reunion on February 15, 1811. There had been almost no priests on the island since the Revolution and for the most part the French colonists could hardly be termed practicing Catholics. Le Vavasseur's own religious upbringing, then, left much to be desired. As a child, he gave evidence of a rather pleasant character, highly emotional but considerate enough to feel spontaneously sympathetic toward the slaves on his father's estate.

At the age of ten they sent him to school in the capital, St. Denis, and he did rather well for the first few years. Then as he developed into a temperamental teen-ager, he began to find the routine excessively monotonous. When some less sheltered classmates started taking him with them into town, he soon learned that dancing with the local girls involved considerably more charm than wrestling with a geometric theorem. It was not long before his teacher gave him up as hopeless.

Just then a priest arrived from France. He was Father Warnet, the future Superior General of the Holy Ghost Fathers. He immediately set about preparing the boys for their First Holy Communion. The instructions affected Frederic profoundly. With his usual reckless ardor, he now plunged into the practice of asceticism. In the retreat that preceded Holy Communion he maintained such absolute silence that he would not even speak to his mother. The poor lady was impressed no end and that confirmed him in his unbalanced pursuit of perfection. It even led him into a case of persistent scrupulosity.

After the great day, his demonstrative piety continued unabated. When he stayed at his grandmother's he shared a room with several cousins who were also schoolmates. They were amazed to see him crawl out of bed before dawn to go out in the woods and pray. At such times, he would become terribly wrought up trying to experience an emotional love for God. Moreover, when he prepared for confession, he would shut himself up in a room for hours on end, perusing pious books and doing his best to make actual tears flow in sorrow for his sins.

His completely irreligious father was mightily perturbed by all this nonsense and decided to put a stop to it. Unable to distinguish between the authentic and the specious elements in Frederic's piety, he moved to obliterate all such ideas from the youngster's mind once and for all. Accordingly, he sponsored a series of dances and parties for his son, but the poor boy did his best to avoid them. Instead, he preferred to spend his time instructing his personal servant in the elements of the faith and running off to distant parts of the plantation to baptize dying slaves.

Even the old grandfather seemed bent on torturing this scrupulous lad. When Frederic stayed with him he would take books down from his well-stacked shelves and ask his grandson to read aloud. Sometimes it would be a romantic novel, and when Frederic reached a love-scene he would stammer and blush and hurry on to less obnoxious parts of the text. Since novelists interlard their stories with generous quantities of such material, one can easily see that the young reader must have been in frequent agony.

When Frederic reached eighteen his father decided to send him to the *École Polytechnique* in Paris. Studies had been going a little better now, and the boy's proficiency in mathematics warranted an attempt at engineering. Old Le Vavasseur was not too particular as long as there was no question of the seminary. "Become what you like," he said in bidding farewell to his son. "Be anything at all — even a gangster — but whatever you do, don't become a priest."

Upon his arrival in Paris, the lad took up residence with Professor Millet at Versailles and on the very next day he attacked his studies in the same wildly passionate way he did everything else. He shut himself up in his room and never left his books except to go to class or down to meals. No one around him seems to have had the wisdom to curb either his unhealthy preoccupation with academic pursuits or his ill-advised practices of asceticism. Everyone stood by in breathless amazement, as if watching an acrobat on the flying trapeze and knowing that sooner or later he would come hurtling down. Before long, overwork brought on severe headaches. Then the whole episode came to a climax when he failed hopelessly in his courses. At that point, his confessor recommended that he join the famous Sister Rosalie who was then working so hard among the poor in Paris. During most of the ensuing year, therefore, Frederic tried to regain his physical and emotional health by assisting this remarkable woman in her far-flung charitable activities.

For some years, thoughts of the priesthood had been flitting through his mind. Each time they appeared, however, he thought of the uproar such a move would make at home and the idea would vanish quickly. Now the thoughts had fused into a desire, and the desire had grown swiftly in intensity. Not yet daring to write his parents, he went to Stanislas College and enrolled in the higher classical program there. Despite headaches that prevented his reading more than a page at a time and weakness that necessitated his leaving class for a breath of fresh air every half hour or so, Frederic resolutely pursued the course.

At last he wrote home and told them he wanted to be a priest. It was good timing. Just then his sister was engaged to marry a bright young man who was quite able to take over the management of the Le Vavasseur estate. Frederic was somewhat surprised, therefore, at the readiness with which his father granted permission. (It must be admitted, however, that the old man wept when he first saw him in a cassock.)

Frederic now began his philosophical studies at Issy and it was there he met Francis Libermann. Two more opposite temperaments can hardly be imagined, but Libermann soon recognized beneath the wild impassioned exterior of this Creole, a wealth of robust good will, a courageous spirit of sacrifice, and a fund of straightforward honesty. The maturity and masterful poise of the convert Jew quickly began to pervade Le Vavasseur's unbalanced character and bring peace to his troubled soul. Before long they were quite good friends, though their friendship was to run a stormy course. Frederic himself admitted candidly some years later: "I left the seminary with a feverish desire for the good, an exaggerated concept of perfection, a severity that was in absolute contrast to the virtues which seemed to constitute the very essence of our beloved Father's personality. In a word, I was at the opposite pole from him in the spiritual life."[1] These two men built their relationship on an electrical sort of attraction and, as might be expected, disturbances sometimes occurred.

Eugene Tisserant completed the triumvirate. On his mother's side, he was the grandson of General Bauvais, chief Brigadier of the Jacmel District in Haiti. General Bauvais devoted his life to fighting for interracial justice. Two other generals had charge of the rest of the island colony, and when civil war broke out between them, Bauvais refused to take sides. He packed up his family and left for France. On the way, a storm wrecked the ship and, since there was only one lifeboat, its occupants had to be chosen by lots. He and his children were among the lucky ones, but he forced his wife to take his place and then, as the dory pulled away, he stood on the deck waving his handkerchief till the ocean swallowed him from view. One of the daughters thus rescued grew up in Paris and married Mr. Tisserant, a druggist. Their son, Eugene, attended Charlemagne College, worked for a while in his father's pharmacy, and then entered the seminary of St. Sulpice.

Eugene Tisserant was far less impetuous than Frederic Le Vavasseur, but his resolve to work for the disenfranchised of this

[1] N. D. 3, 424.

earth was just as ardent. He had a great devotion to the Blessed Virgin Mary. In fact, he was one of the first to frequent the Parisian shrine of Our Lady of Victories. By strange coincidence, on February 2, 1839, both Tisserant and Le Vavasseur went there to see Father Desgenettes, the shrine director and the founder of the Archconfraternity of Our Lady of Victories. Each of them asked that he include the salvation of neglected souls in their respective countries among the intentions to be prayed for at the shrine. Father Desgenettes could not help being edified by the apostolic sincerity of the two young clerics. He brought them together and amazed them by explaining that they had been working, unknown to each other, toward the same objective.

The flame of enthusiasm leaped higher. Father Gallais, Le Vavasseur's confessor, did nothing to snuff it out. Then Libermann suggested that his old friend Father Pinault be consulted. The holy Sulpician listened, thought for a long time, and then suggested that it might be well to look toward the eventual formation of a religious society through which priest-members might labor for those neglected people in far-off places in whose welfare Tisserant and Le Vavasseur showed such interest.

Through all this, Francis Libermann stayed on the periphery of things, refusing to become involved. Frederic had gone to Rennes and spent a few weeks there scattering the sparks of his enthusiasm with wild abandon, but even when he guardedly suggested that potential missionaries like himself might wish to be trained by Francis in the Eudist novitiate, no apparent reaction was elicited. Libermann was not ready. The will of God had not yet made itself clear and until it did, no amount of persuasive eloquence would induce him to lift a finger. His father's unforgettable charity to any poor wayfarer inclined him to sympathize with the noble objectives of his friends, but they had specific goals — to work for the poor wretches of Haiti and Reunion — and his vision of the future lacked such precision.

Nothing daunted, Le Vavasseur flew on to the heights. With the same uncompromising drive that made him turn his back on the pleasures of social life when he made his First Holy Communion and impelled him to suicidal application when he decided to become a great Parisian scientist, Frederic now launched into plans for a religious congregation of priests that would save through prodigious ministry every last outcast on his native island. To his way of thinking, the life of these missionaries could not be too severe. They would have to practice the spirit of sacrifice and mortification to the hilt, making themselves subservient to the slaves and spurning worldly goods with eager abandon. They would organize as the Society of the Holy Cross and anyone who wished to join could make his novitiate with Libermann at Rennes.

Even when this terrible enthusiast came with a list of other seminarians who shared his zeal and wished to be counted in, Francis refused to budge. He knew of the plans and, while he did not reject them outright, he counseled moderation. Then, to avoid a needless dispersal of energy, he urged Tisserant to fall in with Frederic's proposal (at least for the beginning) rather than start a splinter movement of his own in behalf of Haiti. But all the while he kept looking for a sign that might point the way to God's will in his own regard. It did not appear.

He understood, of course, that very few would take Le Vavasseur seriously. The explosive Creole had many traits that would provide abundant source material for ridicule and criticism. Nonetheless, the light of grace kept reminding him that God calls whom He wants with little regard to even tempers and nicely balanced characters. The man thus chosen needs only to follow inspiration and brave the indignation or the laughter of those around him. *"Viriliter age et confortetur cor tuum"* [Act like a man and take courage, 1 Par. 28:20], Libermann wrote. "I hope the Lord will bring to realization the plan with which He has inspired you for His greater glory. . . . They will call you foolish, rash, and proud, and they will make countless other uncomplimentary remarks about you. Even fair-minded persons will regard the whole thing as the dream of a young enthusiast and they will insist that it cannot possibly be realized. . . . But even if the best and wisest people oppose it, carry on with the project as it is before God."[2]

Just about this time, Francis' problems at the novitiate were coming to a head. Suffering cruelly from a growing uncertainty and spiritual aridity, tortured by repeated clashes with Father Louis, and seriously disillusioned by some of the novices, he began

[2] N. D. 1, 638 f.

to wonder if he was in the right place. Here he was, an invalid permanently barred from the priesthood, nothing more than a sign-post to his charges and a questionable one at that. A feeling of uselessness began to gnaw at him. He felt like a corpse in a mausoleum, a corpse prematurely and unwillingly buried because an indefinable urge told him there was still work to do for God and souls. Perhaps the professors at St. Sulpice could help him. He took off for Paris during the holidays and sought their advice, but the trip was wasted. All of his old friends at the seminary welcomed him kindly, but no one could give him any clear direction. Tired, depressed, and ill, but fully resolved to surrender himself to God's good pleasure, he went back to Rennes to work and wait.

"The whole time I spent . . . at Rennes," he observed later, "was a period of misery and torment for me. . . . I spoke and taught and did my best to inspire fervor, but my words were dead. . . . During the first year that is what threw me off stride and confused me. The second year, my problems really became serious. Worries occasioned by my job as director of novices overwhelmed me so badly that I never imagined I would have to go through such torture. . . . But I must honestly say that my greatest agony stemmed from an inner conviction that I was useless to the Church. This realization was accompanied by a simultaneous craving to do something for God's glory and these contrasting moods literally tore me apart. Father Louis, of course, made things even worse. I used to keep up my courage by reminding myself to put my faith in Our Lord and His Blessed Mother to whom the Congregation was dedicated, arguing that they would protect the little society and straighten things out for it. After a while I had to admit that this was sticking my head in the sand and that, while I let the years go by waiting for a change to take place, I would stay there without anything worthwhile to do, and my life would pass away, I would wear out physically and in the end be good for nothing at all. . . .

"That was the state I was in when I went to Paris during the summer vacation. There I found some consolation but no real advice. I went back to Rennes . . . resolved to creep back into my little tomb and never leave it again if that's the way God wanted it. I began to think that Our Lord wanted me to stay there and get ready for death. . . . Somehow, though, I couldn't throttle that burning desire to do something for Christ and His Blessed Mother. Through it all, I felt a gnawing pain at seeing myself so utterly useless and a mounting fear that the few days left to me would pass before I could accomplish anything."[3]

Toward the end of September, a seminarian by the name of de la Brunière came to visit Francis at Rennes. He was a deeply religious young man, a nephew of the Bishop of Mende and the heir to a substantial fortune. He came of a noble family, was endowed with considerable talent, and knew his way around in both ecclesiastical and worldly circles. When he took fire at the prospect of helping Le Vavasseur and Tisserant establish their proposed organization, they and their associates had gone so far as to talk about entrusting him with seeing the project through and, perhaps, of making him superior of the new institute later on.

De la Brunière was keen enough to detect Libermann's uncertainty during their meeting. He sensed the pent-up frustrated energy of the man, and he had no trouble in eliciting an expression of real sympathy as he outlined the objectives once again. Why then, he asked, outright, was Francis so reluctant to cooperate? Didn't everything point to the fact that Providence was beckoning him down a new road? Why bury himself here when his energies could be employed productively elsewhere? Francis thoughtfully stared off in the distance. He did feel some attraction for the plan; that was true. But was it really the will of God? Without rejecting or accepting the proposition, he said good-bye to de la Brunière and begged for time to see some indication of Heaven's design in the business before making his decision.

Nearly a month afterward, Libermann had two extraordinary experiences. They occurred on the 25th and the 28th of October. On each occasion, a clear view of the future seemed to be laid out before him and he saw precisely how God wanted him to fit into the new undertaking. Later, when he talked to Le Vavasseur about it, he spoke with such cryptic caution that Frederic did not catch the full import of the conversation. The emotional Creole had a fondness for baroque elements in the spiritual life; he could only imagine special graces that were accompanied by various external phenomena. Tisserant, however, subsequently designated that his-

[3] N. D. 1, 674 f.

toric moment as the beginning of Libermann's vocation to become the founder of their new society.

Following hard upon this new insight into things, Francis once more displayed that resolute determination which always effectively counteracted his natural timidity when the will of God was clear. From that moment, he set down a fixed and well-calculated program of what had to be done. With hardly any further pressure from the others, he took over the direction of all planning and immediately made it known that, before anything else was done, they would have to consult the Holy See. It was perfectly clear to him that pontifical approval would have to be obtained at all costs.

Running parallel with this new-found drive, however, was a mood of black pessimism. How could he think of going to Rome on this mission, he who was so poor and insignificant, a spiritual guide who had failed, a novice master who had done more harm than good, an epileptic with a broken body, contorted face, and halting speech! What was he thinking of? And those who had been so good to him — the men at St. Sulpice, his friends at Issy, the people at Rennes — none of them had been able to hear the clear call of God in his soul. They would surely think him foolish, or proud, or even a victim of hallucinations. He foresaw it all and it oppressed him mightily. Then, suppose he reached Rome. What could he do? He, an epileptic barred from the priesthood, penniless, with no family support and no livelihood. Would anyone listen to him? Indeed, there had been light on two days but the darkness was closing in. Only a penetrating shaft remained, urging him on into an unknown future.

Now he began to think of Father Louis. He would be left without a novice master again, and perhaps some vocations would be lost to the Eudists because of this sudden departure. After all, it had not been too bad. The novitiate had given him a measure of solitude and quiet. Hadn't he always wanted to be away from men and their complicated transactions and their dreadful arguments? And here he was, rushing into a new sea of troubles, jealousies, and disputes that might be far worse than those he was leaving behind. His anxiety was so oppressive that it began to show up physically in his walk and general demeanor. Collapse seemed perilously near, but God continued to spur him on. His young associates had asked him to draft the new constitution. Still he hesitated. Then at long last, Father Pinault came to the rescue.

Many a time before, both in St. Sulpice and afterward, Father Pinault had been a tower of strength. Once again, Libermann, crushed under the weight of God's mission, racked by agonizing insecurity, heard his encouraging voice. He told Francis to give Father Louis proper notice and then go ahead with his plans. That decided it. Libermann arranged to leave for Rome with de la Brunière in December, 1839. Then he sat down to write a long and sorrowful letter to the Eudist superior.

Rennes, Nov. 30, 1839

My dear Father,

In the presence of Our Lord Jesus Christ and His Holy Mother, I humbly beg your pardon for any offence this letter may give. I admit quite frankly that I have been concerned and seriously worried for more than a month now over the effect this announcement of my intentions may have upon you, but there is no alternative. The love of Christ is our prime consideration. Even if it were a matter of my own life and the lives of all who are near and dear to me, I would still have to sacrifice everything to His will.

By this time you have surmised, Reverend Superior, what I have in mind. I have prayed for guidance and I have consulted the wisest, holiest men I know. All are unanimously agreed that I must leave this congregation, an organization that I will love and cherish for the rest of my life. I have hesitated and thought about this for a long time because I wanted to be of some use to this little society, but I never could give myself a good reason for staying on.

Dear Reverend Father, what will happen to a poor fellow like me when everybody leaves him to his own devices? For a while I shall find some outlet in the new work that we are planning. But after that? No one but God knows. I am openly admitting my wretchedness and misery to you. The realization of it has sometimes led me to behave strangely, but I have never succumbed completely, thanks to the grace of Christ. He alone is my strength and my only hope. After Him comes His holy Mother who is my mother as well.

My feeble, timid, and cowardly character has often been sad, depressed and desolate in His presence, aware of all the humiliations and contradictions that were ahead of me, but the thought that Christ is my strength and support gives me an indescribable courage. For that reason, I console myself with the assurance that life is short and that the good Lord will sustain me with His love and mercy till He finally calls me to Himself.

I am telling you this, dear Father, to make you realize that I am not leaving this congregation to seek honor and satisfaction elsewhere. You can easily see what opposition and ridicule are in store for me, but that will not deter me. I'm doing what God wants. He will help me carry the burden of difficulties that will surely weigh heavily upon me. He knows quite well that I do not ask exemption from sorrows, crosses, humiliations, and reverses. The only thing I ask is the grace to bear up under it all and to be kept in His love and holiness.

And now, my dear Reverend Father Superior, I have a favor to ask of you: please don't try to keep me from going. Why break the weak insignificant reed that is already so badly mutilated? God has given the command. My mind is made up. Further discussion would break my heart but my resolve would never change. I am ready for anything now.

Dear Father, give me your blessing before I go, and pray that Jesus and Mary will not forget about this poor fellow. I hope they won't, for they know that I love them even more, and that I'm ready to give up everything for that love.

I have decided to leave next Monday. It is important and necessary that I do. You know the state of my nerves. I very much fear that the sadness of parting and the pain I am causing all the wonderful people in this house will bring on a serious upset. But, may Our Lord's will be done in that area also. I'll do my best to prevent such an accident.

Goodbye then, Father. A last fond farewell. Once more, please give your blessing to this poor unfortunate. In the love of Jesus and Mary, I will remain throughout life.

Your most unworthy son and servant,
FRANCIS LIBERMANN[4]

Father Louis glowered bitterly at the letter. With an involuntary grimace he dismissed the whole thing as the fanciful lucubration of a sick mind. Then he sat down and wrote a few short biting sentences to the effect that Libermann's decision was an insane delusion inspired by the devil and all stemming from selfishness. Then he followed it up with a personal interview in which he did his best to make Francis change his mind. The younger man listened with bowed head and tear-filled eyes, but no amount of threats or entreaties could induce him to reconsider, though the emotional strain must have been unbearable. "I was so touched," he wrote afterward, "by the sorrow I was causing Father Louis and the

[4] L. S. 2, 295 f.

others in the house . . . that I cried bitterly right in front of Father Louis. I was really in bad shape, but I left in spite of it all."[5]

Once back in Paris, Libermann went straight to Father Pinault and again he found the same warm welcome, the almost supernatural confidence, and the steady encouragement he needed so badly. No wonder Francis subsequently inscribed the name of Pinault with his own hand on the list of the Society's special benefactors and followed it up with this explanatory note: "From the very beginning he encouraged the first members to overcome their difficulties and follow out their plans. He has had to take a good deal of abuse for the interest he showed in our work for the poor Negroes, but he stayed with us. He does that habitually when God's interests are involved, and he has no fear of the persecution he may have to undergo as a result of it."[6]

Francis saw quite clearly that his actions were creating something of a furor. From a purely human point of view, the project did look foolhardy and unlikely, but a mysterious inner force carried him onward. "I felt just as keenly as those who were interested in me," he confessed, "that this enterprise was beyond me. I think I can say in all honesty that it was not pride or ambition that drove me to undertake it. After all, I understood better than anyone else the difficulties I would encounter. Humanly speaking, I was sure that in my hands this work would die aborning. That possibility haunted me. But somewhere inside me an intense and persistent urge propelled me ahead in spite of my misgivings. My fear of failing God and neglecting a soul-saving work made me deaf to the wisest advice on the other side. Now I find it humiliating that I dared to embark on such a difficult project without any material, intellectual, or moral support."[7]

---

[5] N. D. 1, 676. [6] N. D. 3, 390. [7] N. D. 9, 271.

CHAPTER ELEVEN

THE COURAGEOUS ADVENTURE

Francis went to Lyons first, then to Marseilles where de la Brunière was to join him. Once more he was the restless wanderer, lonely and miserable in his quest but full of a deeply confident peace in the knowledge that it had to be this way. That mysterious ambivalent facet of his character ran like a thread through his life. At home, unlike his brothers, he had driven himself to an almost fanatic study of the Law and the Commentaries; at Metz, he disappointed his liberal companions by sharing their ideas but refusing to emulate their conduct and finally by breaking away to throw himself into the strange new world of Catholicism. At the seminary, instead of following his naturally timid bent and losing himself in the crowd, he seemed to prefer the stormy blasts of the mountain-top to the easy calm of the valley. At Stanislas, he might readily have promised to work for a while in the home missions; instead, honest conviction forced him to sacrifice free board and lodging. In the seminaries of St. Sulpice and Issy, he braved the criticism of his colleagues to carry on the work he felt impelled to do. At Rennes, just as the newly restored Eudists began to look on him confidently as one of their number, he threw security aside like an old worn-out coat and started off into uncharted seas once more with only God's will as his compass and God's grace as his sail. Always and everywhere he was like a man goaded on by an inner voice, drawn by an inner light, and cutting every mooring that threatened to tie him down securely before his course was run. Yet, concomitant with the voice and the light, there flowed through his career a dark forbidding current of natural uneasiness, insecurity, and self-distrust.

When he reached Lyons, he stopped at several places and asked for a night's lodging. The astonished householders simply stood in the doorway, gazed at the pale Jewish features, listened to the stammering request, and then closed the door as they murmured excuses. There was no hope of hospitality until he reached the Ozanams. They welcomed him graciously. Frederic Ozanam, a professor at Lyons, was later to become world famous as the Father of the Poor in Paris. Like Libermann, he was called to answer the needs of the time. His family took in every transient, just as the old Rabbi had done many years before in Saverne, and this poor tired traveler, whose face twisted painfully when he tried to talk, had come to the right door at last.

During the few days he spent at Lyons, Francis did some visiting. First he went to the superior of a religious house to discuss his plans. That reverend gentleman listened disdainfully to the curious recital and then, when he felt he had heard enough, he summoned up a sardonic laugh and swept from the room, leaving his astonished visitor alone and miserable. Madame Rémond was next. Though she and Libermann had never met, a long series of letters had been exchanged, and the pious lady had treasured the guidance they provided. In fact, she read and re-read each one while she rocked her children to sleep. Now the maid came to tell her that a young cleric was at the door and wished to speak to her. She was shocked to see the bowed figure, hat in hand, mumbling something that she could not catch. She begged him to come in and asked what she could do for him, but the voice that answered was so weak and halting that she missed the reply entirely. On the assumption that he needed help, she pressed some money in his hand. With downcast eyes and a gesture of thanks he accepted it and walked toward the door. As he left the room he turned around, looked at her for a long time, sighed deeply, and then disappeared. Only later, when the maid told her she had fogotten to announce the mysterious caller by name, did she learn that her guest had been Libermann.

De la Brunière met Francis at Marseilles. The two of them stayed with Father Perrée, but not for long. Soon they were on their way to Rome. They sailed on January 1, 1840, and landed at

Cività Vecchia six days later. Twenty-four hours after debarkation, they arrived in Rome. De la Brunière had bought the boat tickets; now he paid for their quarter in a *pension* where French ecclesiastics lived. They were in Rome at last, but they had no recommendations of any sort beyond a letter from de la Brunière's uncle, the bishop of Mende. It was addressed to a Greek Archbishop, rector of a Roman College, who welcomed the two pilgrims very kindly but then went on about his business because he could not help them in any way.

Francis started out by probing the attitude of Roman officials. He found the atmosphere far from favorable. Postrevolutionary developments in France had caused grave misgivings in the Vatican. Inventive French minds were bursting with plans for restoring and strengthening religion at home and proposals were pouring over the Alps. Already in 1837, when Dom Guéranger came to Rome with plans for a new institute, Cardinal Sala had remarked somewhat testily: "Not a day passes without some request coming in from beyond those mountains for the approval of rules and new congregations. In France there are only founders."[1] This was the situation into which another founder was about to inject himself.

Monsignor de Conny, the old friend from St. Sulpice, was now living in Rome. Libermann went to him and gave him a full account of developments thus far. De Conny listened politely, made up his mind that the whole thing was ridiculous and dangerous, and promptly set about warning everybody he could regarding the foolhardy scheme and its proponent. It was a bitter lesson in diplomacy for Francis. Thereafter, he always observed a cautious silence about his projects and advised others to do the same.

De Conny seems to have been successful in arousing two influential French Jesuits, Fathers de Rosaven and de Villefort, against Libermann. Then he stirred up Father Vaures, the eminent Franciscan Penitentiary and a friend of the Pope himself. All these men agreed that the convert Jew was a dangerous individual who would bear watching. His fanciful ideas might lead young minds astray and his quiet manner might be simply a ruse to get himself ordained. Father de Rosaven in particular took upon himself the task of defending the Church. Availing himself of that exaggerated eloquence

[1] N. D. 2, 3.

which some people feel they must use when they wish to be emphatic, he roundly berated Francis as a man whose unlimited ambitions were leading him far from the holy will of God.

Once more, Dr. Drach provided the only ray of consolation. He was now working in Rome as librarian of the Congregation of the Propagation of the Faith. He understood and sympathized with the young convert and encouraged him to go on despite the opposition. Like a special grace of the Holy Ghost, he appeared at the two great turning points in Libermann's life. Only he and Father Pinault seem to have had the courage and vision to stand forth and give their support when all the world had turned its back.

In a short time Dr. Drach arranged for an audience with Pope Gregory XVI. The pontiff, a former monk, was a man of deep spirituality, filled with wisdom and zeal, more priest than statesman, and inclined to such conservatism that he usually frowned on change and innovation. Francis, de la Brunière, and Drach knelt before him. The conversation was brief, but as they withdrew, the Holy Father allowed his hand to rest on the curly head of the serene little Jew. It was a gesture of affection, a kindly caress for this suffering child of the Church. He detained Dr. Drach for a moment after the other two had left and asked about the young convert. When Drach had ended his brief account, there was a long silence in the ancient hall. Then, Gregory rose and said: *"Questo sarà un santo"* (This man will be a saint).

On May 11, 1840, Francis handed Bishop Cadolini, Secretary of the Propaganda, a carefully-worded memoir. It did not seek approval for a new foundation. It merely asked if Libermann could in good conscience continue with his planning. It made no secret of his epilepsy and his consequent ineligibility for orders. It did state, however, that the illness was gradually improving and that no one had ever given a final verdict disbarring the writer from the priesthood.

Eight days went by. No reply came from the Propaganda. Libermann went to see Bishop Cadolini again. The Secretary received him politely, but all he would say was "You must become a priest first. Then we will discuss matters further." Francis diffidently asked what the Propaganda thought of his plan, but Monsignor was too much of a diplomat to commit himself. He stated with some directness that the Propaganda does not deal with simple clerics. "Once you have become a priest I shall tell you," he concluded. And the interview ended there with the memoir still lying on Cadolini's desk. Once more, Francis came home with disappointing news for the now impatient de la Brunière.

He described the painful experiences of this period in a subsequent letter: "For a span of six months no one approved my proposal. In Paris, Lyons, and in Rome, everyone to whom I spoke rejected the idea. Only Father Pinault went along with me, and even he gave the impression of having certain reservations. . . . But even if the whole world had been against me I would have gone on. The arguments used by my opponents didn't seem to be good enough to make me change my mind. Most of them, especially those who were good and wise, had a bad opinion of me personally. They suspected my plan was the product of ambition or something equally bad."[2]

De la Brunière now grew restive. He had imagined things would go more smoothly. Certainly he had never expected all these reverses. Everything that gave him a certain amount of prestige and influence in France dwindled to insignificance in this strange place. There was so much purple around on all sides that he made no impression whatsoever when he told people his uncle was a bishop in faraway Mende. The other seminarians had indicated their desire to have him head the group when it was organized, but this foundation business was a risky and enervating affair. He saw less good in it. Besides, criticisms of Libermann were mounting to a formidable crescendo. Had he perhaps been mistaken in regarding the poor fellow as a saint? Somehow Libermann looked different now. He was a sorry little wretch, deformed by his sufferings and confused by an interior darkness. How could the venture succeed with him playing such an active role in it?

Just then de Conny had another "convincing" talk with de la Brunière. Moreover, Father de Villefort made excellent use of the difficulties Libermann had made known in the course of spiritual direction to unsettle the hesitant seminarian still more. At length the rich young man turned his back on his companion and went home to France on March 25, leaving Francis to carry on alone.

[2] N. D. 2, 151.

It is fully understandable, then, why the lonely survivor of the expedition wrote dejectedly: "I have had to suffer a good deal from my colleague. He saw how they despised me and how helpless I was. He was tempted to turn against me and the project that had previously interested him so much. Then he started to oppose me at every step and to use every means at his command to hurt me. Finally, he left me flat and went back to Paris."[3]

"The good Fathers were prejudiced against me. They acted as if I were seducing him and they stopped at nothing to get him away from me. The one who gave me the most trouble is the one who was (and still is) my confessor. He used everything I told him in direction to turn my companion against me. At that moment I learned that men of God can go to extraordinary lengths when they think they're promoting God's honor. I just can't justify such conduct. My only consolation lies in the fact that they did what they did out of a desire to honor God. I said to myself, 'If Our Lord is satisfied with their conduct who am I to be unhappy about it?'

"Nevertheless, I was strongly tempted to be uncharitable toward those people and the things they were doing. This lasted two days. Then I went straight to my confessor and told him everything I had been thinking about. At the moment we seem to be pretty good friends."[4]

This universal opposition was helping Francis to detach himself more and more from himself and from the passing world around him. It was a death struggle that prepared him for the strange bliss of a purified soul that is no longer bound to anything in creation but lives with an inner freedom for God alone. "There are no better means," he observed, "than crosses and contradictions. When our nature is attacked on every side, it realizes the danger. Then it rises up in rebellion and fights desperately. That is why we must make use of this moment to let grace win the victory. Do not try to find out if you are right or wrong, or if others are fair in opposing you. Do not analyze their motives. Attack the enemy [self-love]. You will have help to weaken, crush, and kill it. But act like a clever politician. Take advantage of your chance. Ignore the pain. It is merely the forerunner of a joy and happiness that imperfect and worldly souls can never fathom. Amid that great peace of the perfect, Christ's

[3] *Ibid.* [4] N. D. 2, 146 f.

kingdom is established in our souls. Only then can we be truly useful for His honor and capable of doing serious and worthwhile work."[5]

Now that de la Brunière was gone, Francis stayed by himself. He was so poor that he barely subsisted on the little bit of money he received from his friends. Nonetheless, he was happy to share the poverty of Christ. He left the *Pension* and moved in with the Patriarca family. They rented rooms to foreign ecclesiastics and their house was a poor little establishment tucked away in the *Vicolo del Pinacolo*. He asked for the cheapest room they had and assured them that he would require no service of any kind beyond the midday meal. Papa Patriarca hesitated, but at Libermann's gentle pleading he finally gave in and showed him two small garret rooms. One was a storage place for odds and ends and occasionally a poor farmer slept there when he came to town to sell his produce. The other, equally small, was free if Francis wanted it. He could take over both for a few *lire*.

The room he chose was humble indeed. A man could not stand erect in it except at the door. From there the sloping rafters dropped sharply toward the eaves. It had a little window that let in not only the elements but a flock of pigeons as well. Though these gentle creatures winged their way through the open window at his approach, they became his faithful friends as time went on. Francis stood in the doorway and sniffed the subtle fragrance of the ancient wooden beams. Then he laid out a straw mattress and a threadbare blanket on the floor. There was an old table there already and a rickety chair stood beside it. He placed his crucifix on the table and hung a picture of St. Francis of Assisi on the wall. Then he laid out his library: a bible, a missal, and a copy of the *Imitation of Christ*. Once more he was at home. As he wrote to Father Pinault, he did not find it lonely at all. The company — meaning the pigeons — was excellent.

He got up early every morning and attended several Masses in the neighboring churches. When he returned, he agreed to take a cup of unsweetened coffee but nothing else. After that he would read and write until time for dinner at one o'clock. Then more reading and writing until it was time for his customary egg, crust of bread, and glass of water.

[5] N. D. 2, 454.

Before long, Papa Patriarca came under the spell of this impoverished but happy boarder. He told the neighbors that his home was blessed — he had a *santo* in the house. He was always after Francis to take a better room at the same price, but his odd little guest preferred the loft which he shared with God and the pigeons. When summer came, his garret became an oven that shimmered in the Roman sun. The next winter it gave little protection against the piercing cold. But Francis never complained. He was always the same: quiet, friendly, ready to help, filled with a mysterious joy. Now and then, his hosts would hear him say feelingly: "If I didn't love the Good Lord I would be a most ungrateful man. He has done so much for me!"

For relaxation he played with the Patriarca children. As a matter of fact, all his life this pure and simple soul showed a special fondness for children. And they reciprocated. Even Rafaele, the little *bambino* in the cradle, gurgled with delight as soon as he came near. When Francis climbed downstairs to join the family, everyone seemed happier. Signor Patriarca grew expansive. With typical Italian verve he would launch into animated stories of the time he spent in the Napoleonic army. He was proud of his sergeant's stripes and felt sure that he would have risen to be a general if his mother had not insisted on his returning home. But his eloquence really reached its full potential when he talked about his illustrious ancestors — noble patricians and ferocious soldiers who symbolized everything that was truly admirable. One of them had served in the First Crusade. Francis had only to go to the church of San Gregorio. There he would see the name gloriously emblazoned on the wall. The stories grew steadily more incredible. At last Francis could no longer keep a straight face. He burst into a hearty laugh that echoed through the house. It was a scene that came to be repeated often during those peaceful happy months.

Even in the midst of that peace and happiness, however, Libermann wondered if his stay in Rome made any sense in the light of his chilly audience with Bishop Cadolini. On occasion he asked himself if it would not be wiser to go back to France, for after all, de la Brunière had sent him 400 francs for the return trip. He did not know that in the meantime his memorandum had been transmitted to Cardinal Franzoni, Prefect of Propaganda. His Eminence had been discreetly gathering data on its unknown author and the reports coming in from Paris were surprisingly favorable. Moreover, at one of the meetings of the Sacred Congregation they had taken up the memorandum and discussed it at some length.

On July 6, 1840, Cardinal Franzoni wrote Francis a letter in which he stated that the Propaganda wished to encourage him in his plans, although it could not yet give any expression of approval regarding the proposed institute. That question would be examined at a later date. In closing, he expressed the hope that God would give Libermann sufficient health to be ordained. Since no forwarding address had been left, the messenger had great difficulty finding the Patriarca household. He finally ferretted out the address and left the letter. One can imagine Libermann's joy and gratitude when he read it. He sat right down and sent the good news to Paris.

All his friends at St. Sulpice were equally elated. Bishop Allen Collier happened to be visiting there just then, looking for priests to staff his island diocese of Mauritius. This proposed foundation looked like a good source of man power for his mission. He discussed the matter with Father Garnier. Since the good Sulpician rector was considerably more at home in the streets of Paris than in the stretches of the Indian ocean, the islands of Reunion and Mauritius were all the same to him. He called Le Vavasseur to talk things over. The Creole seminarian soon made it clear that he and his associates had no plans for anything but Reunion. While the rector was getting something of a lesson in geography and the bishop was sitting back enjoying it hugely, Le Vavasseur rattled on excitedly. Bishop Collier grew interested. The idea still had possibilities. He offered to give the project his episcopal backing if the new foundation would direct its sights to Mauritius rather than Reunion. Father Garnier and the other advisers of the group agreed that this was a good solution to many difficulties.

Meanwhile, Francis waited peacefully in Rome. It was a long time since he had had any attacks and new hope began to dawn. Nonetheless, he remained where he was, watching and praying. Father Pinault recommended strongly that he spend the time writing a provisional rule for the new society, but as soon as he set pen to paper, his mind went blank. Le Vavasseur insisted on calling it the Congregation of the Holy Cross. Tisserant was equally adamant about dedicating it to the Holy Heart of Mary. This matter of the title would have to be decided before anything could be done on the rule. Libermann began a pilgrimage to the seven basilicas of Rome, asking for light and guidance. Before it was over, he felt sure that Tisserant was right: it should be the Congregation of the Holy Heart of Mary.

Now his pen flew over the pages unhesitatingly. When the first draft was completed, he found it surprisingly coherent. It displayed an extraordinary amount of logic and unity. Better still, it went beyond the limited scope which Le Vavasseur and Tisserant had originally assigned to it. They had been concerned only about their own little islands. Libermann widened that aim and announced in Article I that the institute's purpose would be "to announce and establish the Holy Gospel among the poorest and most neglected souls in the Church of God."[6]

Obviously, it is not possible to care for all the neglected souls in the Church simultaneously. One must make a choice and limit his activities to one area at a time. That is why Francis went on to single out the Negroes in the islands as the special and immediate objective of his society's apostolate. This was the "special work," but naturally not the exclusive work of his group. "The specific aim of our mission," he wrote, "the task of our predilection, must be the poorest, most despised, and most neglected souls."[7] And "if the time should come when the Negroes are no longer the most abject of men, what is to stop us from going to the assistance of that part of the Church which is then the most neglected and despised?"[8] Had Le Vavasseur or Tisserant been the author of that Rule, it would surely have fixed the purpose of the institute more rigidly. Divine Providence inspired Libermann with a much broader vision.

As the text proceeded, he began to devote special attention to the way his priests should conduct themselves in their work. One by one, these simple prescriptions built up a sketch of his ideal religious priest: a cultured, lovable figure, a gentleman in the best sense of the term, an embodiment of Christ's charity who tactfully and gently approaches those in need. "They will avoid as detestable short-comings," he warned, "any manner of speech or action that

[6] N. D. 2, 236. [7] N. D. 3, 93. [8] L. S. 2, 484.

gives the impression of haughtiness, scorn, or contempt, for this approach is all too often used when people are dealing with the lower classes. . . . They will bear patiently, quietly, and kindly the vulgarity, the faults, and even the vices of these poor fellows."[9]

Francis had suffered so much himself because of his Jewish ancestry, his nervous affliction, and his utter poverty, that he could write with understandable feeling about treating the unfortunate ones of this earth with delicacy and sympathy. With him, it was all a matter of supernatural love for even the faintest reflection of the Creator in His creatures. "Genuine love," he contended, "always has a ready smile for others. It spreads joy and consolation without a hint of artificiality." "Even among ourselves, we should always show respect and esteem, never indifference." "The way you look and talk are important. If you are not careful about your tone of voice, your facial expression, and your phraseology, you can destroy much of the good effect of your words and actually run the danger of being misunderstood."[10]

Francis had formulated his Rule without interruption. By September it was ready. Still there was no further news from the Propaganda. Unwilling to let the precious days go by in idle waiting, he began to write a commentary on the Gospel of St. John. He felt the work would do him good and he chose that particular Gospel because it is there that Jesus speaks most inspiringly about the hidden splendors of the inner life. In the silence of that lonely attic, the light of God glowed more radiantly than ever and made this simple cleric increasingly sensitive to the meaning of each word and deed that the evangelist recorded. Every phrase sparkled with significance, no detail was cast aside as superfluous. In those exalted moments of insight, Francis set down on paper all that he saw and felt. The result, though unfinished, was a luminous document of mystic experience.

For a long time now, Libermann had dreamed of going on a pilgrimage to Loretto where, according to legend, the holy house of Nazareth is preserved. He had proposed the trip some months before, but his spiritual director dissuaded him on the grounds that the Propaganda might make some move just when he was absent.

---

[9] N. D. 2, 257.
[10] N. D. 2, 283, 297, 302.

After all this waiting, however, it seemed safe enough to go. In November, 1840, Francis started off on the long journey on foot. It took a whole month.

On the way, he prayed silently. There was still so much uncertainty about the whole business. He was unsure of himself even in respect to his own destiny. There were times when he felt strongly drawn to a work that promised to do so much good for souls. Then again, the longing for solitude and contemplation would return stronger than ever. All through the long months of negotiation and waiting, every time some new threat arose to jeopardize the new foundation, he had experienced a quiet thrill of hope that God might grant his wish for a life of silence and prayer after all. Then a new dream began to take form. Perhaps the Good Lord simply wanted to use him for organizational purposes and then, after someone else more capable than he had been found to develop the work, he could withdraw to his beloved solitude and look after his own poor soul.

The life of a founder had little appeal if one examined it seriously — the thousands of little worries, the endless conversations with people who came to lay their complaints before him, the desk weighted down with letters and documents that ceaselessly clamored for attention, the eternal knock at the door, the sleepless nights in which one tossed in a restless endeavor to find answers for problems that would not be put off — all these and more were the ghosts that his realistic imagination conjured up. Indeed, the mountain caves beside the road looked ever more attractive as he walked along in his patched and threadbare cassock.

At last he knelt at the little house where, tradition has it, Jesus and Mary and Joseph lived and prayed during those quiet happy years at Nazareth. At this shrine of the Holy Family, this reliquary of the purest contemplative life ever lived, he laid bare his soul. Would he become a priest? Must he renounce the solitude he longed for so ardently? In the silence of his heart the answer came back, clear and unmistakable. Yes, despite difficulties, he would be a priest. And he would found a congregation. The elements of joy and sorrow mingled their usual bittersweet contradiction in his soul. Opposing currents of exaltation at the prospect of being a priest and dread at the anticipation of a founder's lot made his tears of gladness sting with painful aftereffects.

On the way back to Rome, he sought shelter as usual wherever a village door was open to him. In one of the homes where he stayed for the night, a little girl lay desperately ill. The hand of death was already heavy upon her and the terrified parents saw it clearly. In their wild grief they turned to the silent guest who prayed so devoutly and begged him with typical Latin impetuosity to cure their dying child of the fever that had kept her crying night and day for more than a week. Without a word, Francis approached the bed and gazed for a long time at the pale little form lying there and sobbing so pitifully. Her mother and father moaned softly in the shadows. At length he turned slowly and said, "I picked up some seeds from a tree in the course of my pilgrimage. They say they're good for sick people. Put them in a glass of water and let her drink it." "But *Reverendo*," exclaimed the father, "she hasn't been able to swallow anything. Not even water." "Do you have faith?" asked Libermann, "That's all that counts." Then he dipped his finger in the glass they brought and moistened the child's tongue. Immediately she stopped crying and went to sleep. When he left the next day she was completely cured.

On December 15, an exhausted and emaciated Libermann appeared at the door of his old landlord. Mrs. Patriarca clutched up her apron and rocked from side to side in astonished and pained recognition. *Dio mio,* the man before her was a wreck. His cassock and mantle were all in tatters and shreds, his shoes hung in pieces around his swollen feet! She chattered reprovingly as he slowly climbed the stairs to his attic room where the faithful pigeons were waiting for him like old welcoming friends and the familiar fragrance of those ancient rafters settled on him like a distillation of refreshing balm. A boundless nostalgia flowed over him. Memories of the happy days he had spent there in undisturbed quiet made his longing for a life of solitude surge back with greater force than ever. Yet he knew that the fragile peace of those hours would never come again. Mary had breathed her message to him at Loretto and he must not turn a deaf ear to her call.

On the shaky little table lay a letter. It was from Samson. "I paid a visit," it said, "to Bishop Raess [Coadjutor Bishop of Strassburg] on the occasion of his installation. He asked a lot of questions about you . . . and when he heard about your difficulty in being ordained, he told me he would like to impose hands on you himself. He expects you to come as soon as possible so that he may confer the subdiaconate on you."[11]

Libermann's heart pounded wildly. Here it was at last. The great good news that was so long in coming, the sacred invitation that he sometimes thought would never arrive. And yet, beneath the keenness of his joy was the old dull pain, asserting itself more insistently as the death knell rang for his dreams of solitude and contemplation. Both Father Vaures and Father de Villefort, previously so antagonistic, now recognized the hand of God in the affair and urged him to forego his mystical inclinations and hurry off to Strassburg.

With a tugging at the heart that re-echoes in his letters long afterward, Francis left both Rome and solitude, never to find them the same again.

[11] N. D. 2, 32.

CHAPTER TWELVE

THE PRIESTHOOD

Bishop Raess was a thorough man. He sought information from every available quarter about this convert he was taking into his seminary. At first, the reports disturbed him very much. They pictured a sly adventurer whose gift of intrigue was set off in strange contrast by neurotic manifestations of epilepsy. It was anything but reassuring. His Excellency began to wonder if he had not spoken too quickly.

Oddly enough, Francis reacted with equanimity to these developments when he learned of them. By this time he almost expected people to have misgivings about him. It no longer affected his peace of mind. He simply submitted to the prelate a short résumé of his situation and his plans. On the basis of this document, Bishop Raess made further inquiries, this time of the Sulpicians in Paris. Their recommendation was favorable and the atmosphere cleared speedily. Libermann was admitted to the seminary without further ado. Just then Bishop Collier of Mauritius wrote that he would accept Francis into his jurisdiction. Bishop Raess consented and preliminaries were concluded.

Francis entered the Strassburg seminary on Shrove Tuesday, February 23, just in time for a Mardi Gras celebration that the students were holding. As part of the fun, one of them climbed on a chair and mimicked a rabbi. For young Libermann it was a painful moment, touching off as it did memories of his father over in Saverne and tearing open the still sensitive wound that their old conflict had left him with. Fortunately, he had learned to deal with the painful past. Not too long ago, when life situations aroused the image of his father, a rush of emotions would carry him to the brink of a seizure. Recently, however, his nervous attacks had become less frequent and less severe because he had learned to bring his feelings into line with the new perspective that grace had given to his life. Thanks be to God, on this first night in a strange seminary he could still find it possible to let the incident pass without losing his composure and making a spectacle of himself, but the hurt was deep and lasting nonetheless.

Greatly matured by suffering and opposition, Francis now concentrated quietly on preparing for holy orders. He had learned the lesson that every original man must learn if he wants to avoid being needlessly misunderstood by the less gifted minds that surround him. Unimaginative characters feel threatened by concepts and ideals that differ from the mental structure they have developed against the unexpected and the unpredictable. Their intentions are not bad. It is merely a case of their being genuinely frightened and insecure when something new opposes their established ideas. The creative personality becomes aware of this only by degrees, for when he is young he does not realize his peculiar endowments. Ideas arise so spontaneously that he expects every other mind to function in the same way. He cannot fathom the anxiety he is evoking in more rigidly organized people. He is inclined to express himself openly and to regard frankness as a virtue. Later, he begins to understand that ready expression without elaborate and reassuring explanations can cause mounting nervous tension and unconscious anxiety in his fellowmen. He sees at last that frankness must be moderated by charity and that he must occasionally be silent and evasive in order not to threaten the defenses of his brethren unnecessarily.

This new realization caused Libermann's behavior in Strassburg to contrast noticeably with the way he had conducted himself in the seminaries he had previously attended. In a letter to Tisserant he gave evidence of his new outlook: "When you have occasion to talk with other Fathers, do so with moderation, cordiality, openness of heart, but not openness of mind. Say pleasant things but don't be over-communicative. In matters of the spiritual life, never advance your own opinion. Always give the impression that you fully approve the conduct of those with whom you are talking and of people around you generally. . . . When they try to instruct you in your way of life, listen calmly and kindly to what they have to tell you and don't let on that you disagree. Then afterwards do what you are convinced is right before God. When they criticize you, do not answer directly. . . . Avoid the question by means of a short, friendly and agreeable word. When your pastor himself talks to you about your personal life and tells you to change your behavior, reply in generalities. Do not adduce reasons to justify your conduct. In general it is important . . . never to give detailed information about your conduct and never to reveal the principles that govern your spiritual and priestly life."[1]

It must be understood, of course, that young Father Tisserant had just received his first parochial assignment and, with his highly demonstrative character and his flair for romantic asceticism, he almost invited conflict and controversy. It was to protect him against this that Libermann counseled a degree of reticence beyond what he practiced himself. On occasion he was still given to spontaneous reactions as is evident from the reply he gave one of the seminarians who asked for an evaluation of the practice sermon he had just given in the refectory. In those days, emotional eloquence was the rule. Rhetorical flourishes, sentimental sweetness, and resounding pomposity surrounded pulpit oratory and paralyzed the genuine expression of solid thought. The seminarian's effort had followed this contemporary style and now he looked to Francis for a word of enthusiastic commendation. His disappointment at the following critique must have been great indeed. "When we preach," observed Libermann, "we ought to do so with sincerity. We shouldn't try to startle our audience. . . . I once heard about a priest who tried to make his listeners cry. He ended up making them laugh."[2]

The exaggerated emotionalism that passed in his day for art and literature left him cold. His clear and subtle mind rebelled against its artificiality and by way of reaction he was led to use strong language when he spoke of contemporary aesthetics. Long before existential trends of thought brought their influence to bear on the field of art and philosophy, he turned by preference to an authentic portrayal of things as they are.

His tolerance and boundless charity came to the fore time after

[1] N. D. 2, 468 f.
[2] N. D. 2, 409.

time. When a student told him with evident admiration how eloquently the great Massillon had spoken of the small number of those who were predestined for salvation, Francis promptly asked: "Is that sermon really approved by Rome?" His love for people made such an outlook repugnant to him. Soon after, he wrote to young Father Tisserant: "Handle sinners with the greatest kindness and consideration, never with harshness or rigor. Without hurting them, make them fully conscious of the evil they are doing, but always express yourself in kindly fashion. Except on rare occasions, don't scold them with severity. . . . Don't set down rigid precepts. I am not a theologian and shouldn't be talking to you this way, but I can assure you rigid principles are ruinous for souls."[3]

There in Strassburg he could visit Samson, Isabel, and the children rather frequently. They were all overjoyed when he came. His good humor and quiet easy nature made a lasting impression on all his little nieces and nephews. Imperceptibly, that subtle serenity communicated itself to the Jewish household where hot-blooded Eastern temperaments occasionally clashed in an exchange of biting words. When Uncle Francis came, no one seemed able to escape the net of peace he lovingly threw around them. "When we saw him," they wrote later, "angry words died on our lips."[4]

One of the boys, a fiery little fellow of seven, once flew into a rage that lasted all day. His brother had hurt his feelings and nothing served to dispel the storm. He was bound to avenge himself at all costs. That evening, Francis gathered the children about him as usual for night prayer. Everything went well till they reached the part of the Our Father which begs forgiveness in the same measure that we mete it out to "those who trespass against us." Quietly, Uncle Francis leaned over and whispered: "My boy, you cannot ask the Good Lord for this without condemning yourself, for if you refuse to forgive, the Good Lord won't like you any more and He won't forgive you either." It worked. The little hothead rose from his knees, slipped over and apologized to his brother, and then, beaming triumphantly, came back to his place to finish the prayer with the others.

Theodora, one of the nieces, listened wide-eyed while the maid

[3] N. D. 2, 476 f.
[4] N. D. 2, 404.

told her some nightmarish tale about a woman who had swallowed a snake. Visions of the horrible, slimy, twisting thing going down a human gullet haunted her to such an extent that she became terribly upset. Eventually, convulsions set in. Doctor Samson did his best to pacify her, but nothing he did had any effect. In desperation he called Francis, and as soon as the little girl found herself on her uncle's knee and heard his soft, reassuring voice, she relaxed and forgot her terror. The convulsions ended immediately.

Francis was ordained subdeacon on June 5, 1841, and received the diaconate later that same year on August 10. The experience overwhelmed him. He who had been poor and outcast and misunderstood for so many years, now beheld the Lord flooding him with gifts beyond measure. He stood like a saint among the ordinandi, his heart completely surrendered and his head bowed low in humility. "I can still see Mr. Libermann standing before me in the big cathedral choir during the ordinations," one of his classmates later recalled. "It was touching to see his peaceful attitude, the sanctity of his face, his holy abandonment. He was holding in front of him the vestments with which the bishop was to clothe him, but the way he held them, or — how shall I say it — the way he seemed to offer himself with those vestments, reminded me of the statue of a saint."[5]

The very day after he was made a deacon, he wrote to Dr. Drach, the man who had sustained him in every critical moment so far. "Our Lord," he said, "has now enriched me with His gifts and graces. I never would have believed that I could get so far. I can assure you that even on ordination day I could still hardly believe it was real. I finally do believe it because I have such a vital awareness of the grace that was granted to me. One has to receive that sacred character to understand what I mean. From now on, the fact of receiving and possessing that gift is not going to be so important as making it bear fruit and not burying it like a wicked servant. . . . I know that I may no longer seek my rest or turn back. . . .

"Please be good enough to convey my respectful regards to His Eminence, Cardinal Franzoni, and His Excellency, Bishop Cadolini. Tell them, I beg you earnestly, that I am firmly resolved to work

[5] N. D. 2, 420.

with all my strength from now on and that I will not remain idle any more the way I did during the year in Rome."[6]

Vacation began after the ordination ceremonies. Francis stayed with Samson, but during the course of the holidays he went to Paris and conferred with his friends about establishing a novitiate for the new congregation. His idea was to begin in Strassburg. Its proximity to the German border and the consequent possibility of attracting German members from two nationalities at the very outset would give his foundation that supranational character which he so much desired. His Jewish origin, rooted in an Alsatian background, left little room for narrow chauvinism. His early years, spent in a changing atmosphere of Hebrew, German, and French cultures and seasoned by orthodox, liberal, and Christian influences, gave him a breadth of vision that no single land could circumscribe.

Finally, his concern for the training of priests had begun to focus on the educational needs of the German clergy. Father Tisserant points this out in a memoir that was corrected and approved by Libermann himself. It tells us that Francis planned his first foundation near Germany, "with the desire of becoming personally useful to that country by cooperating in the education of holy priests." "I had begun," he told Dr. Drach, "to take measures for coming in contact with the priests of Germany. . . . It was with profound regret that I decided to leave Strassburg, for I had hoped to be of some use to the German clergy which has a poor reputation. . . ." The same thought was expressed in a letter to Schwindenhammer: "As for Germany, I have to give up on that. It hurts, but what can I do? Our Lord has not judged me worthy of so great an enterprise."[7] For the founder of a missionary congregation to be sighing regretfully after educational endeavors might seem strange, were it not for the fact that, unknown to him, Providence had inspired him with strivings that would find their fulfillment only in the future when he and his men would enter the old Society of the Holy Ghost and become part of its academic tradition.

Right now there were friends in France who offered such an advantageous arrangement that Francis could hardly pass up the

---

[6] N. D. 2, 495 f.
[7] N. D. 2, 376; 3, 65, 192.

opportunity by establishing his novitiate elsewhere. The once troublesome novice from Rennes, Father de Brandt, was now secretary to Bishop Mioland of Amiens, and he was in a position to arrange for Libermann's ordination to the priesthood and for a property that might serve as a first foundation. The ordination was scheduled for the Ember Days of September. The house was a former convent boarding school near Amiens, at a place called La Neuville. Bishop Mioland would welcome the group into his diocese and give them the property for a start. How could anyone decline such generosity?

Francis was thirty-nine years old now. Serious epileptic seizures had left him, but minor symptoms of his nervous affliction still persisted. Even his crabbed, irregular script betrayed the fact that some disturbance yet remained. "My health," he wrote, "is much improved. It is three and a half years since I had an attack and the lesser nervous spells are diminishing. Still, I am not cured. I am not yet free from speech difficulties. For that reason, I shouldn't take a chance on preaching for a while."[8]

On Saturday, September 18, 1841, Bishop Mioland kept his word. He ordained Francis in his private chapel. "This morning I was ordained a priest," we read. "God knows what I have received on this great day. And only God knows it, for it cannot be conceived by man or angel. *Pray,* all of you, that it may be for His greater glory, for the sanctification of souls, and the growth of the Church that I have been allowed to become a priest. Beg Our Lord to accept me as a sacrifice for His honor, for I must devote myself to it from now on."[9]

During the little dinner after the ceremony, he impressed the bishop mightily by the supernatural joy that streamed from him. Later that day, however, when the diocesan Vicars and some Jesuits came for a meeting, the subject of Libermann came up and developed into a heated discussion. They described him as a visionary enthusiast from St. Sulpice and Rennes, an emotional crusader who was ever concocting new plans and schemes, a dreamer who veered ambitiously with every wind of circumstance. "Sorry to say so, Your Excellency, but your good nature has been imposed upon. The

[8] N. D. 2, 493.
[9] N. D. 2, 497 f.

man you ordained cannot persevere anywhere. He causes trouble wherever he goes. You have made yourself responsible for something you are going to regret."[10]

Bishop Mioland was understandably perturbed. That evening he received a visit from the Sulpician novice master at Issy. Preoccupied with anxiety and regret, the prelate soon found himself asking Father Mollevaut's opinion. He knew that the old priest had known Francis for some years. How did he feel about the ordination? It must have been a great relief when the aged novice master leaned forward and said with a tone of deep conviction: "Your Excellency, what you did today is the finest thing you've done in your whole life."[11]

The bishop's faith in Libermann revived, but all the other diocesan authorities except Father de Brandt kept their faces set against him. Thus it would be for many years, not only here in Amiens but throughout France. Suspecting him as a dangerous innovator and fanatic, they would consistently oppose him and his undertakings. It would finally culminate in a great conflict with the somewhat Gallican archbishop of Paris. And although His Grace of Paris would never overcome his suspicion or abandon his antipathy toward Libermann, it is one of history's amusing twists that decades later several Parisian archbishops would owe their training to his spirit because his sons would be their guides in the illustrious Pontifical French Seminary in Rome.

Francis said his first Mass at the convent of the Sisters of Louvencourt. It was a greater thrill than he had ever dreamed of. "Since my ordination," he wrote, "I go each morning to kneel before the throne of the Most Holy Trinity. I offer the Holy Trinity the worship of the entire Church. . . . I ask for the graces and the help that the Church needs. What a miserable intercessor I am, yet I have with me the Sacred Victim of sacrifice. In His company we are always heard.

"The happiness of offering the Most Holy Sacrifice every day is great indeed. One's soul is filled with joy. But when I think just

---

[10] Maurice Briault, C.S.Sp., *Le vénérable Père F.-M.-P. Libermann,* Paris, 1946, 94 (hereafter quoted as Briault).

[11] N. D. 2, 424.

a little about myself . . . my weaknesses, my constant wretchedness . . . I scarcely dare to kneel on the altar-steps."[12]

One week after his ordination, he sang his first Solemn Mass at the miraculous shrine of Our Lady of Victories in Paris. The pastor, Father Desgenettes, assisted him. The first members of the new congregation took part in it also. In the group, a young priest was praying fervently to the Blessed Virgin for guidance. After Mass he went to the sacristy and talked long and earnestly to Francis. Then and there his mind was made up. Father Bessieux added his name to the growing list of candidates. The work was about to begin.

---

[12] N. D. 3, 65.

CHAPTER THIRTEEN

THE BEGINNINGS

The stage coach from Paris to Amiens jolted merrily along the road. In it, Libermann, Le Vavasseur, and Collin were sitting together and their high spirits contrasted sharply with the impersonal reserve that settled in customary fashion over the other passengers. The three young clerics had good reason to be gay. They were going to La Neuville to occupy the house that Bishop Mioland had given them. After all their planning, all the reverses, and all the heartaches, they were at last ready to make a formal beginning.

Le Vavasseur was particularly voluble. With great gusto he was telling about his experience in a stagecoach the week before. It appears that this highly emotional extrovert had been lulled to sleep by the rhythmic beat of the horses hooves and the muffled hum of the flying wheels. A lady and her daughter sat beside him and, as his head bobbed lower and lower, he began to dream that he was hearing confessions. With the oils of priestly ordination still fresh upon him, he saw the confessional surrounded by penitents whom his ardent zeal had won back to Christ. To give them confidence and banish their anxiety, he was making a special point of treating them kindly. At that moment of the dream, a young girl was hesitantly trying to put her self-accusation into words. Le Vavasseur mumbled aloud and the other passengers smiled.

Their mirth increased as he loudly began to say again and again: "Tell it, my child. Don't be afraid. You are speaking to a kind and sympathetic father. Just tell me everything that's bothering you."

His fellow passengers tried to look out the window and suppress their snickers with a discreet cough.

"Go on," he kept insisting, "confess what's on your mind. There's no reason to be afraid."

At that point, the company burst into gales of laughter and he woke up wondering what had caused the uproar.

"Monsieur l'Abbé," said the lady, "I believe you have been busy hearing my daughter's confession for the last half hour."

Le Vavasseur's hasty apology was drowned by the guffaws of his fellow passengers.

At Amiens they left the coach and asked directions to La Neuville. Then they hurried down the dusty road because it was growing late. As a matter of fact, darkness had already fallen when they pushed open the heavy oaken door. After a brief stop to catch their breath and light a lamp, they set out on a tour of inspection. The garden could wait until daylight, but they had to see what sort of accommodations, if any, there might be inside. It was a strange trio that walked through the rooms — Libermann, the quiet, mature, and moderate leader; Le Vavasseur, the quick and volatile Creole who fancied himself a heroic pioneer; and Collin, a jovial little Breton who saw fun in everything.

God bless the good Sisters of Louvencourt. They had gathered together whatever furnishings they could from various sources. Among the acquisitions, three secondhand beds smiled a bright welcome to the newcomers. They had been painted a fire-engine red and the three clerics stared at them for a moment of awestruck silence. Then Frederic exploded. "Look at those beautiful beds!" he shouted at Libermann. "Is this the way we are going to begin? And if we do, where are we going to end? We'll die out before we've gotten under way. Let's burn them right away."

Little Collin stood by, hugely enjoying the scene. To keep it going, he began a mock defense of the poor innocent beds that Le Vavasseur had condemned to the fire. With exaggerated eloquence he pleaded for a stay of execution, for some drop of mercy's gentle rain. Then, when he saw that Frederic had the extrovert's customary disdain for anyone else's histrionics he swung to a more serious vein and observed that the riotous color, far from enhancing the beauty of the beds, made them downright repulsive. Besides, he was tired and wanted to use what Providence had accorded them. Le Vavasseur still ranted on.

At last, Francis had to make his first decision as superior of the new house. Delicately tacking between the prosecutor and the counsel for defense, he ignored the disputation on aesthetics and quietly observed that they all needed sleep and that they would have to make use of what they had. The fate of the beds could be postponed to a more propitious hour. By this time, however, Frederic was beyond the sweet call of reason. They could do what they liked. He would do no sleeping in a frivolous blood-red bed. With that, he snatched up a mattress, staggered downstairs, and spread it out on the dining-room table. It was a serio-comic routine that he insisted on following for a number of nights thereafter.

Next morning, they worked out their daily rule. After meditation, the two priests would say Mass at the Holy Family Convent in Amiens. Mr. Collin, still a seminarian, would serve them. Then they would come home for breakfast. At this juncture, Frederic blew all valves again. "Did you ever hear of such an idiotic thing! An apostle of the poor and neglected having breakfast! One meal a day; that's what we get. Nothing in the morning and nothing in the evening. That's the way new foundations should start out." When the tirade finally subsided, Francis softly repeated his prescription of three meals a day and then went on with the rule.

Not long after, the young man in charge of the kitchen placed on the table some salad and eggs for breakfast. Le Vavasseur cast a lynx eye on the menu right away. That was one of the good points about sleeping in the refectory; you could keep up with such items. He promptly summoned the criminal from the kitchen and ordered him to take these things hence. Dry bread and beer would be quite enough. The poor *cuisinier* quickly disappeared into the kitchen with the offending platters. To obviate any further trouble, he withdrew behind the stove and brought on a prodigious case of indigestion by consuming all the salad and all the eggs. After all, he was not an apostle of the poor and neglected.

When it came time to discuss the provisional rule and the commentary which Libermann had written, really serious difficulties arose. The whole idea of founding a congregation for abandoned souls had, it is true, originated with Tisserant and Le Vavasseur. But because they found it impossible to compose their differences and solve their problems, they had left the execution of the plan up to

Francis. With his customary reliance on the grace of God and his natural good sense, he emerged from the organizational process with something quite removed from the narrow limits of the two little French-speaking islands of Haiti and Reunion.

What Frederic, Eugene, and Francis first thought or first found interesting is much less important than what God intended as the end result. There are times when Divine Providence arranges things so that the initial goal becomes subsidiary, almost swallowed up by a greater work that it initiates. Thus, for example, St. Ignatius and his first Jesuit companions dreamed of going to the Holy Land to live like the Apostles and convert the Saracens; they ended by kneeling before the Pope and offering themselves for the most pressing needs of the Church wherever these might arise. Similarly, St. Francis of Assisi heard the challenge of the Sultan and moved to take it up, but before long he was assigning a different field of missionary activity to each of the early Franciscan provinces in Italy. The vast sweep of present-day Jesuit activities and the worldwide gamut of modern Franciscan enterprises are developments undreamed of by Renaissance and medieval planners. Yet the Spirit of God, who hovered over the primal chaos and whose function it is to remake the face of the earth, kept these saintly founders from unduly circumscribing their aims, lest a narrow view of the present paralyze their organizations in centuries yet to come. Theirs was the gift of receptivity to the promptings of the Eternal Wisdom which "shapes our ends, rough hew them how we will."

Some privileged souls enjoy this charismatic grace to a high degree. Libermann was one of them. Through the purifying years of suffering he had become more and more divorced from wholly human calculations and grew increasingly attuned to the inspiration of the Holy Spirit. His mind became a ready instrument in which no earthly overtones disturbed the full resonance of God's touch. No wonder then that human planners regarded him with dismay and indignation when he resolutely followed a line of action that he would have been hard put to justify rationally. The ultimate reason for his conduct was that the Eternal willed it so.

This quasi-intuitive tendency came to the fore quite frequently in the many little skirmishes he had with his collaborators during those early days of the foundation. Their ideas were not his and the conflict between their reasoning and his inspiration, between human and divine planning, plagued him seriously at this initial stage. It caused him grave disappointment when they thwarted his program for training the German secular clergy. On that occasion he yielded to the pressure of his friends. Later, the divergence came to a climactic clash over their merger with the Society of the Holy Ghost, but by then he would yield no longer.

Aside from the supernatural element in Libermann's *modus agendi,* a very natural source of conflict lay in the radically different temperament of Le Vavasseur. The poor misguided ascetic argued bitterly over every point of the rule as they went along, doing his best to impose a routine of spectacular but untenable severity. True, it was the fashion of the day. But long before St. Therese of Lisieux propounded her "little way," Father Libermann had effectively disposed of the rigid and self-conscious asceticism that found such favor among the spiritual guides of his time. Except for its masculinity and greater applicability to the active life, his doctrine is typically Theresian. It embodies a surprising degree of psychological refinement and emphasizes in a special way the dangers attendant upon excessive religious tension.

He saw little value in extreme and external mortifications for the members of his Congregation. He refused to consider such things as strokes with the discipline, penitential chains, hair shirts, sleeping on wooden planks, and fasting on days other than those appointed. He mistrusted the unhealthy atmosphere in which these practices are apt to flourish and he was particularly apprehensive about their effect on young people. He saw that all too often they end in pride, conceit, nervous tension, and a distorted scale of spiritual values.

Perfect and ready surrender to God's will at all times and under all circumstances provided the only key to holiness that Francis ever needed. "In order to go to God with your heart," he maintained, "your mind must be undisturbed, indifferent. Keep it quiet. Do things simply, without too much analysis. If you really want to please God and intend to be in full agreement with His Will, you can't go wrong. It is important for you not to spend time trying to find out exactly what is agreeable to Him or what pleases Him most. Act like a child that is fond of its father. It can't analyse or figure out what its father likes most. . . . It does the first thing that comes into its head. It gets the idea that Daddy will be pleased and then goes ahead and does it. Why not do the same? Sometimes the child makes a mistake. So will you. But that doesn't matter. God knows you meant well . . . and that pleases Him. It's essential for you to develop this unconcerned way of doing things. It will improve you much quicker than any self-conscious striving for perfection."[1]

"All your mortifications are nothing," he insisted; "all your prayers are unimportant; all your good works are worthless. That's not what Our Lord wants of you. He wants your heart, your whole heart, without question or reservation. I pooh-pooh your good works and I'm totally unimpressed by your mortifications. I ask only one thing: your heart. It's not for me. I don't want it. It's for Our Divine Lord Himself."[2]

Of course, with such an approach to the spiritual life, Francis came into immediate opposition with the prevailing thought of his day. In entering the new road, he had been led solely by grace and experience for, outside of Holy Scripture and some lives of the saints, he read hardly any ascetical literature. As he admitted himself, "in this matter I am almost completely without such knowledge as is gleaned from books. I have done almost nothing in the line of spiritual reading."[3] Yet he set himself calmly and squarely against contemporary opinion because he knew in his heart that he was right. Le Vavasseur, with his tragicomic exaggerations, was the Don Quixote of a bygone age. Libermann stood on the threshold of a new.

Frederic's ever recurring petty grievances soon fused into an attitude of fixed opposition. Francis bent over backward to placate him. He offered to sacrifice the explanatory text of the Rule, but it was all to no avail. Le Vavasseur confessed later that "bitterness had set me against the good Father and eroded my confidence in him. . . . Again and again I thought of leaving him. . . . Every time I came in contact with him, the temptation reasserted itself. During recreation, for example, I was always at loggerheads with

[1] N. D. 4, 105. [2] N. D. 4, 315. [3] N. D. 4, 190.

him. As soon as he opened his mouth, I was ready to contradict whatever he might say."[4]

Eventually, the antagonism reached such a pitch that Le Vavasseur fastened on the idea of joining the Jesuits at nearby St. Acheul. At the moment, this would have been particularly embarrassing because the Jesuit Fathers had not been enthusiastic about the arrival of the newcomers in the first place. Their superior, Father Sellier, had actually gone to the bishop and told him that he had taken a group of intriguers into his diocese. Subsequently, when he was better informed, he showed enough magnanimity to reverse his stand and speak quite favorably about them to the relieved prelate. Nonetheless, an irresponsible attack on the part of Le Vavasseur at this time might have confirmed the wild rumors that were circulating about the little group.

Here again, Libermann displayed that profound respect for the individual temperament which always characterized his dealings with others, even the most refractory. When Frederic bared his soul in one of those repentant and self-analytical moments that occasionally took possession of him, Libermann's consideration and delicacy kept him from taking unfair advantage of the situation. As Le Vavasseur wrote afterward: "The good Father didn't say much to me, but what he said was full of kindness, love, and wisdom. At that critical juncture, he took special care to convey to me only what God inspired him to say. He kept himself out of it entirely. He limited himself strictly to fostering the grace of God in me without in the slightest way exercising any personal influence over my will. Anyone else would have leaped at the chance to dominate me. He did nothing of the kind. He dealt with me so humbly, so considerately, and so respectfully, that I find it hard to describe it. . . . He never said anything that might have influenced me one way or the other."[5]

It is significant that this deep respect for the personality and the inclinations of the individual came to the fore so strikingly at the very outset. Francis attached such importance to it that it became the hallmark of his congregation. He foresaw it as the permanent and distinguishing possession of a society wherein everyone

[4] N. D. 3, 425.
[5] N. D. 3, 425 ff.

would cultivate a reverence for the character traits, the natural and supernatural endowments of his fellow members, avoiding with an alert sensitivity anything that might harm or jeopardize individual development. Through the establishment of an atmosphere of mutual tolerance in which each personality unfolded spontaneously in the manner and after the fashion that God intended, Libermann envisioned his congregation as one of the most vital and flexible groups of the Church. It would be an ensemble of truly original natures that were encouraged to reach their full potential uninhibited by a repressive and stereotyped pattern. Then and only then could it do its best work for the missionary, social, and educational programs of the apostolate.

Tensions eased somewhat at La Neuville when Le Vavasseur left for Reunion. He and Francis had agreed that his departure would be best for all concerned. Before embarking, he spent the whole night in prayer at the shrine of Our Lady of Victories in Paris and at the end of it he made a solemn promise not to sever relations with his confreres. It was a generous act that rose in all sincerity out of the calm that long meditation had evoked. Yet the temptation was destined to return at least once more before he achieved permanent serenity.

Libermann did not send him away stigmatized with the brand of perpetual uselessness. As soon as Frederic was settled in Reunion and a measure of equanimity had been restored, Francis promptly reintegrated him into the general administrative procedures as if nothing had happened. "My very dear confrere," he wrote, "the little disturbance of a year ago seems so remote now. I would like very much to spend a few hours with you. Write to me often. Tell me quite frankly what your ideas are at the present time. I'm very fond of you — much more so than you may be inclined to believe. I shall not undertake anything worthwhile without contacting you first, unless things are too urgent to permit an exchange of letters. At all events, I shall constantly keep you informed of everything."[6]

Eugene Tisserant now came from Paris to join the novitiate at long last. Hitherto, the archbishop had been so violently out of sympathy with Libermann's undertaking that he flatly refused to allow Tisserant, then an assistant at the Shrine of Our Lady of

[6] N. D. 3, 301.

Victories, to leave for La Neuville. Although less fiery than Frederic, Eugene was a child of his environment also and he functioned with a severity that was diametrically opposed to Libermann's unruffled peace. Even as a young priest in Paris, his almost savage asceticism brought him so close to exhaustion that his pastor, Father Desgenettes, had to intervene. Moreover, his highly emotional character was further handicapped by a not too generous degree of ability. Francis was not at all uncharitable when he wrote, "He has a wild imagination and a narrow outlook that is not very reliable."[7] After a brief period of preparation, Tisserant set sail for Haiti.

Another pioneer who went off to the missions was Jacques Désiré Laval. He was a young physician who had occasionally thought of the priesthood before writing his dissertation on articular rheumatism, but after a few months of practice, he grew so lax that hunting and partying held more attraction for him than attendance at church. As he recuperated from injuries sustained when he was thrown from a horse, he had plenty of leisure to think, however, so he made his peace with God, entered the seminary, and did parochial work in Brittany until such time as a missionary opportunity would open up. Laval had met Francis at St. Sulpice and when the new foundation began to operate, he received his confessor's permission to join the group.

Just then Bishop Collier was leaving for Mauritius. Fr. Laval went with him, but not before he had transferred ownership of his real and personal property to the new society. From 1841 to 1864 he lived and labored on his remote island and came to be universally regarded as a saint, a veritable Apostle of Mauritius. At his death, thousands of Catholics, Protestants, and Moslems came to pay their respects. A half-dead tubercular girl was carried in and placed beside his casket. She touched his hand and was instantly cured. Many of the bystanders reported that a fragrance of roses seemed to emanate from the corpse which, incidentally, showed no signs of decay despite the suffocating heat. More than 40,000 persons followed his body to the grave. Since then a daily stream of pilgrims can be seen visiting his burial place. From dawn to dusk, Negroes, Europeans, Creoles, Indians, Chinese, and Moslems crowd around the tomb and bring so many flowers that an attendant is

[7] N. D. 4, 187.

kept busy removing them constantly to make room for new bouquets. To this day, on the anniversary of his death, the number of visitors ranges from thirty to fifty thousand. In 1919 Pope Benedict XV signed the document by which the process for his beatification was introduced.

By this time, the Congregation of the Holy Heart of Mary was functioning with a certain measure of security. Francis actually began to think of foundations outside of France so that a wider scope of influence might be attained. With the vast stretches of England's colonies in mind, he frequently dreamed of branches in Great Britain and Ireland. According to his scheme, these foundations would develop into autonomous provinces, loosely federated under a somewhat decentralized administration. Regarding Belgium, for instance, he wrote: "The new work will be as it were, a sister of the already existing work; it will be an integral part of it and will have the same spirit, follow the same Rules, be directed by the same general administration. Just as the French branch, it will have a share in this administration and be represented in it by a fixed number of members. But in addition it will have its own special administration, with a Superior and a Council charged with this administration. The French branch will be similarly organized. . . .

"With respect to the missions, the same system would be followed. The communities established there will be staffed exclusively from the house in Belgium; they will report directly to a Belgian member representing these houses in the General Council of the Congregation. He will be in charge of their immediate direction and report about them to the Council and to the Superior General. The same system will be followed in the French Missions."[8]

Again, writing about a foundation in Great Britain, he said: "They can be sure that they won't discover any national prejudice in me. State this as strongly as you can for the benefit of Father Philips. You know that I'm completely without a trace of it."[9]

He grew as enthusiastic over the possibility of an English establishment as he had been in opening his novitiate for German candidates in Strassburg. He even proposed to go to England himself and wrote accordingly to Father Tisserant who was still a curate in Paris: "If you can spend a few days here after Easter, it will

[8] N. D. 9, 9, 4 f. [9] N. D. 3, 136.

help a lot. Then I can go to England. . . . This British business seems to me more important"[10] than union with the Holy Cross Fathers.

Despite all this enthusiasm on Libermann's part his friend wrote from Paris, insisting that he postpone the "English business" for the present and concentrate on La Neuville. Thus another one of his major objectives was thwarted. Had he been able to follow his own inclinations, things might have been quite different. He would have had a house on the German border in which both French and German vocations could have been welcomed. Then the new society would have devoted itself from the very beginning to training the German clergy. Soon thereafter, his foundation would have spread to England and Ireland and then to Belgium, Spain, and Portugal. It would have been international in character with a combined missionary and educational aim. But his associates objected strongly to any such extension, whether geographic or purposive. Only when they merged with the Congregation of the Holy Ghost did his plan — and God's — see its full fruition.

Meantime, life went on. And with it went the little cares as well as the great. The kitchen boy left much to be desired. It was clear that Francis would have to dismiss him. When the kindly but firm announcement was made, the lad stared, thunderstruck. He very deliberately sat in a chair beside the stove and refused to budge. "I never expected this. I'm satisfied here. You can't fire me!" Libermann smiled and left the room. The next morning he went back, reaffirmed his decision, and offered to pay for the work that had been done. By this time, the *cuisinier* had grown somewhat more manageable. He tearfully gathered together his personal effects and then went to say good bye to Francis. Along with the clothes, he had some money that he had brought with him. All of it was packed in a bag which he opened and held out. "Take whatever you want, Father," he said. "It's to pay you for all the happiness I've had in being with you."[11]

Jean Boisdron succeeded him. Le Vavasseur was still there at the time of his arrival, so he took the slightly retarded youngster under his wing with the clucking solicitude of a mother hen. Every morning the bustling Creole invaded the kitchen and energetically

[10] N. D. 3, 153. [11] N. D. 3, 370.

dedicated his efforts to teaching the principles of spirituality to this well-disposed but rather dense pupil. The lessons were accompanied by enough oratorical clamor to fill a large lecture hall and the imperturbable young man submitted to Frederic's holy violence without a murmur, letting every pearl of eloquence bounce harmlessly off the protective armor of his impenetrable skull. Le Vavasseur finally gave up, but not before he had observed the boy's ability to sing. When he left for Reunion, he took Boisdron along and installed him as a church cantor there, a position which the former cook filled until his death with far greater distinction than he had been able to achieve in the kitchen.

Now it was decided that the members of the community would handle the feeding operations, and Francis spent so much time over the fire that Collin, the novice, had to come to the kitchen for his conferences. Despite divided attention, however, Libermann seems to have demonstrated some culinary ability. Of course, his reputation in this respect was considerably enhanced by the fact that memories of Le Vavasseur's efforts were still painfully present to everyone in the household. Frederic used to simplify matters by boiling enough carrots to last for a whole week; then somehow he resented it when, after two or three days, the sorry mess began to cover its shame with a velvety green mold.

As the number of novices grew, the supply of potential cooks increased. Mr. de Regnier was the first to be appointed. He struggled valiantly, but after nearly a week, he came asking for a change. "Father Superior," he said ruefully, "I'm doing that kitchen job entirely too well. I do it while I'm saying my Office, I do it while I'm saying my rosary, I do it while I'm saying my other prayers. My mind is on it all the time."

Next it was Mr. de Saint-Albin. Francis and de Regnier briefed him on his duties and then left him to his own devices at eight o'clock on the first morning. With a true beginner's fervor, he started by recommending his kitchen to God. His eyes were still on the crucifix above the mantelpiece when the clock struck eleven. Terrified, he discovered that the fire had died and that nothing was started for the noon meal. He rushed to the community room where Libermann was about to give a conference to the other novices and whispered hoarsely: "Father Superior, I forgot about my work.

When you left, I began to pray before the crucifix. Then time went by without my being aware of it. There's nothing ready for dinner. Even the fire is out!" Francis smiled understandingly, gathered up his notes, and quietly announced to his audience that the conference was canceled. Then he went back to the kitchen and got things going. The dinner was served on time as usual.

One day, a novice cook poured kerosene over the salad instead of olive oil. There was a guest for dinner, Father Ducourneau, and he loved to recall the incident many years later. As a visitor, he was given priority and with the first forkful he detected the error. Then he sat back silently to enjoy the fun. As he toyed with his food, he watched furtively while the others helped themselves to the atrocious salad. It went down the table and his eyes opened wider and wider when each one began to wade into the offensive mixture with considerable appetite. After all the variation of cooks and menus, they were supremely indifferent to outlandish flavors. Only Mr. de Regnier appeared to have retained some trace of discernment. He took one mouthful and choked. "For goodness' sake!" he sputtered, "There's coal-oil in it!" Whereupon the visitor burst out laughing and the momentary tension was broken.[12]

Word soon got around that the group was living in barbaric severity and abstemiousness. While this was not exactly true, it gained currency from Le Vavasseur's rigoristic diatribes and from the too ready tongue of the Sister Portress at Louvencourt. Any time she brought something for the kitchen, she would wait until the cook was otherwise occupied and then steal a glance at the list which Frederic had posted beside the oven. It was not intended to be a complete menu. Since soup and meat were taken for granted, only carrots, cabbage, and other daily variables were noted. As the self-appointed news agency for her convent, the portress transmitted that edifying data not only to her community but also to any visitor who happened along. Soon Bishop Mioland warned Libermann to be more humane and not to impose absolute vegetarianism on his young charges. While it was easy to explain the mistake to His Excellency's satisfaction, Francis could not help feeling that there were enough antagonists around to take quick advantage of every chance to discredit him. He was right.

[12] Cf. N. D. 3, 382 ff.

The Venerable Francis Libermann (1802–1852). Founder of the Congregation of the Holy Heart of Mary. Second Founder and Eleventh Superior General of the Congregation of the Holy Ghost.

The old *Judenhaus* of Saverne where Father Libermann was born.

Dr. Samson Libermann (1790–1860).

Dr. David (Paul) Drach (1791–1865).

◀ Internal and external views. Father Libermann's garret in Rome as reconstructed on a *loggia* of the Pontifical French Seminary.

La Neuville, near Amiens, where Father Libermann founded his Congregation of the Holy Heart of Mary.

◀ Father James Laval, C.S.Sp., the Apostle of Mauritius (1803–1864).

◀ Mother Emily de Villeneuve, Founder of the Congregation of the Immaculate Conception.

▼ Father Amable Fourdinier, C.S.Sp. (1788–1845).

Internal and external views of the Shrine of Our Lady of Victories, Paris.

Father Desgenettes, Director of the Shrine in Libermann's time.

Bishop John Remigius Bessieux, C.S.Sp. (1803–1876).

Sister Sainte-Agnès (Caroline) Libermann (1827–1867).

Sister Marie-Thérèse (Theodora) Libermann (1831–1919).

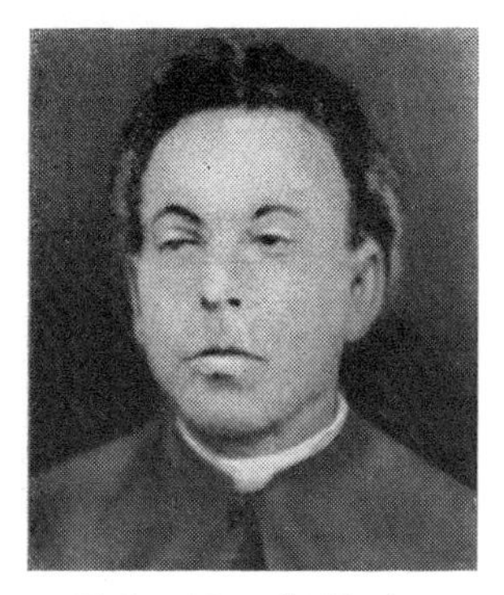

Father Francis Xavier Libermann, C.S.Sp. (1830–1907).

Dr. Henri Libermann (1834–1890).

General Leo Libermann (1837–1923).

Fr. Alexander Leguay, C.S.Sp. (1794–1865).

Blessed Mary Ann Javouhey, Founder of the Congregation of Saint Joseph of Cluny.

Father Louis Barazer de Lannurien, C.S.Sp. (1823–1854).

Father Charles Blanpin, C.S.Sp. (1817–1890).

Father Frederic Le Vavasseur, C.S.Sp. (1811–1882).

Father Eugene Tisserant, C.S.C.M.-C.S.Sp. (1814–1845).

The Abbey of Notre Dame du Gard.

Bishop Aloysius Kobès, C.S.Sp. (1820–1872).

Father Francis Delaplace, C.S.Sp. (1825–1911). Founder of the Congregation of the Sister Servants of the Holy Heart of Mary.

Father Leo Le Vavasseur, C.S.Sp. (1822–1892). Liturgist.

Father Claude Francis Poullart des Places (1679–1709). Founder of the Congregation of the Holy Ghost.

Bishop Alexander Monnet, C.S.Sp. (1812–1849).

Father John Loewnbruck, C.S.Sp. (1795–1876), the architect of the merger of the Congregation of the Holy Heart of Mary with the Congregation of the Holy Ghost.

The Motherhouse of the Holy Ghost Fathers in Paris, which until recently served also as the Holy Ghost Seminary.

Father Nicholas Warnet, C.S.Sp. (1795–1863).

Father Joseph Lossedat, C.S.Sp. (1820–1887).

Father Jerome Gravière, C.S.Sp. (1814–1886).

Father Mathurin Gaultier, C.S.Sp. (1803–1869).

Father Ignatius Schwindenhammer, C.S.Sp. (1818–1881).

Shrine on Father Libermann's grave in Chevilly, near Paris.

CHAPTER FOURTEEN

THE OPPOSITION

The rumors continued. Strange stories of every sort circulated about the little group at La Neuville and the dangerous eccentric at their head. Because they found readiest expression in episcopal residences and seminary rectors' quarters, candidates for the Holy Heart of Mary Society were vigorously discouraged from entering. Francis suffered keenly under the growing mistrust, particularly since his respect for the human personality made him scrupulously careful not to exert undue influence on a possible recruit. "I use absolutely no pressure," he affirmed, "to get candidates. I quietly wait till God gives me work and people to help me do it. It would hardly be fitting for this least of His servants to entice men away from other occupations. . . . When postulants come, I rejoice that the Master is sending laborers into this neglected and needy corner of His vineyard. When they don't, I avoid getting excited.

"The only regret that I feel and will continue to feel comes from the fact that some holy persons imagine they are doing the right thing when they make it hard for me. They have their reasons, of course, for agitating against me. They consider me proud, vain, ambitious, a dreamer, a fool. . . . If these things are true, it is understandable that they should dislike me. But what can I do about it? The Good Lord must want me to be tried like this.

"It is disconcerting to know that my reputation has been blackened before the Archbishop of Paris. I'm sure if he knew the great sadness that oppresses me, he would feel sorry for me, no matter how strong his indifference or contempt may have grown. If His Grace knew how little influence I have brought to bear on the priests of his archdiocese, he would certainly not criticize me for proselytizing activities among them. I assure you that his displeasure is my greatest worry at the moment."[1]

Libermann's instinctive concern was fully justified. The archbishop's antagonism intensified as time went on. He opposed not only Francis, but the Society in general and its plans. He prompted the French Government to request Rome's approval for an arrangement whereby the Ordinary of Paris would have charge of ministering to the spiritual needs of all French colonies. He even had ideas of founding his own congregation to take care of the work involved. Realization of these proposals would have put him in a position to snuff out the little community at La Neuville.

Francis reacted in characteristic fashion: "It is certain that His Grace would do great harm to us by starting that sort of congregation. Then there would be two institutes struggling along and preventing each other's success. I would really be sorry if I were thus to be thwarting the excellent things that His Grace might do for the welfare of French colonial Negroes."[2]

Libermann expressed a hope that the archbishop might accept his priests for the work, but he knew very well that the basis of the whole problem was personal antipathy and suspicion. "The only obstacle at present is myself," he observed. "From all sides I hear that people have been trying for quite a while to arouse suspicion against me among the members of the Archbishop's entourage. If His Grace thinks it wise to delve more deeply into these allegations, . . . I ask nothing more than to appear before him. I shall answer simply and honestly anything he may wish to ask me. I am even ready, if he so desires, to outline in writing the principal points of spiritual doctrine on which he may want to question me. If the obstacles are completely insurmountable, then tell His Grace that the work can go on without me. I certainly wouldn't insist on remaining with the foundation if my very presence jeopardized its success. Should it be successful for the honor of God, it matters little whether the accomplishment is mine or someone else's. Only one thing is important: to find a person who is acceptable to His Grace and has, at the same time, the confidence of my associates.

---

[1] N. D. 3, 224 f.
[2] N. D. 3, 33.

I think that, with God's help, we may find that person in Father de Brandt."[3]

But the Archbishop of Paris remained obdurate. He refused to see Francis and maintained his opposition without knowing him personally.

The Cardinal Archbishop of Arras now conceived an even more violent enmity toward the little convert Jew with whom his colleague of Paris seemed to be having so much trouble. Cardinal de la Tour d'Auvergne was no man to be trifled with. He had heard all the alarming reports about Libermann and now something had happened here in Arras, right under his patrician nose, that propelled him into speedy action. One of his seminarians, Charles Blanpin, had been at St. Sulpice and had now become one of the little band at La Neuville. The boy's mother was a widow, rather well off and painfully scrupulous. Libermann's enemies drew a heartrending picture of this pathetic woman who needed the support of her son so badly but feared to incur the horrors of divine wrath by urging him to come back to the diocesan clergy. They went on to describe young Blanpin himself as a pitiful victim of an ecclesiastical Svengali who spent his time luring unsuspecting seminarians into his web and then keeping them trapped in his outlandish novitiate against their will. The horrible injustice of it all made His Eminence fume with righteous indignation. He ordered the Bishop of Amiens not to ordain Blanpin under any circumstances and then dropped the full weight of his ire on St. Sulpice for allowing such things to happen. Francis wrote a carefully-worded letter of explanation to the outraged Cardinal and ended it courageously with: "After noting what I have taken the liberty to set forth in this letter, Your Eminence will find that our work is very important for the glory of God, and that our existence is neither so precarious nor our conduct so reprehensible as is thought to be the case by some priests whose zeal and wisdom exceed by far their knowledge of the true situation."[4] With this, the skirmish was over but the battle still went on.

Yet, if the older clergy feared and suspected him, the young priests and students of France were enthusiastically in favor of him. Monsieur Dupont, a Parisian seminarian, even asked permission to

[3] N. D. 3, 34 f.
[4] N. D. 3, 341.

copy some of Libermann's writings. Francis' humility rebelled against things like this. "Because I am only your servant," he wrote back, "I cannot claim any rights over myself or what I have written. I belong to everybody and everyone can do what he wants with me according to God's will. But, my very dear friend, I beg you, have mercy on this poor fellow and don't ruin him by handing him over to the demon of pride . . . Monsieur Senez also played this nasty trick on me by copying my writings. . . . Please don't allow others to copy them."[5]

Nevertheless, youth is quick to sense the dawn of something new. Libermann's ideas had a special appeal for his young contemporaries. His letters, notes, and memoranda passed surreptitiously from hand to hand. Their appeal for heroic abandonment to God's will and his inspiring yet peaceful zeal struck such a responsive chord in the unspoiled idealism of their readers that they were widely disseminated despite his protests. Eventually, this caused an uproar at St. Sulpice. Unsympathetic faculty members and students accused him of being a sickly theorist whose novel theological concepts were endangering the orthodoxy of the seminary. Father Mollevaut wrote to counsel greater prudence. Others reproached him bitterly for aiding and abetting the affair.

Then resentment arose on another front. Traces of active Gallicanism could still be found in the France of Libermann's day. They flourished particularly in the liturgy, despite the fact that the Church was interested in fostering Roman usage in rubrical matters. Francis, who was subsequently to sponsor Leon Le Vavasseur's textbook on ceremonies according to Roman pontifical decrees, now insisted that the novices follow Roman practice. When a newcomer arrived with his Parisian breviary, he would quietly explain that a true son of the universal Church should do things as they were done in Rome. Then he would unobtrusively substitute the Roman office for the Gallican breviary. It was a procedure that effectively eliminated undue chauvinism from his community, but it earned him the undying hatred of those who jealously guarded the prerogatives of Paris against any extension of Vatican influence.

Just about then, Father Fourdinier, the Superior General of the Holy Ghost Fathers, declared war on Libermann for seeming to

[5] N. D. 3, 101.

encroach on his domain. The Spiritans had been educating diocesan priests since 1703. Gradually, more and more of their alumni went off to work in the French colonies, where they still maintained a kind of tenuous affiliation with the Society of the Holy Ghost. Although these priests limited themselves in general to caring for the free population by means of regular parishes, and the Holy Heart of Mary Fathers were working among the Negro slaves who had not received much attention hitherto, Fourdinier saw a serious threat in the arrangement. The Spiritans were officially responsible for these areas and, since complications had already arisen through the admission to the colonies of other priests who had not been trained at Holy Ghost Seminary, the Superior General had no desire to compound his difficulties by allowing the visionaries of La Neuville to invade his territories and increase the number of misfits.

Even when the Cardinal Prefect of the Propaganda wrote to Fourdinier and asked him to permit two of Libermann's men to work in the colonies, he voiced considerable mistrust in his reply. "Your Eminence, I am not at all convinced that those priests . . . will achieve what we expect of them. . . . It is said that they are dependable priests, but . . . they are young people of whom the majority are not even ordained. . . . Should we not be a bit astonished that they are volunteering for our colonies when they have just begun and are so few in number?"[6]

Libermann did not discount this opposition on the part of the Spiritans, for they had a long and distinguished history and their influence in Parisian chanceries — both ecclesiastical and governmental — was considerable. Francis knew that Fourdinier would do his best to wield that influence against the Holy Heart of Mary group, but he also knew that Rome functions with a wisdom gleaned through centuries of experience. It diagnosed the petty jealousies, the intrigue, and the gossip, and in the end it stood by the frail God-centered man who was fighting with his back to the wall.

The Cardinal Prefect sent him full powers to appoint two priests for the island of Reunion, a gesture that was all the more surprising because Francis had made no move to secure the apostolic letters for this purpose. Then the Internuncio received him kindly and

[6] N. D. 3, 541.

spoke for nearly an hour about the work of the Congregation of the Holy Heart of Mary. After that, the prelate accompanied Francis to the door and said, "Have courage, Father Libermann. Have courage for such a beautiful work." It was another ray of sunshine in an otherwise dismal period of contradiction.

As was usual at such times of strain, his feeble health reflected the torment in his soul. Occasionally during Mass he would suffer racking nervous spasms. Then Collin, who served him most of the time, would take a firm hold of the chasuble to keep him erect. Abdominal cramps were a perpetual torture. He wrote to Dr. Samson about them: "There is still something wrong with my intestines. . . . Every morning I have two or three spells of nausea. . . . Sometimes the indisposition lasts all day. . . . I think it's due more to nerves than to anything else. . . . I have a wretched body. I'll have to do what I can to drag it with me until the end. When its time has come, the Good Lord will do with it whatever he sees fit."[7] Now too, the old headaches came back with greater frequency than ever. Often he could not do any work because of them. It is an excuse that appears over and over again in his correspondence.

Perhaps most tormenting of all, however, was the tyranny of routine and extraordinary business. He who had yearned to live as a recluse now saw his beloved silence and solitude cruelly torn from him by irksome correspondence, troubled novices, anxious visitors, official documents, and the thousand great and petty concerns of administration. Yet there was an unwelcome sort of loneliness in all this hectic activity. "I have no one here," he admitted. "I don't dare approach the Jesuit Fathers, although I am on rather good terms with them. I am afraid of getting embroiled in something from which I might find it difficult to extricate myself later on. Father de Brandt is of some assistance in things with which he is familiar, but for the rest he just says 'Yes' to everything I propose. The young men who are with me have no business experience whatsoever. It's hard if you have only yourself to rely on when serious decisions have to be made. I go along taking all the precautions I can. Then I place my trust in the Lord."[8]

---

[7] N. D. 3, 219.
[8] N. D. 3, 294.

There were times when the temptation to run away from it all pressed heavily upon him. Like the Curé of Ars who longed to flee from his crowded confessional and find rest for his soul, Francis occasionally looked back with nostalgia to the silent little attic in Rome or the quiet roads of Umbria. At such moments he was overcome with a desire to entrust the direction of the Society to someone else. Once, when he saw the chance to unite his little group with the Congregation of Holy Cross, he very nearly succumbed to the temptation. Preliminary negotiations were about to start. Then he learned that the Holy Cross Superior, while he was prepared to accept the men, was not inclined to take on the work to which Libermann's community was dedicated. After a brief correspondence and a few preliminary conversations had served to spotlight the problem, both parties abandoned the idea. The promise made at Loretto came back to haunt him. Full of shame at his cowardice, he again decided that it was better to live with the contempt of men than to betray God's mission.

Through all this manifold suffering, Libermann displayed no bitterness whatsoever. He was still the compassionate priest with the warm human heart. He remained always cheerful, kind, and serene, although he observed once that it took a good deal out of hypersensitive people like him to avoid being influenced by even such minor things as vagaries of the weather. If so, nobody noticed it. "His conversation was so animated, so paternal, and so kindly, that recreation periods seemed to end too soon," writes a contemporary. "We were always at ease when we wanted to talk to him, but we liked it better when we could hear him speak." "During recreation, he kept us interested, spoke to each one present, and made sure that everyone had a chance to say something. He had absolutely no trouble engaging in the conversation, no matter what the topic."[9]

Another reported: "It is really impossible for me to describe the way in which this good Father received me and the fine impression he made on me during our first interview."[10] This ideal of politeness and cordiality was one that he recommended to his sons. When he found it necessary to send a difficult character to the missions,

[9] N. D. 3, 379; 4, 55.
[10] N. D. 3, 378.

he wrote to those confreres who were already there: "When he acts according to his temperament he is quite inflexible, stubborn and contrary. . . . At such times, don't be severe with him. Let the bad moment pass and then, at a more opportune time, take the matter up with him privately. If you treat him with consideration, confidence, and real charity, you will bring him along and help him to overcome his faults."[11]

---

[11] N. D. 4, 129 f.

CHAPTER FIFTEEN

TROUBLED SOULS

At La Neuville, Francis became the true patron of destitute people of all sorts. One of his confreres quite frankly admitted: "I never witnessed so much activity, solicitude, gentleness, kindness and devotion. The Reverend Father kept himself frightfully busy with the poor and especially with anyone who was seeking peace of mind."[1] "There was a constant stream of visitors, particularly of the emotionally disturbed, because they had discovered his reputation for giving consolation, encouragement, advice, support, ease of conscience and a sense of security. . . . He had an extraordinary insight and an ability to detect the source of the trouble as well as to apply the proper remedy. In the course of his therapy, he maintained an unruffled considerateness. He listened to every tale of woe with imperturbable patience, whether the teller was poor or rich, first or last. Many came from Amiens and the surrounding countryside. The renown of his holiness and effective spiritual guidance spread quickly. . . . Yet, in spite of the constant interruptions he went immediately as soon as he was called to the parlor or confessional and never kept anyone waiting."[2]

The poorest and the richest — he was ready to receive the privileged of this earth, for he understood that they can be as neglected as the disenfranchised. Francis had no ingrained prejudice in behalf of the externally wretched as is often the case with romantically inclined saviors of the proletariat. He recognized that one can be exquisitely dressed, refined, and scholarly, and yet carry around

[1] N. D. 4, 47.
[2] N. D. 4, 54.

with him a heart that is breaking with unhappiness and sin. Less perceptive individuals, even those who professedly work for God, are often so bound up with material appearances that they confuse spiritual realities with externals. In their mind, neglected souls are those who live in squalor and degradation. They look on the more richly endowed members of Christ's Mystical Body as outside the pale of their ministrations. Libermann never made this mistake of reverse snobbishness.

The Sisters at La Neuville had a large orphanage for girls. As its spiritual director, Francis spent as much time as he could among the orphans. He spent many of his recreations with them, amusing them, telling them stories, and doing everything in his power to make them feel wanted and loved. One of them was a fifteen-year-old, named Clémence. She was a shy, sensitive youngster who never knew her father and who had been repudiated by her unnaturally cruel mother. After a brief sojourn at her grandmother's she landed in the orphanage at La Neuville, emotionally disturbed and suspicious of everyone. Soon after, her anxiety reached a truly critical pitch when her mother wrote to say that Clémence was not her daughter at all.

Libermann bent every effort to comfort the desolate child. Out of fear that the heartless woman who now repudiated her might later see some advantage in claiming her again, he induced Father de Brandt and Father Cacheleux to help him adopt her. Through the kindness of this strange procedure, Clémence found the first bit of security in her brief but turbulent life. She herself declared later: "Father Libermann provided for all my needs as far as he could. I am embarrassed when I think back over all his kindness to me. He was so friendly that it made me forget my troubles."[3]

As the months passed and Libermann's guidance began to take effect, Clémence became calm and self-assured. Eventually, she told him that she would like to be a nun. For an illegitimate child, however, that was going to be extremely difficult to arrange. One convent, it is true, offered to accept her, but its affairs were not in the best of order and Francis refused to let her go. Why should an underprivileged girl have to submit to such things? To his mind, she would be better off in the orphanage than in a badly

[3] N. D. 3, 388.

governed community. Still insisting on a respected and well-organized convent, he searched far and wide for one that would take her. Every door closed gently but firmly on the illegitimate child. When Clémence cried in desperation that her vocation would be thwarted by something that was not her fault, Francis Libermann replied reassuringly: "If it were necessary to found a cloister for you alone, Our Divine Lord would do it for you out of His goodness."[4] At long last, there was a break in the resistance, and the happy orphan girl took the veil.

Clémence was but one of many. Another, eighteen years of age and most attractive, caused him no little concern when she was setting out for Paris. He wrote to a lady there and explained the case. "I know very well that Paris is dangerous for a pretty young girl. . . . This one would like to get a job in a shop where cottons, laces, embroidery and similar materials are sold. . . . She's a good girl, full of faith and religion. She's gifted in many ways: good manners and almost too much beauty. That's what makes me apprehensive about her going to Paris. . . . What she really needs is to be placed with a devout family, to be settled in a milieu where she can practice her faith without let or hindrance in moral safety. . . . You will be doing a good turn for one of my penitents."[5]

Once when he was in Paris staying, as was his custom, at the Hotel Strasbourg, one of his acquaintances came and asked help for a youngster he had found alone and abandoned in the city. Francis promised to see that she was taken care of right away. He returned to La Neuville, begged the Mother Superior to take her in, countered all the arguments against it, and met the last frantic objection that there was no extra bed by even sending a mattress to the orphanage. Then he rushed off a letter to Paris: "Hurry up and send the girl you brought around to the Strasbourg Hotel yesterday. They will give her a nice welcome at the orphanage. They didn't have a mattress to spare but I ordered one for them. . . . Send her by coach."[6]

They were often strange, forlorn, and difficult people, these unfortunates who sought his help. In many instances they had no one else to turn to, because those they consulted feared to appear ridiculous in the eyes of colleagues and superiors. It takes courage

[4] N. D. 4, 343. [5] N. D. 4, 266 f. [6] N. D. 4, 426.

to assist society's outcasts, for their eccentricities can easily prove embarrassing and disappointing to the one who befriends them. Human respect will lead him to give them a wide berth unless his moral fiber is of the heroic stamp. Libermann's was. Human respect exercised little influence over his actions. The opinions of others played no part in his life when the welfare of souls was at stake. Despite the danger of ridicule, he resolutely went ahead, dispensing guidance and consolation to anyone, no matter how abnormal, who sought his help.

Already regarded by several bishops and many priests as an unbalanced zealot himself, and fully aware that a wider acceptance of this opinion might well mean the end of his life's work, he nonetheless refused to betray those who turned to him as their last hope. Moreover, he demanded the same courage in others. "You should," he urged, "despise that fear or timidity which leads us to think, act, judge, and speak to the detriment of those who deserve so much of our sympathy. We are naturally inclined to protect our reputation and assure our self-esteem, but we should be prepared to sacrifice everything for the spiritual welfare of these poor devils. We must resign ourselves to having others regard us as stupid, superstitious, and ridiculous, rather than leave off helping these unfortunate souls. . . . I myself have given in to this weakness occasionally. . . . God knows how severely I shall be punished for it. . . . I hate to think of it. . . . I really will deserve it, for when we act that way, we are really wolves in the flock who tear to pieces the poor, weak sheep for our own ease and comfort."[7] Indeed, for him, as for St. Peter, it was better to serve God rather than men.

Through the happy confluence of inspiration, exceptional talent, and the effects of his own neuro-physical affliction, Francis became one of the few who could recognize the role of divine grace even in the neurotic, the disturbed, and the unintegrated. His writings are full of precious analyses in which full attention is devoted to that all too frequently neglected dimension of grace. Some religiously inclined observers seem to rule out the possibility of intimate union with God in cases of pronounced aberration. They seem to detect some irreverence in attributing even a slight degree of holiness to the mentally or emotionally ill. Libermann, on the other hand,

[7] N. D. 4, 364 ff.

always looked for potentialities that might be exploited, even though he knew all too well the handicaps under which he was working. That is why he said about one client: "I don't think she has acquired a single virtue. She's in no condition to do so. At least that's what I'm inclined to believe. Nonetheless, her will is wholly pointed toward God. If only she didn't go about blindly impelled by attractions, repulsions, or antipathies."[8]

In this fashion, he developed over the years a special doctrine for those who devote themselves to the care of such unhappy souls. His letters grew into a paeon of charity, a valuable summa of spiritual guidance, a fountain of wisdom for our own day when work among the neglected has become an organized profession. The psychologists, social workers, nurses, and all the ranks of mobilized interest need inspiration and encouragement if organized charity is not to become the great fiasco of our century. The death of love, the loss of human sympathy could bring on a quick fulfillment of the Scriptural prophecy: "And the charity of many will grow cold" (Mt. 24:12). Francis Libermann's teachings and example could go far toward staving off that tragedy.

That Francis wanted his followers to emulate this example is evident from the words of Father Louis de Lannurien. Functioning as Libermann's confidant and personal secretary, de Lannurien appreciated the scope of things with a clarity of vision that is all the more remarkable because it lacked the historical perspective on which we can call. After the Venerable Father's death, de Lannurien penned a long memorandum dated July 28, 1853. He did so at the request of his confreres, who wanted to preserve for posterity whatever ideas the secretary might have gleaned from his close association with Francis. Among other things he wrote:

"It is evident that his first mission consisted in the foundation of an apostolic work to help the most neglected souls. Libermann added that, for the moment, Divine Providence was sending us to help the poor Negroes as the most abandoned people. In the same Provisional Rule he stated that those who remain in Europe must also take care of souls there. Thus, from the days of La Neuville on, special attention was paid to social works, such as those for the Savoyards and those for orphans. After that, when the Bordeaux

[8] N. D. 4, 336.

job was accepted, a decision was made not to confine the Congregation to the abandoned souls of Africa in particular or even the missions in general. Rather, it was decided that the Congregation's work extends to every sort of apostolic activity among the neglected, whether in Europe or overseas, wherever personnel is badly needed."

Libermann himself justified his involvement in such things quite simply: "These works are not against the purpose or the spirit expressed in the Rule. True, in the beginning we did not think of them, but this does not prove that God did not want them. Here is my plan: The work which we will undertake in Europe will be concerned mainly with the salvation of the working class, sailors, and soldiers. . . . We will begin our establishments in the principal ports serving our missions, such as Bordeaux, Marseille, Toulon, Brest, Nantes and Lorient."[9]

Since Francis formulated such declarations with considerable prudence, we may assume that they were set down only after lengthy reflection had fully ripened these concepts in his mind. He knew that, in committing them to writing, he was leaving behind a record for posterity.

---

[9] N. D. 9, 288. The "Rule" referred to here is that of the Holy Heart of Mary.

CHAPTER SIXTEEN

HUMANITY AND HOLINESS

One of the commonest misconceptions about holy people is the impression that they walk with their heads in the clouds, blissfully unaware of the little gems of beauty and the contrasting blobs of ugliness that lie about their feet. Popular apotheosis has mistakenly raised them above mundane considerations and it has often removed them irrevocably beyond the pale of that peculiarly human characteristic, a sense of humor. Through some false alchemy of the spirit, those unfamiliar with saints would make them not a little less but a little more than the angels. With a perverse revival of Manicheanism, they refuse to believe that humanity and holiness are quite compatible.

The whole literature of hagiography gives the lie to such a distorted idea and Libermann's writings in particular are redolent with a warmth and quiet humor that is all the more marvelous when one thinks of the suffering hand that committed them to paper. Once when his niece Pauline showed some concern over her younger brother's antics, Libermann wrote soothingly:

"It's understandable that you are worried about Francis. I figured things wouldn't go so well this year. But there is no need to be peeved at him on that account. I don't believe it's really his fault. If he doesn't study as hard as he should, it's because he has not yet learned how to put his mind down to it. Maybe, too, he is not ready for that kind of study. It's perfectly natural not to like school if you're not good at it and if you have to work hard for what you get.

"Besides, little Francis has an easy-going character. His main trouble seems to be that he gives up too quickly. So I say again what I told you so often when I was home with you, nobody should scold him too much and nobody should let him know that they think he's stupid. They should talk nicely to him and encourage him with kindness. When they lose their tempers and shout at him they just cause him to freeze up inside. They discourage him when they let him see how bad they think he is.

"Daddy will never be able to be patient with poor Francis. O.K., then you should be the go-between. Try to console the poor lad when they nag him and whisper to him that you know he can do better if he wants to.

"Try not to lose your temper with him. Always be sweet and kind. Don't cross him. To make him like you, never say anything nasty. In that way you will save him a lot of trouble when he grows up."[1]

About the same time, Dr. Samson Libermann was encountering serious financial difficulties. He had no Jewish patients because they regarded him as an apostate; very few Catholics went to him because they were prejudiced against a Jewish doctor. Thus his practice was limited mainly to a few Catholic institutions. The melancholy situation began to make him gloomy and irritable at home. Before he reached the danger point, Francis moved in with a word of fraternal advice: "Give yourself and your whole family over to the Providence of God . . . but don't try to ignore your family's needs. God certainly doesn't disapprove of your concern, but you should take your distress in stride. Make every effort to preserve that equanimity which is so threatened by all this sadness.

"When reverses make you feel discouraged or bitter or annoyed or impatient, raise your thoughts to God and His Blessed Mother. Humbly make an act of submission to and confidence in God. Then quiet down for love of Him."[2]

For Caroline, another of his nieces, Francis had an "exceptional sympathy." He searched around until he found a boarding school where the moderate tuition would enable her to attend without being a burden on the poor physician back in Strassburg. As a personal favor to him, the Sisters at Louvencourt took her in with-

[1] N. D. 3, 50 f.
[2] N. D. 4, 90 f.

out asking much in return. In fact, the Mother Superior felt so sorry for Dr. Samson that she even promised to accept the three younger girls later on. It was an ideal arrangement, because Uncle Francis was nearby and could keep an eye on the little scholars from his vantage point at La Neuville.

When Caroline arrived, everything seemed new and strange to her. She must have succumbed to a very bad case of homesickness, for Libermann was soon reporting the pitiful story with mock seriousness: "Last Sunday, the Headmistress observed that she was feeling very low, so she told her to go ahead and have a good cry. Caroline very dutifully did so. She climbed into the hayloft and cried her eyes out. It did her a lot of good. The next day I visited her. She was still full of tears, but it was a pleasure to see her weep. She cried and laughed at the same time. Tonight she came to spend the evening with me and solemnly assured me that Daddy had promised she wouldn't have to stay in exile for more than a year."[3]

Then he wrote to her sister Mary: "Caroline is doing fine. This evening she came over for two hours and a half. The weather was nice, so we walked in the garden. She's homesick. Since last Sunday she must have shed at least half a liter of tears. You can't feel sorry for her because she laughs right in the middle of a sob. If only Mary were here, she told me today, then I wouldn't be homesick. So what? Everybody has to carry his cross. Caroline insists, though, that hers is heaviest of all. Today, her grief was diminishing. When she was here yesterday, it flowed like two little streams."[4]

Soon after this, Caroline's first report appeared. It was literally nothing to write home about and Uncle Francis saved the day by saying so in a letter to her father: "She's terribly upset about her report because she thinks she could have done better. She'd like to be first in class. She gave me the offending card to send on to you, but I didn't think that would do much good. I'm sure the next report will be a lot better."[5]

When Isabel, his sister-in-law, sent a little keg of preserves for the girls at school, Francis delicately intercepted it. "I have given the keg of preserves," he said breezily, "to my orphans who are also under the care of the good Sisters at Louvencourt. I was afraid the little ladies of the boarding school might not be too keen for it

[3] N. D. 4, 402. [4] N. D. 4, 407. [5] N. D. 4, 470.

because they're not used to that type of food. Then Caroline would have felt embarrassed because they would have kidded her right and left about it. I wanted to spare her that embarrassment."[6] Caroline was certainly a lucky girl to have such an understanding uncle nearby.

The same sort of gentle solicitude was extended to the rest of the family. Even little Hank, another nephew in Strassburg, must have glowed with pride as he trotted off to grade school knowing that Uncle Francis expected great things of him for, with a strong appeal to natural incentives, Libermann had written about the little fellow, urging that he study real hard so he could come home laden with honors. In a sentence obviously meant for the big ears of a little pitcher, he drove home the point: "Pretty soon Hank will be coming home from graduation carrying a pile of books. Perhaps Mama should send Clerc along with a big hamper to help carry home all the prizes Hank is going to win."[7]

Felix, the bookbinder in Paris, occasioned more serious concern. He had his employees working on Sundays and he was not getting along too well with his wife. "I was with them last Sunday," Francis wrote. "The binders were hard at it in his workshop. I'll write to him about that as soon as the big rush is over. Maybe then he will go back to a six-day week. For the rest they're not doing too badly. At the present time they're getting along pretty well. Christopher and Adolph were the principal cause of the disorder there — I mean the spats between him and his wife."[8]

Poor Christopher. He was in America now and things were going rather badly. His wife was sick, he was nearly bankrupt, and he had fallen away from the practice of his faith. He was bent on returning to Europe in hopes of enlisting some support from his brothers. As a matter of fact, Samson was already wondering if Francis might not take the poor fellow in as a Brother or at least as a domestic. The reply came back quick and definite: "It's quite certain that I shall never accept as a Brother anyone like our poor Christopher. If I did, I would fail in my duty. Nor could I take him as a domestic. He couldn't live with us. He doesn't have enough faith or piety. Besides, he would always be doing whatever came into his mind and he wouldn't observe the rules that are the

[6] N. D. 4, 471. [7] N. D. 3, 221. [8] N. D. 4, 68.

accepted things with us. That would wreak havoc with our community. . . .

"Nonetheless, as soon as he arrives, we've got to do something right away to get him a job. As yet I don't see how. Incidentally, how is he going to manage the return trip? It takes three hundred francs for the ticket alone, not counting the other expenses. I don't know what to do. His wife is still sick and he has sent for money to take care of her."[9]

Thus it went, the seriousness and levity, problems and pleasantries, all blended in the typical rhythm of a very human existence. In the light of Libermann's manifold sufferings, his writings contain amazingly frequent references to joy and laughter: "A soul that belongs to Our Lord must preserve cheerfulness in heart and serenity of mind." "Don't be sad. At your age gaiety is a necessity. Joyful characters are always the best." "When you feel like laughing, go ahead and laugh! I like it so much when you laugh." "Be open, light-hearted, simple, and cordial to everyone." "Be cheerful, and laugh heartily."[10]

Once he wrote about a little girl from La Neuville who wanted to be a nun. "Little Adele," he observed, " . . . is lively enough and yet truly modest. But she's laughing all the time. She seems to have a fine character and appears to be excellently fitted for the religious life."[11]

His sly good humor comes to the fore again in a letter addressed to a Mother Superior who exhibited more than usual anxiety over the dowries her novices were to bring with them. He had lined up two candidates for her convent, one with a dowry and one who, he hoped, would be able to live on what he called the provisions kept in the storehouses of Divine Providence. Then suddenly he pulls himself up short with a tongue-in-cheek apology to the financially-minded Mother Superior who might not appreciate such levity. "Forgive the pleasantry," he added innocently. "As the proverb goes, 'He who is hungry doesn't appreciate a joke.' "[12]

In dealing with an unhappy priest who blamed all his trouble on the fact that he had been ordained too young, Libermann shot back: "That's like bemoaning the fact that Adam committed his

---

[9] N. D. 4, 221 f.
[10] N. D. 4, 430; 3, 107, 171, 121, 290.
[11] N. D. 4, 288.
[12] N. D. 4, 120.

original sin and caused all our problems." About the same time, when he was trying to do something for a much-disturbed girl who lacked a sense of discretion, he analyzed her situation rather pointedly: "Her special virtue, her peculiar grace, lies in being simple as a dove, but she seems to lack the prudence of the serpent."[13]

Another religious superior seemed to be pursuing a most unenlightened policy with a highly gifted novice. In order to develop the girl's humility, she was going to great lengths to depreciate the candidate's natural abilities even while she was exploiting them. Libermann cautioned her against the inherent artificiality of such a procedure. "Don't go out of your way to ignore or despise the girl's natural talents and then make use of them while you are putting on a great show of not noticing them. Moreover, I don't think you should subject her to fabricated humiliations or try to give her the impression that you have a low opinion of her . . . as we occasionally read in the lives of some saints. She has a keen mind. She'll soon discover what your real motives are. By that very fact it won't do her much good. In the end, you will do nothing more than give her a good laugh."[14]

The same easy trust in common sense carried over even into matters of conscience. He had little use for the black and white distinctions of right and wrong that mechanically determined guilt or innocence without reference to circumstance, situation, and character of the person he was advising. And out of his mighty awareness of the richness and complexity of human existence, he developed a conviction that makes his ethical doctrine sound surprisingly modern in its psychosomatic overtones. "Learn to know the temperament and character of people," he maintained, "without judging or condemning them, and try in this manner to make it possible for yourself to associate with anyone and to gather experience for the future."[15]

He startled one of his clients by conveying to him this amazing bit of assurance: "I shall begin by telling you something that may tend to shock you a good deal. From the very outset, I've had serious doubts about the enormous crime against purity about which you spoke and for which you seemed to think there was no pardon. From the very first line about the mortally sinful character of that

[13] N. D. 4, 136, 278. [14] N. D. 4, 139. [15] N. D. 4, 172.

act I had my doubts. Now that I've read and re-read the case again and again, I am ready to stand by my conviction that there was no serious sin involved because you didn't reflect enough to give consent with a perfectly free will. Perhaps you might be smart to use natural means in dealing with this problem. A blood-letting, a plaster, or a laxative taken on the advice of your doctor or an experienced therapist might take care of all your temptations."[16]

Pious ears might have found it offensive to hear Francis recommending a purgative in place of a blessed candle, but modern research in endocrinology has certainly endorsed his view that moral problems often trace their origin to a physiological derangement. Even at present, there are still people who fail to arrive at a proper synthesis between the natural and the supernatural and who, on that account, live in an atmosphere of tension that is wholly foreign to and even destructive of true spirituality. Although he lacked the scientific data available to us, he can never he accused of limited vision in this regard.

Somewhat later, when he became involved with the guidance of Mother Emily de Villeneuve's community at Castres, his letters center in part around the question of religious authority. One of them to a superior is so clearheaded that it deserves quotation *in extenso* here:

> You are the first servant of your community. . . . You may object on the score that your authority should be respected. I answer: it is not your authority that ought to be respected but that of our Divine Lord who is in you and whom you represent to your Sisters.
>
> But, you argue, how can I govern a community if my authority is not respected?
>
> I do not deny that it should be. Your Sisters ought to have the greatest respect, but not for you — you are nothing — but for Jesus Christ, their Master, whom you represent.
>
> If one of them ever fails in her dealings with you, be sorry for it and pray a good deal for her because she has failed in regard to Jesus Christ. But do not, on any account, seek to avenge your own authority and, much less, become angry and hold spite against her. . . . On the contrary, develop a gentle concern for her and try to bring her around to her duty. In the meantime, while you are doing what you can to that end, keep concentrating on the inner condition of that Sister and choke back any resentful memories of what she did to you. If you allow yourself to reflect on the affront, you run the danger of acting out of self-love. . . .

[16] N. D. 4, 243 f.

Your first reaction will lead you to use the wrong approach. A second look at the case will enable you to find the proper way.

The calm and moderate approach is the one most in line with the spirit of Christ.

Always remember that mildness and persuasion reach the heart, but harshness and rigidity cause only an external change.

If we want to guide people, we must learn how to bend and adjust ourselves to them. We have to align ourselves with their individual psychological make-up, respect them at all times, and assume whatever manner is best suited to their various dispositions. That is what St. Paul means when he says "Be all things to all men."

Put up with the evil for a long time, and if there are times when you think you can't stand it for another minute, put up with it again. In the end you will see that you did well.

Always remember that rigor and open opposition breaks people who are not well disposed. They are rarely cured by it.

Keep in mind what I told you in Paris: most souls are lost through discouragement. Among virtuous souls especially this is a common problem. Support and encourage them and you will see how Our Lord will help you.

One who has committed a fault is often scolded and persecuted on the pretext of preventing her from repeating the offence. Actually, our motive is often quite different; we are just giving vent to impatience. We are too weak and imperfect ourselves to put up with the weakness and imperfections of our neighbor, but we try to make ourselves believe that we are acting out of zeal.

Pay special attention, dear Sister, to one fault that seems to be rather common among superiors of women's communities. It consists of a kind of antipathy toward characters that conflict with their own and a number of pet peeves regarding certain faults and ways of acting. As a result of this, they are quick to judge such characters unfavorably and to be particularly severe in dealing with their shortcomings. They give in to coldness, indifference, bad humor, and sternness in dealing with such people.

As far as you can, avoid contradicting others. Trials are for perfect souls. We should bring the imperfect ones along within the scope of their potential and try through kindness to stimulate the full realization of that potential.[17]

From all this it is evident that the luminous rays emanating from La Neuville had begun to spread a new warmth in the chill world of formation. Their span of influence would increase with the passage of time.

---

[17] N. D. 4, 293 ff., 325.

CHAPTER SEVENTEEN

PIONEERS

By now things were in rather good running order in the new foundation. Some young men had already completed their training as members of the society and new candidates were constantly applying for admission. Oddly enough, despite widespread calumnies, the difficulty was not one of finding vocations but of finding a territory in which they could put their energy and enthusiasm to work. The early outlook of Fathers Tisserant and Le Vavasseur had gradually widened with the development of the Congregation. It now embraced all neglected souls throughout a great part of the French colonial empire. Only Father Fourdinier, the Spiritan Superior General, stood in the way of its fulfillment.

Over and over again we find Libermann writing: "Tell Father Le Vavasseur that Father Fourdinier has not changed in our regard. He would destroy us if he could." "Father Fourdinier is always very much against us. This holy man would be a menace to us if he had a great deal of influence. He's doing what he can to ruin us, and he's doing it with the best of intentions and out of zeal for good. I believe he's misled by a fear of the harm we might cause the Spiritans. God has put him in charge of the Congregation of the Holy Ghost and it's only natural that he would be inclined to defend it against those he fears." "Father Fourdinier is a holy man. He has won his case and I am not angry because of that. . . . He has already made many moves to have our men barred [from the colonies]. At last he's been successful. . . . As long as the kingdom of Our Lord is preached in that unhappy country, that's all right by us. It's not at all necessary that the good be done by us alone."[1]

Since the Spiritans wielded sufficient influence in governmental circles to exclude from the colonies these "Libermannists" whom they regarded as dangerous and visionary upstarts, Francis went to pray at the shrine of Our Lady of Victories at Paris. On the way out, Father Desgenettes caught up with him. They were old friends, this quiet convert Jew and the kindly pastor of the shrine church, and they paused on the stone steps to chat for a while. Libermann frankly admitted that he was in trouble.

"How is that?" asked the older priest sympathetically. "Do you need money?"

"No, Father," said Francis. "The Blessed Virgin sees to it that we get along that way. But we have no place to send our young priests. The way is blocked on every side."

Father Desgenettes did his best to offer consolation, but he was surprised to note that Libermann seemed to have little need of it. The man was actually lighthearted, as if it was the Blessed Virgin's problem now. A few moments later, when they were sitting near the old pot-bellied stove in the rectory, Francis stared pensively into the fire and observed in matter-of-fact tones: "I feel sure we will soon have a mission." The words startled Father Desgenettes somewhat. They rang with such confidence that they sounded almost prophetic.

That same evening, after Libermann had returned to La Neuville, so many pilgrims swarmed in to see the old pastor that he completely forgot about Francis and his problems. It was far from his mind the next morning when he went into the sacristy and found a newly consecrated prelate waiting to say Mass.

Bishop Barron was a slim young Irish-American who also had a problem. The hierarchy of his country, particularly the Bishop of Charleston, had expressed some concern over the welfare of liberated slaves that had been sent back to Africa. Rome directed the Council of Baltimore to do something about it, and Father Barron, then Vicar-General of the Philadelphia diocese, was chosen to lead a little band of volunteers on the first expedition to Liberia.

His was not the first missionary assault on Africa. Jesuits, Capu-

[1] N. D. 6, 323, 336, 472.

chins, Carmelites, Augustinians, and others had worked and died there four centuries before, and their activities had been extensive. Yet despite their prodigious labors, hardly a trace remained of their apostolic campaign and virtually none of the Negroes remained Catholic. The Council of Baltimore turned first to the Jesuits, then to the Dominicans, and finally to the secular clergy in general when it resolved to do something for the repatriated American slaves. None of these groups found it possible to respond at that time. Only Father Barron and a New York priest, Father Kelly, answered the call for volunteers. With them they took a young Irish layman, Denis Pindar.

Upon their arrival in Africa, Father Barron surveyed the situation and found that there were very few Catholics among the former slaves in Liberia. The missionary potential in surrounding areas, however, seemed unlimited. He went to Rome and presented a full report of his observations to the Sacred Congregation of the Propagation of the Faith (the Propaganda). In due time he was consecrated bishop and named Vicar Apostolic of the Two Guineas, a gigantic tract that ran five thousand miles along the coast, had no limits to the interior, and embraced roughly what we now know as Senegal, Gold Coast, Nigeria, Cameroons, Congo, Angola, and S. W. Africa. And he with one priest and a layman to help him!

Father Desgenettes listened with rapt attention to this amazing story and agreed with the bishop that additional man power was his first and crucial need. Then he went off to say Mass at the shrine altar — the same altar where he once had heard the mysterious voice urging him to consecrate his church to the Immaculate Heart of Mary. Toward the end of the Holy Sacrifice, he stopped in his tracks. He had suddenly remembered Libermann's bent figure before the fire and the eyes staring into the flames as he said: "I feel certain that the Holy Heart of Mary is preparing a field of work for us."

Bishop Barron was still at the high altar when Father Desgenettes came back to the sacristy. After unvesting, the old pastor paced up and down excitedly. He could hardly wait to tell the good news. Then, after the first outburst of enthusiasm, he rushed off to call Francis back to Paris.

The meeting, of course, was a profoundly happy one. Bishop

Barron promised to visit La Neuville and when he did the place and the men impressed him favorably. Before long, his future collaborators were selected and preparations were made for the journey. A colonial doctor in London recommended September as the best time for departure. It was decided that Libermann's men would leave then and the Bishop would follow one month later with Mr. Keily, a seminarian, and an Irish carpenter, John Egan, in tow. Accordingly, seven members of the Holy Heart of Mary Congregation traveled to Bordeaux, the port of embarkation. They were Fathers Bessieux, de Regnier, Audebert, Roussel, Bouchet, Maurice, and Paul (not to be confused with James) Laval. Theirs was a tragic odyssey, as their diary bears witness. They kept a detailed record of events much as the crew of a crashing plane scrawls every terrifying item in its logbook up to the last minute, hoping at least that some other pilot will profit by the gruesome data.

In the absence of Libermann's sense of moderation and his aversion for romantic extravagance, their wild unreasoning fervor quickly reasserted itself. Father Bessieux stopped at a foundling home in Bordeaux and enlisted three additional recruits, Andrew and John Fabé and Gregory Sey. Francis worried a good deal about that when he got the news, for these were men without special religious or missionary training, picked up at the type of place that often houses questionable characters. It was too late to do anything about it. The boat was ready to sail.

In a few days, the postman brought a package. It was the clock that Libermann had bought for the group. On his own, Father Bessieux had decided to buy a couple of hourglasses instead! Next came the insurance cancellation. Francis had insisted on providing the expedition — much to their disgust — with twenty-four tons of supplies and he very wisely wanted to insure them. Bessieux, however, preferred to rely on Divine Providence. It was more supernatural and, incidentally, it saved money.

Libermann sat at home shaking his head. He had done his best to inspire these generous fools with a spirit of moderation and reasonable respect for natural means, yet they were scarcely out of sight when they forgot everything he had taught them. With a sigh he thought, "It's poor old Le Vavasseur all over again." The future certainly did not look very bright.

On the morning of September 13, 1843, the two hundred and fifty ton warship, *Les Deux Clémentines,* hoisted her sails and moved slowly out of the harbor. The young missionaries lined the rail watching the coastline recede and then went down to the miserable quarters which they shared with the ship's boys and a number of dogs. Even with their eager spirit of mortification, they could not keep implied complaints from creeping into the diary: "When Father Roger or any of the other members of the Total Abstinence Union leave for the missions, it would be well to dispense them from their pledge. The food is extremely salty and the drinking water is brackish and unpalatable."[2]

For the first few days out, the captain showed as much politeness and consideration as seamen were accustomed to accord their passengers in those days. He even went so far as to have one of the cabin boys whipped for shaving the crown of his head in imitation of the Fathers' tonsure. It took a great amount of tearful protest on the youngster's part and vigorous intervention by the priests before the irate master of the vessel was convinced that the prank involved no insult, active or passive. Later on, when a deadly calm settled on the sea and the sails drooped languidly, the captain's volatile temper veered unexpectedly toward his clerical passengers. He attributed much of the bad luck to these black-robed figures he had taken on board at Bordeaux and his lurid curses echoed through the still air from stem to stern. The blazing sun seemed to share his prejudice against black cassocks. It beat down mercilessly upon them until they changed in self-defense to ribbons of less obnoxious purple.

Finally *Les Deux Clémentines* put in at Gorée, the French island settlement off the coast of Senegal. The captain's watch dropped over the side and while he vainly tried to recover it with the aid of local divers, Bessieux and his companions went ashore. By this time they had learned enough of the tropics to change their heavy felt hats for more sensible straws, but the treacherous sunlight must have bothered them nonetheless for we find them reporting in their journal that "We notice our umbrellas were made of poor material; they are fading." Another entry indicates that the unrecovered watch had heightened the tension on board ship: "The captain's temper is

[2] N. D. 5, 187.

growing more and more dreadful. He is annoyed when we laugh and appears to want us to be silent all the time. Once when some of the confreres were talking rather loudly, I heard him say: 'Those damned babblers,' . . . He blames us for the slow progress we've been making and says we are so selfish that we don't worry a bit about the poor schedule we've been keeping."[3]

When Cape Palmas finally hove into sight, Father Kelly and Denis Pindar were waiting on shore. It was a happy meeting, despite the fact that the joy of the occasion was dampened by difficulties of communication. The Frenchmen did not speak English; the American and the Irishman did not speak French; and they all spoke Latin with such heavy French, American, and Irish accents that even that *lingua franca* failed as a vehicle of fluent expression. Nevertheless, they set out on their first formal attempt at missionary activity. First they all sent out a call to the natives of surrounding villages. Then they dressed a number of little Negroes in Mass servers' cassocks, clothed themselves in liturgical vestments, formed into a procession headed by a cross, and marched on singing the *Exsurgat Deus* and the *Magnificat*.

Apparently, the audience approved highly, for Father Audebert wrote: "The Negroes expressed their admiration by shouting so loudly that it was impossible to make oneself heard." When they began to recite the Litany of the Blessed Virgin, however, the air of enthusiasm seems to have waned. Undaunted, one of the priests opened a large, gilt-edged bible and read a passage from it. Then Father Bessieux preached in Latin about original sin while Father Kelly gave a running English translation that was laboriously translated into the local dialect by a Negro interpreter. It was hardly an efficient procedure. The crowd threatened to melt away unless there were more singing and marching. Consequently, the Fathers reported, "We were obliged to return. We sang as we went, never losing our courage."[4]

Naïve enough, but in this clumsy procedure there was evidence of an approach that the failures of yesteryear had never used. First, these men presented themselves as God's representatives solely, not the emissaries of a European government. Second, they went directly

---

[3] N. D. 5, 202 f.
[4] N. D. 5, 208.

to the natives, without cloistering themselves as chaplains of a garrison on a French settlement. Finally, they couched their message in the African's own tongue.

Yet in other things, they lacked even the semblance of wisdom. Ignoring the murderous sun, they went about wearing their dark and heavy woolen cassocks. Even the nourishing provisions that Francis sent along lay untouched while they struggled vainly to live on a ridiculous version of the native diet. With mechanical fidelity to accidentals, they refused to adjust themselves to the peculiar circumstances in which they found themselves and forgot entirely the clear sense of relative values that Libermann had tried so hard to instill in them. The inevitable tragedy ensued.

The recruits from the foundling home were the first to fall ill. All three, John, Andrew, and Gregory, soon lay burning up with fever. Then Father Maurice collapsed, to be followed shortly by Father Audebert and Father de Regnier. When the last sacraments had been administered, de Regnier summoned up his failing strength to write a letter of farewell to Libermann in faraway France: "I am going to bed. Father Bessieux also has the African fever. Gregory is half dead. Pray to my good Mother Mary for me and for the others. If I had to start all over again, I would do it a thousand times over for the love of Jesus and Mary whose mercy towards us is really admirable. Don't worry. When there's nothing more to hope for from men, Mary will show herself.

"I beg you, dear Father, if my heavenly Mother comes to take me, please write to my cousin. Tell him also that I wouldn't change places with anyone for all the money in the world. Only one thing is necessary; the rest is nothing but misery. Tell him to break the news to my parents.

"Farewell, my dear and respected Father; whether we live or die, we belong to God and Mary.

"Your child who commends himself to your prayers, de Regnier, missionary and son of the Holy Heart of Mary."[5]

Gregory lay delirious in the same room where Father de Regnier died. He never knew that his companion had stopped breathing. It was Father Roussel, wretchedly sick and exhausted himself, who had to dig the grave. He lowered the body into the hole just as the

[5] N. D. 5, 263.

fever struck him full force and was hardly able to make his way back to the bed that Father de Regnier had relinquished a few moments before. Gregory regained consciousness just when this second victim passed away, and he asked weakly if it was Father de Regnier they were carrying out. Father Bessieux assumed the unenviable responsibility of telling him the full story.

Denis Pindar was next. He was felled by a sunstroke and died almost instantly. That was the end of Father Kelly. His courage snapped and he fled home on a passing American ship. When Bishop Barron and his two companions arrived on the first of March, they found only a gaunt little band of half-dead survivors supporting each other as best they could.

On the way out, His Excellency had met the French commandant, Bouet-Willaumez. They discussed the apostolic venture about to be undertaken, and the Frenchman urged a tripartite division of the territory into Assinia, Bassam, and Gabon. When the bishop announced this plan to his fever-ridden missionaries, they looked at each other in mute agony. It meant abandoning the graves of their confreres and leaving all that they had built up at the cost of so much misery. Nonetheless, obedience called. Fathers Maurice and Laval were to accompany the Bishop, the seminarian Keily, and Egan the carpenter to Assinia; Father Bessieux and John Fabé would stay for a while at Cape Palmas and then follow the others to Assinia; the rest were supposed to set out for Gabon.

This latter group boarded the *Églantine* on the following day. Gregory, still too weak to manage for himself, was carried on board by the others. Thus began a horrible voyage. The ill-tempered, tipsy, foul-mouthed crew made life unbearable for them, but no amount of torture could quench their zeal. "How many people live on these coasts!" they marveled. "Pray the Lord of the harvest that he send laborers. Lord, prepare the hearts of these poor people. Infuse in me the virtues necessary for this beautiful vocation of making Your name known to those who know it not. Thanks be to God for this great gift!"[6] Thoughts like this, no matter how highflown they may sound to modern ears, must have been a very necessary source of inspiration in those weeks of ribaldry when cursing sailors threw the

[6] N. D. 5, 228.

emaciated missionaries out of their hammocks and subjected them to a variety of other indignities.

On their arrival at Assinia, the crew engaged in one last refinement of cruelty by unloading so carelessly that the missionaries' belongings were dumped pell-mell into the surf. The journal records that event with melancholy resignation: "Everything has been soaked and ruined with sea-water. Much of it is so spoiled that it can be written off as useless. *Fiat voluntas tua.* Thy will be done!"[7]

From Assinia, Father Audebert, Father Laval, and "Brother" Gregory set out on foot for Bassam. Shivering with malaria, they found on their arrival that the accommodations would be the same as those they had left: a blockhouse full of French soldiers and Africans in the service of France, the latter with their numerous wives and all of them splitting the air with shouts, ribald songs, and pounding dances. The missionaries had literally nothing, not even a change of linen, for the little luggage they had managed to salvage in the debarkation fiasco had been stolen during the overland journey. Worse still, their purse was as empty as their prospects.

Bishop Barron and Father Bouchet made the same trip shortly after, but on board the *Églantine.* It was a dreadful voyage during which Captain Gence forced them to drink salt-water coffee and eat beans while he enjoyed an abundant and varied menu in his own cabin. When Father Bouchet died a few days later, Gence refused to give him the usual honors attendant upon burial at sea, allowing no prayers, no shroud, and no ballast to settle the body gently into the ocean. He simply dumped the corpse over the rail and sneered: "Now you'll see what a nice foot-bath that fellow will take." Ultimately, when his own crew turned against him, Captain Gence ended his malicious life with a bullet through his head.

The bishop finally got to Bassam and found his men there in dire straits. They had no altar breads with which to say Mass nor any flour with which to bake new ones. Father Audebert was bravely carrying on though dysentery was sapping his strength, Gregory had received Extreme Unction once more, and Father Paul Laval looked close to death. Since the young seminarian Keily had just succumbed to tuberculosis over in Assinia, the bishop decided to run

[7] N. D. 5, 271.

no more chances with his men. He followed the advice of a passing doctor and took steps gradually to collect all the sick and dying missionaries in the hospital at Gorée. They got Father Laval as far as Assinia, but by then he was much too sick to go any farther. He died in a few days. Father Maurice, Andrew Fabé, and John Egan reached Gorée alive, and as soon as they had recuperated sufficiently, they went back to Europe. Egan died off the coast of Ireland, Father Maurice traveled to Rome and obtained permission to leave the Congregation, and Andrew Fabé disappeared somewhere in France.

Back in Bassam, Father Audebert and Gregory lay dying in a wretched hut. In his last agony, the priest fell from his bed and remained prostrate on the earthen floor. Utterly helpless, Gregory watched his eyes grow dimmer and dimmer until a last long sigh left them blank and expressionless. For a day and a night he watched beside that broken body in the steaming hovel. At last, with a supreme effort, he dragged himself over, prepared it for burial, and called for native soldiers to take it away. He followed it out and waited till the clods of earth began to pound sickeningly over the bloated corpse. Then he staggered back to his hut.

Waves of fever coursed through his emaciated frame. From time to time he would drag himself to the military post for food and medicine, but by and large the next six months were spent on the pile of filthy rags that passed for his bed. On rare occasions, he managed to reach Father Audebert's grave, picking wild flowers on the way and placing them reverently over his companion's tomb. Then came the great day when his black neighbors began to shout that a boat was coming up the river and a priest was at the rail. It was Father Bessieux who had left Cape Palmas to search for the others. His companion, John Fabé, had gone stark mad and died on the way home to Europe.

Panting with excitement, Gregory implored the Negroes to row him over to the riverboat in a canoe. It was a short but perilous voyage. The canoe capsized twice and Gregory's powerless form had to be pulled out of the murderous current on both occasions. Finally, they hauled him over the rail, unconscious, more dead than alive. Bessieux looked down into that bony face, all covered with sores and river mud, and his broad shoulders began to heave with sobs. Softly, through choking tears, he promised this inert hero that his sufferings were over, that they would send him back to the wonderful man in La Neuville of whom they had spoken so often, there to find peace and rest and health again. But Gregory's eyes were open now, and he shook his tired head. He would never, he gasped, leave Father Bessieux alone, even if it cost him his life.

So they sailed on to Gabon together. When they landed, the commandant showed them their lodgings — the rear of a lumber shed, ten by six, walled off from the rest of the warehouse by a barricade of barrels. This they now subdivided by means of a bed-sheet partition into a tiny chapel on the one side and a living cubicle on the other. It provided some shelter at least until the commandant was able to bring to Gabon the little frame house that had been intended for Bishop Barron. Father Bessieux was welcome to it now, because the bishop was already on his way to Rome where he would submit his final report and ask to be relieved of the superhuman task.

All through the harrowing months that preceded, Bessieux wrote letter after letter to La Neuville but none of them ever reached their destination. Libermann's regular messages of encouragement fared no better. Not one of them arrived either. The strain of not knowing began to tell on Father Bessieux. He imagined all sorts of things — that he had done something unpardonable, or that the Society had failed and left him to his own devices in the jungle. "This is the eighth time that I have written to you," he observed ruefully, "and as yet I haven't received even a postcard from our beloved community. I don't know what to make of the complete silence that has lasted over the past two years. Maybe something I am totally unaware of has made me look bad to you. . . . Gosh, how I wish for one of your letters and how I long to have a confrere.

"The absolute silence you've been maintaining in my regard makes me think that I am to blame for something serious and that your charitable silence indicates the hopelessness of correcting whatever is wrong." "A number of ships have come in since I sent my last letter, but they haven't brought me the one thing I'm anxiously looking for. Perhaps what I'm so impatiently awaiting is still hidden in your heart. No matter how great and severe may be the punishment you are inflicting on me, I admit I deserve it and I accept it willingly."[8]

Then one evening, as the stifling heat slipped off into the blackness of a tropical night, a ship came up the river and cast anchor at ten o'clock. One hour later, its courier arrived at the little wooden house with a packet of letters for Father Bessieux. Gregory had already gone to bed, but he was soon awakened to join in the excitement. They knelt before the Blessed Sacrament and said a quick prayer of thanksgiving. Then to the letters. Through tears of joy they read the news. The Congregation was not dead at all. It was growing rapidly. Young and enthusiastic recruits were ready to come to their assistance. Libermann's fatherly consolation fell on their souls like a soothing balm. Spontaneously, their heavy baritones rang out in the tropical night as they chanted the *Magnificat.* Though it was now past twelve, all thought of sleep had disappeared. They spent the remainder of the night talking about the letters and rereading every line.

For his part, Francis had been living in harrowing uncertainty. His initial forebodings over the hourglass episode had grown more and more disturbing as the months went by without the slightest information concerning his missionaries. His uneasiness became an obsession that he could not shake off even when he went to bed. By his own admission, he was unable to keep Guinea out of his thoughts. Widespread and vicious rumors did not help matters. People were criticizing him for his wild ambition to start evangelizing Africa after centuries of death and failure had proved the futility of the task. He knew his enemies were willing to pounce on every reverse to accuse him of irresponsibility and fanaticism. They would exploit the least tragedy to prove his readiness to sacrifice young lives for his own self-aggrandizement.

He stifled the gossip wherever he could, even taking cognizance of a letter from two girls in a boarding school at Nantes: "The rumors you hear going around are unfounded. . . . I've had no news for a long time, a fact that I regret very much. Don't believe the bad news that you're picking up through hearsay. Around here in the Amiens, Nantes, and Montpellier area, I remember that

[8] N. D. 5, 286 ff., 291, 294.

people were saying our missionaries had been shipwrecked. As a matter of fact, they had an excellent trip. After that, some insisted that the natives had burned them."[9]

He found it hard, however, to keep up a brave front. One week later, we find him writing to a friend: "For quite a while now I've been expecting news from Guinea, but none comes. . . . The missionaries there must be suffering a lot because hardly anything was properly organized. . . . I am even afraid that there will be great losses precisely because they haven't enough experience with the country. (Don't say anything about this to anyone; it might start trouble.) The pioneers will pay heavily for that experience and pave the way for their successors. May God be praised no matter what He has in store for our missionaries."[10]

On October 8, 1844, in the midst of a retreat that Francis was preaching to the novices, Bishop Barron's letter came. It brought crushing news: the failure of his enterprise, the death of his sons, tragedy everywhere. Libermann stood with the letter in his hand, paralyzed with anguish, blinded by a mist of tears. Yet even as the immense flood of grief surged over his sensitive being, he held tight to God in a spirit of absolute surrender just as he had learned to do long ago in all the sufferings of his tortured life.

After the retreat ended, the cloister bell rang and the seats before him began to fill up. Francis knelt for the *Veni Sancte Spiritus,* then rose, cleared his throat, and addressed himself to the ordeal. Outwardly calm and controlled, he looked into the faces before him and broke the highly charged silence with the stark announcement that five of the original seven were dead. Then his voice trembled. Emotion got the better of him. "It is Satan who has done this," he rasped. "He wants that unhappy country of Guinea for himself. But he shall not have it! I will not and cannot send my men to the charnel-house again. You will have to request it, you will have to demand it of me, else I shall go myself."[11]

He had trained his men well. These many months he had been instilling in them a courage and enthusiasm equal to even harsher developments. No sooner had he reached his room than a vigorous knock at the door roused him from his meditations. A pair of shining eyes peered in. Shy but determined, the young priest asked to

[9] N. D. 6, 351. [10] N. D. 6, 353. [11] Briault 160.

be sent to Guinea immediately to take up the fallen torch. Scarcely had he gone when another knocked. Then another and still another. They gave him no peace. They begged and pleaded and argued until he was forced to issue a formal command against their importuning. "All of them begged to be sent to Guinea," he wrote. "I had to forbid them to torment me any more with the request."[12]

Along with the weight of sorrow that bore down so heavily upon him, the mysterious pressure of his sense of historic responsibility for the millions of African natives lay as lead on the shoulders of this European Jew. He could not capitulate. He must keep a tight rein on his vulnerable sensitivity. He had to accept his destiny no matter what it cost. No hesitation; no looking backward. He knew he stood at the crossroads. If he shrank back, Western Christianity would shrink back in his person during that hour of decision. "I see very well," he sighed, "that I shall have no rest or comfort in this world. There will be cares and sorrows till the end of my life. Very well. I am ready for anything. But I cannot abandon so many wretched people whom God appears to have committed to my care. How can it be that the Divine Wisdom would choose poor men like us to undertake the hardest and most taxing mission? I cannot imagine. I shall not analyze it. I do not understand it at all. But that is no reason for slackening my efforts, for I cannot see things in any other light. Congregations that were much larger and wiser than ours did not want to assume the burden of these missions."[13]

"O unhappy land of Guinea! I feel as if I were carrying all of it in my heart. The misery of those poor souls oppresses and overwhelms me. Shall we turn our back on them? Never. That won't do. I am more hopeful than ever." "The one lasting impression after this tragedy is a burning desire to be with my two confreres who are fighting in the breach."[14]

Without knowing it, and certainly without seeking it, Francis was growing in stature as a figure of great significance in the development of history, for the Church's development is the history of mankind's salvation. Under the impetus of the Holy Spirit, this sickly but indomitable man, always longing for solitude, was being propelled into the forefront of a movement, giving new direction to the

[12] N. D. 6, 511. [13] N. D. 6, 313. [14] N. D. 6, 510, 310.

current of missionary activity, despite apparently insurmountable obstacles.

Even Haiti, the object of Father Tisserant's apostolic dreams, poured out a stream of calumny against him and his men in the first flush of its anti-French republicanism. It identified the Church of Rome with the colonial past and regarded anything pertaining to it as a threat to new-found liberty. Yet Libermann's attitude was firm here also: "I would regard it as failing Our Lord and His Holy Church if we abandoned that country." "Let the conviction grow on you," he wrote, "that if we want to do good we must expect constant contradictions at every turn. I'm sure things will be all right in Haiti. Don't worry about what the newspapers say. Intelligent people know well enough what value is to be put on the screaming of journalists."[15]

Vituperation and catastrophe closed in on him from all sides, but he remained firm. His odd combination of natural timidity and counterbalancing resoluteness had been apparent from the beginning. He displayed unshakable steadfastness in youth when the overwhelming father-image threatened to stunt his personal development, he showed it in the seminary when resistance hampered his work of spiritual renewal, he called upon it in Rome when universal opposition seemed to be nullifying his efforts, he used it in protecting his feeble young society when adverse reaction in high ecclesiastical circles almost guaranteed that it would die aborning. Now, he unveiled it again in his determination to open Africa to Christendom even though centuries of failure seemed to condemn the venture to almost certain ruin.

He remained himself, unafraid to deviate from previous and contemporary thinking by his emphasis on objective planning and organization. Through it, he led the way for later socioecclesiastical researchers by engaging in prescientific observation, writing down his data in masterful memorandums that expressed his recommendations for an organized apostolate. It was this businesslike approach that finally assured the success of his enterprise, the first permanent establishment of the Church in Negro Africa.

He stood his ground also against the predominant asceticism of

[15] N. D. 6, 77, 455.

his time when it distorted the missionary ideal, centering it in a romantic desire for martyrdom rather than in quietly effective efforts to found the Church in pagan lands. That is why he strove to guard and foster good mental and physical health in his confreres. Calmly and charitably he battled against their endless tendency to relapse into the mentality of the age where they felt more at home than they did in the presence of his progressive insight. It was a struggle that would go on till the end of his life.

Yet the vision and stature of this born leader are indicated best by the fact that the overwhelming needs of Africa never blinded him to broader issues. Keeping mind and heart always open to God's inspiration, and with the Cape Palmas catastrophe still tearing at his soul, he had no hesitation about extending the aims of his Society to include the spiritual needs of civilized countries as well. For most people as keenly aware of the situation as Libermann was, such considerations would have to be buried under an avalanche of human emotion centering on the newly opened continent. The great calm with which he was able to turn a ready ear to the promptings of the Spirit even in moments of such personal crisis demonstrated most eloquently the high degree of interior detachment to which this hypersensitive man had attained. It meant continual resistance, continual estrangement from friends and aides who were unable to keep up with him in his soaring flight on the wings of grace. His life became a lament of solitary courage, a tortured hymn of surrender to the purest of ideals, a pain-strewn epic of faithfulness to a historic destiny that became ever clearer as the years went by and gripped this modest little man all the more cruelly as it grew in scope. Again and again he shrank toward oblivion, but the power of grace drove him on relentlessly. In quiet determination he wrote: "If I paid attention to the agonies I experience in this thorny endeavor, I would flee every moment of the day and withdraw into solitude. Small chance! We are bound to be consumed in sorrow and labor for the glory of the Master. Courage, patience, humility, and trust; then God will get things done with the most unlikely instruments."[16]

[16] N. D. 6, 517.

CHAPTER EIGHTEEN

LIFE GOES ON

The African venture seemed to have failed. Francis' heart was broken. Yet life went on — life with its daily cares, life with its myriad demands on his love and attention.

The family turned to him as usual in its petty difficulties. Pauline, his pretty and vivacious niece, wanted to go to the convent. Since she loved music and singing, he insisted that her musical abilities demanded a community that would appreciate and develop such talents. "If you want me to find a convent for you," he wrote, "tell me exactly how far advanced you are in your musical studies, whether you could give piano lessons, and whether you know any vocal music."[1] He learned that the Sisters of Louvencourt would respect Pauline's gifts and that they would see to their further development during the novitiate. "They are counting, especially," he assured her, "on your talent for the piano. . . . You still have lots of time to increase your mastery of it during the two years of the novitiate."[2]

The Mother Superior also promised that Pauline would not have to bring a trousseau with her, but Francis felt that Samson and Isabel might be too ashamed to take advantage of this exemption because of fear that others might notice Pauline's poverty. For that reason, he wrote reassuringly: "For the rest, don't worry. Nobody will know that the house has supplied the cloth, for that's the customary procedure. Then the Superior sends a bill to the parents. There will be nothing extraordinary in your case, except that you

[1] N. D. 6, 221.
[2] N. D. 6, 287.

won't get a bill. That's what the Superior told me when I insisted that you wanted to furnish the outfit. She pointed out that you wouldn't even be able to pick up the material because you have no precise idea of what is required. She does the purchasing. The only thing left would be to send the bill to Strassburg. No one will even know whether it was sent out or not. There will be no suspicions about it at all."[3]

Once Pauline had entered, Francis saw her every week when he gave his regular Monday conference to the novices. He followed every aspect of her career with much interest. When she was grief-stricken because her brother had forgotten to send her best music books, it was Uncle Francis who came to the rescue. As a postulant, Pauline could not write home freely. He did it for her: "If you haven't sent out packages yet, please include the music books. If the packages have already been posted, send the books by stage-coach."[4]

In all this loving concern, Francis exhibited no trace of that neurotic anxiety and cold disdain which the Jansenists and other reformers experienced in the face of beauty, art, and culture. These negative influences had penetrated seminaries and convent schools to such a degree that even in his day the free and unhampered appreciation of art and culture had not yet returned. The exuberant flowering of creative beauty which sprang up from early monasticism in the imperishable forms of statuary, stained glass, song, and poetry still generated fear and mistrust, and the truly artistic soul could not yet feel as much at home in religious life as he did before the Reformation. Yet in this, as in everything else, Libermann acted with supreme indifference to popular opinion when he was convinced of his position.

Pauline's problems were easier disposed of than her father's. For some reason, Samson was always financially embarrassed. He had so many debts that Francis finally borrowed two thousand francs to pay them off. Then he wrote to urge greater caution in the future: "I hope very much that you won't contract any further indebtedness. If you don't, you will be able to free yourself gradually from the dreadful entanglements in which you are involved.

[3] N. D. 6, 476.
[4] N. D. 6, 442.

It's going to be difficult if not impossible to arrange for any more loans here."[5]

His brothers and sister-in-law seemed particularly anxious to keep up with the Joneses in dressing their children. Libermann sympathized with them in this and gave occasional hints on economical fashions. When Theodora was coming to join her sisters at boarding school, he wrote to warn her parents about sending too many dresses with her. Caroline, he observed, hardly ever wore her formal dresses, for the boarders ordinarily appeared in the simple uniform that the school prescribed. Moreover, Pauline had told him that the winter dresses could be dyed green for summer wear. As for the black silk dress that was recommended, Uncle Francis saw no reason why Mother could not make over one of her own gowns. "I beg of you, for the love of God," he pleaded, "do not buy anything that isn't necessary. If you knew what a fine spirit there is here and how simple life is, you wouldn't worry so much."[6]

He was ready to buy Theodora's stagecoach ticket from Paris to Amiens himself, and he wrote to Father Schwindenhammer (his future successor as Superior General), asking him to stop for the girl at Felix's home in the capital. "Make sure she stays near you during the trip," he cautioned. In the end, through a happy change of plans, he had the pleasure of accompanying the little chatterbox on this last leg of her journey from home.

Once in school, Theodora proved to be such a lively one that Caroline, much to Libermann's delight, was hard put to it to keep her under control. Soon Samson and Isabel received a good-humored report of Theodora's high jinks and Caroline's exasperation: " 'Stop preaching at me. You make me tired with your everlasting sermons!' That's what she answers most of the time when Caroline tries to give her a bit of sisterly advice. That's why I'm asking you not to scold her or let her know that you're aware of her carrying on. Just because Caroline is more serious and sedate and her ways are more settled, it doesn't mean that wild creatures with Pauline's open and jolly character should be the same."[7]

Despite their bickering, Theodora took it very hard when Caroline announced her intention to enter the convent too. Libermann made a special effort to console her: "My dear Theodora, I cannot help

[5] N. D. 6, 475. [6] N. D. 6, 475. [7] N. D. 7, 104.

sending you these few words before I go to bed although I'll have to pay for it with a headache tomorrow. . . . You're finding it hard to give up your sister. I understand that quite well and sympathize with you for it. But, dear child, the more it costs you, the more generous you should be in making this sacrifice to God. . . . I wanted very much to see you yesterday. I searched everywhere around the playground, hoping to find you among the girls."[8] From this it is obvious that Uncle Francis could be grateful for the religious vocation of one niece and still feel for the other in her natural sense of loss.

With his usual respect for the sacredness of each personality, he had bent over backward to avoid influencing Caroline's decision to enter religious life. Some weeks before he had written to Samson that she might be so inclined, but he was quick to add, "I myself never talk to her about it. . . . The Good Lord must call her. . . . He must speak to her heart and guide her in that direction. He alone is Lord of souls. He leads where He wishes. I admit I would be delighted to see her go, but I am resolved never to discuss it with her." Even when his young nephew Francis wrote to him that he wanted to become a missionary, Libermann replied rather definitely: "Don't bother yourself with thoughts about a vocation for the missions. You ought to take up that question only when you reach the subdiaconate. So, you see, you still have lots of time to think about it."[9]

When his brother Christopher died in far-off America it was a double blow, for Christopher had not been practicing his religion for a long time. "It is too bad," Francis wrote to his bereaved sister-in-law, Julie, "that he was so careless about his religious duties. Let's pray for him and hope that God will be merciful to him in spite of it all."[10] Then he proceeded to find work for the widow when she came home to Europe destitute and heartbroken. While he was trying to get her placed, he kept up her courage by writing consoling letters and sending occasional gifts when he could spare them.

And so, life went on. Every day brought its problems, chiefly within the Congregation itself. Powerful opposition to his worldwide views began to build up among his own priests. Their limited vision

[8] N. D. 7, 408 ff. [9] N. D. 6, 476 ff; 7, 198. [10] N. D. 7, 359.

and exclusive concern for their part of the vineyard made them blind to the universality of the Church and deaf to the insistent call of God in their founder's heart. Every time Francis devoted his attention to anything but Africa they protested vigorously. It was a struggle that was to be renewed to the very day of his death, and it plunged him into the kind of loneliness that is always the penalty of leadership. None but Schwindenhammer and Lannurien could appreciate the scope of his intentions and they preserved a record of it in their memoirs. The rest followed him from afar.

When Francis sent missionaries to Australia and kept others home for European works, the men in Africa gave vent to an amazing bitterness. Father Arragon made himself their spokesman and sent back a venomous letter which took advantage of the arrival of a newly appointed superior to point out that he and his confreres in Africa might decide to refuse the new man and elect a superior of their own. Then he went on to tear open old wounds by asking if Libermann still wanted to send his missionaries to their death, adding ominously that this time they would refuse to go. He closed by warning Francis that it would do no good to despise his missionaries, for they would despise him and his pompous councilors in return.

It was a cruel and unfair attack and it upset Libermann seriously. In his reply to Arragon, he took up his own defense: "You say that I want to send my missionaries to their death once more, but that this time they will not go. It's wrong of you to say this of one whose tender concern for you is greater than your parents ever had, one who would rather go to his own death than see you die. . . . In your third observation, you say something dreadful: 'Beware, lest the missionaries who are so low and despicable in your opinion and in the opinion of your pompous councilors despise you in return.' My dear friend, don't allow your rage to get the upper hand. Calm down, I beg you. . . . You are offending God. I shall pray with all my heart that the Good Lord may grant you peace, self-control, docility, and charity. Don't give in to discouragement because you have lost your head. Regain your peace of mind and God will be with you."[11]

Since Arragon had intimated that others were on the verge of

[11] N. D. 8, 147 ff.

mutiny, he then addressed this open letter to the rest of the African missionaries:

You are profoundly melancholy. Perhaps you have lost courage because of me. How can I go on with such a thought plaguing me? . . . I am ready to put up with any trouble or sorrow if it will ease your sufferings any. . . . My greatest sadness stems from the realization that mutual confidence has been destroyed between us, and that you are upset about and in total disagreement with what I've been doing. . . . But why do you scrutinize and pass judgment on my actions? Why do you disapprove of my sending priests to Australia? Please, have more confidence — not in me for I don't deserve it — but in God, who has laid the responsibility for our work on my shoulders.

You realize that my intentions are good and sincere, that I seek only God's glory and the best interests of our endeavor, that I am ready to die a thousand times rather than jeopardize it. You know how I think things over for a long time and pray not only for important projects but even for the smallest move I make for the good of our work. Yet you give in to anxiety and allow yourselves to get upset when I do something contrary to your ideas in an area that does not concern your missions at all. What can I do to keep you peaceful and happy as you walk the glorious pathways of the apostolate? Tell me, my dear confreres, and I will bend every effort to do it, for I would rather die than grieve you. . . .

Please ignore my sadness. Do not grieve over that now. Rather, keep an eye on yourselves that you may always remain faithful to God. . . . I feel sure that any harsh feelings you entertained against me are banished now. You can't remain angry with someone who is so fond of you. You cannot maintain your conviction that I have no regard for you or that I'm neglecting you. I would be a miserable ingrate if I felt that way. After all, you know me well enough not to say such things seriously. That is why I can't believe you really thought so. . . .

One more favor. . . . Don't try to find out who wrote that unfortunate letter. Don't suspect anyone and above all don't condemn anyone. So what? He was all wrought up. He simply and honestly registered his complaints. I ask all of you to do the same when depression or temptation lies heavily upon you. Don't worry about hurting me. I am glad to share your sorrows. Simply watch that you don't offend God.[12]

Again, life went on. Problems within the Congregation sometimes gave place to difficulties from the outside. Suspicion and opposition

[12] N. D. 8, 150 ff.

still bayed at him from every angle. He exercised extreme caution, particularly where publicity was involved. "We have enemies," he noted, "who would like to accuse us of seeking publicity." Sometimes he found it hard to get proper support from the Society of the Propagation of the Faith because, he stated, "distrust . . . has been sown there against me and my priests." Certain government functionaries disliked him. They felt he was a dangerous child of a rejected race defending the rights of another despised segment of mankind. He wrote of a certain colonial officer as one who was "very much opposed to our missionaries. He has fulminated against them in the Colonial Council. He has pictured them as the emissaries of French societies of do-gooders who are out to liberate the Negroes, as nefarious agents who should be expelled from the country as soon as possible. He has told a lot of lies about our Rules and Constitutions. All of this is going to appear in print."[13]

Then too, his spiritual doctrine still generated mistrust in many quarters. His original ideas, his so-called modern views, and his typically personal mode of expression caused him to be regarded as a dangerous author for young people to be reading. A veritable anti-Libermann psychosis broke out in professorial essays and letters. Self-appointed heresy hunters scanned their domain for traces of the highly feared Libermann influence. When young Letaille wrote a short life of Mr. Liévin, a recently deceased St. Sulpice deacon, he used a biographical sketch that Francis had made. Unfortunately, Letaille's little opus seemed to imply that Liévin's way of union with God was the only valid one. In the storm that followed, he was obliged to withdraw his work from publication. Then suspicion swung to the hated man at La Neuville.

"Letaille seems to say," Libermann observed, "that he wrote this brochure on my advice. However, I never said a word to that effect and I knew of the pamphlet's existence only when it came off the press. He saw a little memoir that I had written about Mr. Liévin and that's where he got the idea. It's possible that he made some slight changes in my text and kept the original for the rest."[14]

The rector and professors of the renowned Holy Ghost Seminary added to these complications by doing everything in their power to

[13] N. D. 6, 47, 93, 186.
[14] N. D. 6, 218.

seal off the Holy Heart Fathers from every access to French colonial missions. Before his death, the former superior general of the Spiritans had frustrated every move. Libermann admitted ruefully: "The minister refused me everything." Fourdinier's successor in the generalate, Father Leguay, told Tisserant quite frankly that he had declared "open war on Libermann's Congregation." He accused Francis "of bad faith and indelicacy" because the man had volunteered to take charge not only of Guinea but also of Senegal where the old Spiritan prefecture had been in existence for many years. Leguay went on to prophesy darkly that such foul tricks on the part of "that intriguing hypocrite" Libermann would ultimately bring the Society to a bad end.[15]

Francis knew all this, but he wrote nonetheless: "I am firmly resolved to do everything I can to preserve the bonds of charity with Father Leguay. I don't think I need to justify myself. I honestly believe my conscience is completely clear of all the untrue accusations and the erroneous interpretations others have put on my intentions and sentiments."[16]

For years now he had been living in an atmosphere of slander and jealousy, an atmosphere in which small men perish but great souls grow into heroes and saints. "An apostle," he wrote, "doesn't react like a child. He doesn't engage in self-pity when things go wrong. He has learned to forget himself and to meet his problems head on. He has a heart of stone for his own sorrows, but a deep and tender sympathy when others are suffering." Actually, he was at home in the whirlwind of opposition. He would have missed the storm of accusation and insinuation if it had suddenly ceased. "I am accustomed," he said, "to having people hurt and trouble me. It's my life. Yes, that's my very existence, for when I have no troubles I find I am not serving God or doing anything for Him."[17]

Inexorably, life went on. He who had longed for solitude and contemplation, he who had hoped to walk in the presence of God far from the madding crowd now found every hour bringing new burdens of work and worry. Yet amid the plethora of activities that chained him to his desk, he kept recalling that it was the will of

[15] Cf. N. D. 7, 361, 478 f.
[16] N. D. 7, 327.
[17] N. D. 9, 230; 7, 144.

God that immersed him in a routine he never sought for or desired. When the press of business affairs denied him the human comfort he always derived from writing to his beloved family, he resigned himself to the inevitable. "My time is not my own any more. Everything belongs to the Master whose servant I am. I must do His work before all else. There is no more enjoyment for me on this earth. I must no longer seek satisfaction in the love of those who are dear to me. I may not enjoy it except in my few free moments."[18]

His friends, his confreres, and his clients began to complain about not having prompt replies to the letters they wrote to him. They could not see the mountainous array of letters and documents behind which this horribly tired little man wrote and wrote to stem the tide of troubles, problems, and cares that always threatened to inundate him. With his nervous, almost illegible scrawl, he admitted that his correspondents were justified in their impatience. "I deserve all the reproofs of these good people. That is why I readily and meekly accepted them." When no objection was registered, he seemed surprised. "My dear Sister, I admire your heroic charity. Your frankness nearly gave you away but charity reined it in. When I read your first sentence — even the first words — I said to myself, 'Oh, no! Now I'm in for it.' Then I saw how your charity gave consideration to my weakness. Let me be frank in turn and express my full conviction that I don't deserve such indulgence. I'm guilty, quite guilty, that's certain. . . . I would like very much to exonerate myself, but I'm not sharp enough to find an excuse that will stand up." When four nuns from the convent at Castres saved postage by writing to him simultaneously, he begged to be spared future invasions of that sort. "Please ask your good Mother Superior not to make all of you write at the same time. It will spare me the shame of always being behind in my correspondence."[19]

In the course of a letter, his brother once observed that it was wonderful to see what a responsible position Francis held in the Church. The harried little man behind the loaded desk was quick to demur: "So you think our heavenly reward will be based on great enterprises! You get a kick out of seeing me involved in this business, but let me assure you, you're seeing only one side of the

---

[18] N. D. 7, 61.
[19] N. D. 7, 253, 258, 259.

coin. You can't imagine the heartaches, the grief, and the trouble that this great and thorny endeavor has caused me for nearly a year now, particularly when I encounter the immense problems of the mission in Guinea, a mission that is dear to my heart. When I stop and think that a poor little guy like me is supposed to arouse that country . . . and bring it to God, removing obstacles, surmounting difficulties, finding the right approach . . . and laying a good solid foundation . . . I feel absolutely awful. I sometimes wonder how I can last through such torture and bear up under such burdens. We have to admit that Divine Wisdom is using a mighty small fulcrum to lift a gigantic weight.

"Honestly, if I knew then what I know now, I would have been too scared to undertake a venture that is so far beyond my strength. Now I'm chained to it. I've got to go ahead. I'll carry on until I fold up. Then God will find a stronger and more adequate instrument to accomplish the task.

"As for me, I hope He will have pity and deal mercifully with me. But I hardly think, my dear brother, that it will be because of the great things I have undertaken. They are great enterprises, very great indeed. I am aware of that and it overwhelms me, but that is not what will be rewarded, for God regards the saintly dispositions of one's heart rather than the impressive activities he may have engaged in.

"For my own welfare, let me assure you, I much prefer my cares and reverses to the achievement of brilliant successes. Nevertheless, I shall go along with everything God wants, sacrificing everything for success, even though it is not the success that He will reward. On the contrary, the gratification arising from it is always tainted with some hint of vanity and self-love."[20]

Libermann seems almost envious of this brother who escaped the spotlight of history. Things had changed since their childhood days. Then it was the strong and sure Samson whom Francis admired and relied on and in whose shadow the younger man would have been quite content to remain for the rest of his life. Now, with this sudden invasion of grace, everything was different. His timidity became humility. He grew into a heroic and daring renovator endowed with superhuman courage and tenacity. Meanwhile,

[20] N. D. 8, 5 f.

the same mysterious flow of grace transformed Samson, a fearless and progressive Jew who fought for the advancement of his race, into an obscure physician, shunned by patients, dogged by social misfortune, and distressed over the ordinary expenses of family life.

That is why Francis wrote encouragingly: "Be glad of your condition, I beg of you. You are fortunate enough to be sustained by divine grace in the secrecy of your heart without living in a goldfish-bowl. Adversity and suffering of all sorts will make a soul holy. 'Big deals' reverse the process. Those who engage in major endeavors for God's glory are like accountants and bank cashiers. They add up large sums, talk in big figures, and handle great amounts of money, but when they leave the office, their pockets aren't any fuller. I'd much rather be a little store-keeper with a comfortable nest-egg. The money he counts is his own."[21]

He was well aware that others gained graces through him but that this did not necessarily sanctify him. He compared himself to a telegraph operator who transmits important messages without growing wiser or richer in the process. He had, admittedly, been given a special grace to convey God's message to other souls, but that grace benefited others, not himself. Under no illusion whatsoever, he analyzed it this way: "I believe it has pleased God to grant me a special facility for guiding and passing on to certain souls the truths of salvation. That, however, is precisely what misleads people about me and makes them take me for what I am not and never have been. It is a grace that is purely for others and from which I derive absolutely no benefit."[22]

The most depressing thing he encountered was the frightful lack of understanding even on the part of his best friends. He would humbly solicit their opinion, but each time his well-mentioned advisers came up with quick and superficial answers to questions he had been wrestling with for days on end. To his great chagrin, he found himself obliged to rely on his ingenuity and responsibility for decisions that were to have vast historical repercussions. "I had no one to whom I could go for guidance," he would sigh. "I have never been able to get any help from men in determining the direction I should give such an undertaking. . . . Even level-headed

[21] N. D. 7, 6.
[22] N. D. 7, 178.

people, as a rule, do not sufficiently analyze a plan that is set before them. They give a pat answer without putting themselves in the place of the proponent. . . . Hence I am reduced to figuring things out for myself. For that reason, I have to be on my guard, especially when it is a matter of highly important decisions that run counter to the accepted way of doing business. I have placed my trust in God and Divine Providence has made decisions I didn't dare to make. Nonetheless, my worries weren't any the smaller because I still had to rely on my own views."[23]

While Father Desgenettes, the devoted old pastor of Our Lady of Victories Shrine, was always available, his old friends and spiritual counselors at St. Sulpice failed him when it came to giving advice on matters that required a greater knowledge of worldly affairs than they possessed. They shared the seminarians' cloistered existence to such an extent and came in contact with the real problems of life so infrequently that Francis found he could place no confidence in their appraisal of situations, holy and devoted though they were.

Because good judgment was at such a premium, Francis decided to reserve his ablest men for responsible positions in the European social and apostolic endeavors that he was planning. His idea was to enable them to grow in stature through a vitalizing contact with modern reality. Trained in this way, such confreres could subsequently step into administrative posts in the Congregation and in its houses of formation. Meanwhile, he would always have in Europe a contingent of able men who were familiar enough with the culture of their time to fill vacancies as they arose.

The only contemporary in whom Francis found full understanding and support was the recently beatified Mother Javouhey, a dynamic and fearless woman, who had founded the Sisters of St. Joseph of Cluny. With characteristic vigor (King Louis Philippe called her a "great man"), this holy soul had made daring explorations along the coast of Africa where her Sisters were working. Now she lived in hopes of seeing a congregation of men invade that vast dark country with the cross of Christ. Rather prophetically, she wrote: "We shall wait until the Lord sets His seal on the man whom He has chosen for this great undertaking."[24] When the convert-

[23] N. D. 6, 192. [24] Briault 272 f.

priest of La Neuville became her friend and counselor, she soon saw that it was he who bore the divine stamp.

Her nuns were not receiving a proper formation for the arduous and solitary mission duty to which she was sending them. It worried Libermann. "I was unable to stifle my concern," he said, "when I thought of the two hundred and fifty religious spread through several countries, poorly educated for the religious life, and working in a congregation that was in constant danger of dissolution."[25] That is why he felt it his duty to help Mother Javouhey improve the situation. His guidance and counsel contributed heavily toward the advancement of her organization.

As a matter of fact, the role of restorer fitted Francis better than that of founder. He was like new yeast in the Church, causing ferment and action wherever he went. Nearly everyone with whom he dealt became infected with a new and vital outlook. Whatever his hand touched was changed never to be the same again. The ways of Providence kept moving him ever closer to that great moment when he would take the tired old Congregation of the Holy Ghost, bled white by the Revolution and kept anemic by postrevolutionary pressures, and restore it with a stimulus mighty enough to regenerate and surpass its eighteenth century strength.

Like Libermann, Mother Javouhey had the distinction of making powerful and vociferous enemies, both civil and ecclesiastical. The common cause in which they were engaged soon involved him in her defense. "It seems to me," we find him writing, "that she has been grievously calumniated . . . She has suffered much and has had to put up with a good deal. The humble and docile way in which she bears all this is certainly a mark in her favor." When she asked him to take over the running of her congregation, however, Francis winced at the thought of adding all her adversaries to his own already ample supply. "I shivered in the face of that job," he said, "for it was quite risky for us. We took the chance of running afoul of the Bishop of Autun and, if we had taken charge of the Society, we would have offended a number of prelates in whose dioceses the St. Joseph Sisters were working." Moreover, Mother Javouhey would be taking on his antagonists also. He warned her of this explicitly: "I think, Reverend Mother, that you

[25] N. D. 7, 304.

would be well advised to keep quiet about our discussions. Otherwise you will bring down upon you all the enemies I have in the archdiocese of Paris and elsewhere."[26]

In a kind of holy conspiracy, then, these two powerful figures entered into plans that gave a decisive impetus to modern missionary activity. It all had to be done secretly because they feared that their respective opponents might learn of these discussions and, since each had friends in the camp of the other's enemies, they feared they might end with no friends at all. "I must ask you one favor," Libermann wrote. "Please keep as an absolute secret my offer to have Father Tisserant intercede for you in Rome. I beg you, pay attention to this. I regard this as utterly important for you and for me. Don't say a thing about it to anybody. If this should become known, it might very easily destroy the good impression you made in Rome . . . and the two of us could get into trouble both in Rome and in France.

"Although we place all our trust in God's goodness, we ought to be prudent enough not to jeopardize the good end we are pursuing. Instead, we ought to use the surest means to arrive at success."[27]

Mother Javouhey was a ready pupil. Before long, she was holding up her end of God's underground. Libermann wrote to her: "May I ask you to please find out from the [Colonial] Ministry how things are going with the business in which you have shown such kind interest? I mean the Senegal affair. Have they made up their minds yet about the memo you were good enough to give Monsieur Bouet for transmission to the Department?" Her work in his behalf must have been effective, because he told a trusted friend, "I feel confident that the Minister is well disposed. I'm sure about it, not only on my own account, but also because of what has been done by the Internuncio and the Superior of the Saint Joseph Sisters." Nonetheless, he declined her invitation to occupy a guest room in her convent when he was traveling. "I am most grateful," he wrote, "for your courtesy in setting aside a room for me and I would be delighted to use it, but I think that it would still be inopportune.

---

[26] N. D. 6, 225, 226, 236.
[27] N. D. 6, 355.

Prudence dictates that our collaboration be hidden from the eyes of men."[28]

Subsequently, when Libermann wanted to inform the Congregation of the Holy Ghost that he looked with favor on a merger, it was Blessed Mother Javouhey who acted as intermediary. Had he made the approach directly, it might have put him in a position of weakness and inferiority, thereby adversely affecting the discussions to follow. "I only ask," he prompted her, "that you so present things that they will not suspect me as the author of the proposals. If you wish, you can write them on the pretext that your health does not warrant a personal visit to Father Warnet. Then it would be easier for you to incorporate in your communication those parts of my letter that you want to get across to him."[29] Little by little, through intelligence, natural psychology, wide and sometimes painful experience, instinctive delicacy, and spontaneous courtesy, Francis was developing into a superb diplomat.

The effort took its toll, however. Physical indispositions bedeviled him constantly. His correspondence is full of breezy references to what must have been terrible suffering. "Don't worry about my health. I'm fine. Frequent and somewhat tiring hikes through the mud stimulate me and do a lot of good. It's a tough remedy for a lazy fellow who is inclined to stay in his shell, but what else can I do? I oughtn't to neglect this poor old body. If it has to pay some of the cost, all the better. After all, it should contribute something toward what's being done for it. The bottle of medicine Mr. Tisserant [the druggist] sent me is working wonders for my stomach. For a while I was satisfied just to look at it. That was something, anyway, for we should approach this medicine business gingerly. From now on I'll sample it every time I feel upset. When it's gone, I'll be rid of it. Are you satisfied now? I wouldn't want to be around you all the time. You would be always hounding me to take care of myself."[30]

Monsieur Beauchef, a seminarian, received the same type of reply. "Stop worrying about me. . . . If I didn't have a little pain once in a while, I would forget to take care of my health! You see, this is a little trick of the body, a polite way of asking for some attention. Actually, the ruse works, for I cherish it as if it were a

---

[28] N. D. 6, 356, 248, 258. [29] N. D. 7, 113. [30] N. D. 6, 20.

jewel. . . . Rest easy, I shan't die of it. Probably I'll be around to say a *De Profundis* for you!"[31]

Now and then he let slip the fact that his excruciating migraine headaches were at work. "For a whole month now I've been suffering from a nervous pain in my head. It was accompanied in the beginning by an extreme aversion for food." "My head is still in such a miserable condition that I'm lucky I got through this letter." "Dear Confreres, I hope you will be satisfied with this short note. A wicked migraine hit me when I got to the middle of this letter. . . . I couldn't do a thing for at least thirty-six hours and now I'm way behind schedule. . . . Don't be too hard on my migraine. It's a faithful companion that seems quite fond of me, for it pays me frequent visits. Ordinarily, I offer it a cup of black coffee. Satisfied with that, it normally goes away. But when I forget about the refreshments or don't have time to show it that courtesy, it lets me feel the insult. Don't ask God to take it away. It's quite useful. After all, you are suffering in the course of sacrificing yourselves for God's glory; since I'm not doing anything, at least let me suffer a little. Besides, it looks as though God wants to substitute the migraine for my nervous disease, for the other symptoms diminish in proportion to the frequency of my migraine headaches."[32]

Apparently there was no need to worry about his "visitor's" constancy. Not long after, he wrote: "I have had migraine for two days. That good friend of my soul didn't want me to devote myself to anything else during the two whole days it spent with me. . . . Now at last, at ten o'clock, I am writing this. I've been upset till now."[33]

Moreover, abdominal disturbances further complicated the picture. "As usual during the winter," he observed, "I have had intestinal pains and came very near having peritonitis. I was obliged to give up all work."[34]

Bad health often hampered his activities. We find him saying repeatedly: "I cannot force myself to get down to work . . . either it goes by itself or it doesn't go at all. When I drive myself to it anyhow, I'm not fit for anything after a quarter of an hour." "I was suffering from one of those dreadful migraines. . . . It was almost

[31] N. D. 6, 300 f.
[32] N. D. 7, 39, 18, 125 f.
[33] N. D. 7, 242.
[34] N. D. 6, 17.

impossible to stay up at night to write to you. In fact, I couldn't do a thing."[35]

His attitude in the face of almost incessant distress was sane and self-possessed. There is no hint of that Spartan imperviousness to pain which some people parade externally in order to impress themselves and others with their heroism. Nor do we ever detect in his writing the whimpering air of a martyr looking for sympathy. Instead, he always refers to his sufferings in a perfectly matter-of-fact way, without exaggeration and without undue reticence, whenever circumstances seemed to warrant it.

The young priests who surrounded him had grave fears for his health. They held a secret meeting and drew up a daily schedule that was calculated to protect him from himself.

1. No one will go to Father Superior for confession during the morning meditation.
2. No one will go to Father Superior after night prayer to ask advice or talk about business. We desire, and even demand as far as we can, that the Superior go to bed at ten o'clock and not rise till five in the morning.
3. Every day, Father Superior will have two hours completely free to devote to personal and community affairs. During those two hours there are to be no visitors. These hours are to be fixed by Father Superior and his First Assistant, who is hereby named executor of this decision. Once the hours are determined upon, they shall be made known to the Community.
4. The First Assistant is charged by the Council with the responsibility of watching over all that concerns Father Superior's health. Hence we beg Father Superior to divulge simply and plainly to the First Assistant or his substitute everything that he considers good and useful for the preservation and improvement of his health. We even desire that Father Superior will be perfectly docile in taking every means to achieve that improvement, and we appeal to whatever authority we may have to impose this obligation.
5. The First Assistant is hereby empowered to appoint someone to replace him in watching over the Superior, and he may change that substitute at will.

These then, dear Father, are the intentions of your sons, and we dare say, of the entire Congregation. Our affection for you and our desire to keep you for ourselves and the works of God have prompted us to take these measures and impose this obligation upon you. We know, dear Father, that you will not take offense. Now we

[35] N. D. 7, 105 f, 24.

> can leave you with peace of mind, not worrying about your very precious health. We would be very sorry to think that our Superior would have to suffer because his zeal keeps him from submitting to what his sons have requested as a favor and a consolation. We would be heartbroken. But we know that will not happen. We hope, dear Father, that you will comply with our wishes as you have always done in the past, and that you will always remain faithful to the resolution.[36]

The authors of this document knew how to trap saints. How could anyone reject a request that appealed to docility, obedience, and love? Francis submitted without further ado, although it was strange to let one's self be spoiled by a confrere whom the Council appointed and who exercised his delegated powers to the full.

Libermann wrote about the new dispensation to an absent confrere. "We have three cows, one horse, some pigs, chickens, ducks, geese, turkeys and pigeons. This is all for the good of the house. Our menu is about the same as when you were here. I'm the only one with a special diet. They're fattening me up like one of the boarders listed above whose name I shan't mention for fear of shocking someone's ears."[37]

The confrere who took care of him proved to be the inventive sort, searching far and near for a thousand and one ways to prolong the life of his protégé. "I am the poorest fellow of all," protested Libermann. "Everybody else sits on an ordinary hard chair, but I have to occupy an upholstered one." Just then he realized that it was ten o'clock, so he drew his letter to an abrupt close. "That will be all for now. The clock is striking ten. I have to get to bed. Otherwise I shall fail in obedience."[38]

To one of the signatories of the manifesto, he appended a reassuring footnote to a subsequent letter, explaining why there was a grease spot in the paper. "The oil-stain shouldn't lead you to believe I wrote this late at night. Don't accuse me of unfaithfulness. The good Brother spilled a drop of oil on the stove. I never suspected it when I put my letter there to dry. That was ten in the morning, do you understand?"[39]

As life went on, Francis preserved his good nature and his good

[36] N. D. 7, 517 f.
[37] N. D. 7, 345.
[38] N. D. 7, 346.
[39] N. D. 7, 422.

humor. Indeed, his sense of humor asserted itself more and more. It was a sign of established equilibrium, a proof that he had achieved an inner deliverance from suffering. Grace was increasingly fortifying his weak nature. Years ago there would have been emotional shocks and epileptic seizures. Now he was no longer subject to them. The symptoms still lingered, as his migraine headaches proved all too readily, but the terror was gone.

This growing sense of balance manifested itself in the correspondence he devoted to spiritual direction. It took on a more matter-of-fact tone. Where formerly he had been given to describing human suffering through metaphoric references to annihilation, rending, wounding, and crushing — all suggested by his own neurotic sensitivity — he now turned to more moderate expressions that gave no hint of hyperacute experiences. A more relaxed and secure atmosphere now pervaded his writings and lifted the last veil of melancholy.

Actually, it is difficult for a truly holy person not to be humorous, for he is blessed with a continuous vision of the relation between the things of time and the things of eternity. When a comparatively insignificant affair is blown up into an important event, it becomes grotesque and ridiculous. The resultant discord necessarily provokes a smile in the discerning observer. Anyone who is not a saint tends to magnify little things all during his hectic trip through creation. He resembles one of a group of schoolgirls looking in a department store window and squealing with rapture over some little trinket displayed there. More mature passersby smile benevolently at the great effect produced by so small a cause. Those who are not saints engage in the same excited magnification when they give an absolute value to passing things, and since they are predominant in number and vociferousness on this earth, the truly holy man in their midst is always confronted with laughable situations. But he laughs at himself too. His humility and peace of mind free him from exaggerated ego ideals and enable him to accept in good part his own shortcomings. Libermann's jocose sallies were crystallizations of just such a genial humor. They marked him as a man who had once and for all measured temporal values against eternal norms.

The following letter to confreres in faraway Reunion is typical.

"This year we have harvested over seven hundred bushels of potatoes. We won't sell any. They are all to be devoured by ourselves alone. I'll bet Father Collin will miss La Neuville now, because he was a great potato-eater. But poor little Father Blanpin can congratulate himself on getting out of here just in time; potatoes used to constipate him terribly.

"We are still fattening up three pigs. There is always one in the meat-tub and when he has completely disappeared, another takes his place willy-nilly. Our three cows yield plenty of manure. They earn their keep by the milk they give, so the manure is a pure bonus. . . . We have fifty chickens and forty pigeons. The latter, in my opinion, don't pay very well for their board and lodging. Then too, we have a horse. . . . We could have done quite nicely with a jackass, but they tell me that's not so. Besides our two dogs we have any number of cats, but then there is a still greater number of mice living like queens in the attic on better than a year's provisions."

After this inventory, he turned to teasing Dr. Brunet who, it appears, had left the house with great protestations of faithful correspondence in the future. "He hasn't written us a single line," Libermann complained, "although he promised us a volume." "I am looking forward to an enormous bundle of letters from Dr. Brunet. He must have dropped his promise overboard into the sea. We shall have to haul it out."[40]

A local priest once wrote that Father Lannurien, professor of Moral Theology at La Neuville, had accidentally carried off his umbrella. The identification was not quite accurate and Libermann decided to make capital of it when he replied. "If he were professor of Moral Theology, he might have known that stealing is forbidden. As it happens, though, he's just our professor of dogma."[41]

He had a good deal of trouble with an old pastor who feared that Father Blanpin's inheritance would go to the Holy Heart of Mary Congregation rather than to the parish in which Madame Blanpin lived. Several times he had tried to induce the priest to come to La Neuville and talk things over. At last, when it looked as though the visit might materialize, he wrote to assure Madame

[40] N. D. 7, 118, 376.
[41] N. D. 10, 302.

that her parish priest would be well received. "When the reverend pastor does us the honor of staying with us, we shall prepare the bishop's room for him. Perhaps the episcopal honors thus bestowed on him will make him more favorably disposed to hear our story. We shall light a good episcopal fire for him in that bishop's room, and after dinner he won't even have to go to the kitchen to smoke his pipe. We shall sit before the hearth in his own room."[42]

Warlop, a belated vocation and the first Belgian recruit, had formerly been a noncommissioned officer in the Army Engineers. Since he had a great flair for architecture, he set about building a very beautiful but quite expensive chapel. The altar demanded a particularly heavy outlay for the young community and Libermann laconically reported the pinch to one of his men in the missions: "Mr. Warlop is proud of his altar. He's proud of it only as an architect, not as a bursar." "It's true that our good Mr. Warlop took me by surprise. . . . He trapped me and, what is worse, he doesn't seem to have any remorse about it."[43]

Libermann even had to watch himself, lest his humor be misinterpreted. Thus we find him explaining: "I may have said something jokingly during the excitement of departure day. You know how often I engage in thoughtless kidding without intending to be taken seriously."[44]

Thank God that he did, for in those troubled times at La Neuville the salutary balance of wholesome humor made things a good deal more bearable as life went on.

[42] N. D. 7, 434 f. [43] N. D. 7, 48, 345. [44] N. D. 8, 216.

CHAPTER NINETEEN

COLLABORATORS OF THE FIRST HOUR

From his remote outpost in the Indian Ocean, Father Le Vavasseur watched developments with intense interest and impatient curiosity. Shortly after he had recovered his peace of mind he was again beset by temptations against the colleague he had left at La Neuville. Letters did not come as quickly as he felt they should. Not knowing that many of Libermann's communications never reached him, he fumed and fretted over the silence, convinced that Francis still resented his opposition in days gone by. Now that he was far away, the people at La Neuville no longer needed him. Maybe they felt that they were well rid of him. Or perhaps the whole thing had gone down in failure.

Then suddenly, letters came and reinforcements arrived. Reassured once again, he got himself under control. But it was only the calm before an even greater storm. Word filtered through that Libermann was considering mission fields other than Reunion and Frederic flew into a rage. Once again, wild recriminations burned their way back to France and quiet words of self-defense flowed out from La Neuville. It was an exchange that repeated itself as the years went on. Not only Le Vavasseur, but the missionary bishops of the Congregation in general rose up indignantly each time Libermann ventured into undertakings that even remotely threatened to divert man power and resources from existing operations.

Time after time, Francis stood midway between confreres who wanted to abandon every project not directly referable to the African mission and confreres who concerned themselves wholly with work in more civilized countries. Each camp adhered rigidly to its narrow view. Francis alone, under divine guidance, surveyed the total range of the task that God had imposed on him. He consistently defended any move that met the Church's need, whether in Africa, the islands, or in Europe.

With endless patience he explained to Le Vavasseur: "I personally believe that the apostolic spirit consists more in extending the confines of the Church than in concentrating on a small portion. If we succeed in broadening the scope of the Church's influence . . . I believe we shall have done something that will last for centuries to come."[1]

"Don't indulge in faulty reasoning, arguing that we should first go to what is certain before tackling what is uncertain. If St. Paul had reasoned that way, he could not have done such wonders for the glory of God. We've got to be generous and not entertain such grave fears for our Congregation's welfare. . . . We must not insist on having success assured before we start something. If we aren't entirely dedicated to the service of Jesus Christ and His Church, it wasn't worthwhile forming a society."[2]

Libermann modestly referred to the inner force that impelled him to undertake what human wisdom might have rejected. This appeared to pacify Frederic best of all. He replied somewhat hesitatingly and with a tinge of aversion: "I consider it most regrettable that we are encompassing the earth with our little band. But, what can we do? For as you tell me, you have been driven in spite of yourself to take on so much from the very beginning."[3]

All the uneasiness was not on Frederic's side, and with good reason. Libermann could not help being concerned when he read in one of the letters from Reunion: "As for me, I'm always the same: full of activity, impatience, brusqueness, and sometimes I smash up everything! . . . I am aware that this comes from impatience and irritability. The least little thing that goes against me burns me up!"[4]

Then when Frederic heard that Father Tisserant might be appointed bishop of Haiti, he wrote the following amazing confession: "I felt rather bad when I read that he may get the purple. I would have preferred it to be me. From then on — and even before

---

[1] N. D. 6, 112.
[2] N. D. 6, 76.
[3] N. D. 6, 611 f.
[4] N. D. 6, 534 f.

that — I've been thinking that I may be a bishop some day. Sometimes I find myself day-dreaming about that and the things that go with it, but I do my best to dispel these thoughts. Nonetheless, to sum it up, I feel that such honors would not cause me the sadness and fear that they should if I had enough faith and humility."[5]

On one occasion, Le Vavasseur had quite an altercation with the Governor of Reunion. Then he sent this self-satisfied report to Libermann: "Luckily, in spite of [the Governor's] fury and vulgarity, I never for one moment gave him the impression that I was afraid of him. I shouted every bit as loudly as he did. After exhausting my lungs — for it is really hard to make him see things — I managed to get across what I wanted."[6] One can imagine how Francis, with his lofty ideals of gentility, must have received the news that one of his sons got the point across by outshouting the Governor of Reunion. He normally advocated other procedures that put less strain on the vocal chórds and more emphasis on mutual understanding.

Le Vavasseur was to cause more than mere uneasiness, however. According to Libermann's own words, this cofounder cut him as if he wielded a sword.

It all started over Plessis. He was a youngster just out of La Neuville. When Francis sent him to Reunion, he wrote Frederic a rather gingerly letter, begging him to receive this somewhat difficult character with all the consideration that charity could inspire in him, and to help him gradually overcome his personal difficulties. Frederic was the last man to do something like that. He found Father Plessis timid, confused, upset, totally devoid of initiative, and completely lacking in zeal. With each passing day he grew more irritated with the newcomer. His dreams and ideals evaporated dismally. He, Frederic, would have done things differently. If he had been in charge at La Neuville, luxury would never have insinuated itself. Remember those scarlet beds? And the three meals a day? and the other excesses? This was all due to Francis, with his gentle manners, his refinement, his lax spirituality. No wonder he produced characters like this Plessis fellow. And he thinks he can establish a congregation on such a regime! No question about it,

[5] N. D. 6, 609.
[6] N. D. 6, 624.

he is up there in France spoiling and corrupting what he, Frederic, had begun with the highest ideals. And then he dares to write and plead for understanding and help for this Plessis!

The poor young recruit was sent packing to France, followed by some scarifying letters addressed to Libermann. Then Le Vavasseur stalked off to make a retreat with the Jesuits at St.-Denis. At the end of it, he informed Francis that he had made up his mind for good. He was going to join the Society of Jesus. The only thing he needed to get was Libermann's permission. Once that came, he would carry out his resolve.

While he was awaiting the reply from La Neuville, he met with a tragic complication. Young Father Collin came and admitted having serious doubts about his vocation, alleging that he found it too difficult to stay in a Congregation that encountered so much opposition. As superior of the mission, it was Le Vavasseur's function to support and encourage the younger man. He was called upon to preach constancy just when he himself had decided to abandon the group. Frederic did his duty nonetheless with honesty and thoroughness, adducing many incentives for fidelity that he too might have found useful in a less disturbed hour.

Back in La Neuville, Francis read the wild letter and it cut him to the quick. Here was a friend who wanted to leave because he had gradually become the victim of an illusion and allowed his heated imagination to sway his intelligence. And it was the very man who had taken the initiative in this whole thing, one of its very originators. It was one thing to be ridiculed and despised by outsiders; it was quite another to be betrayed and abandoned by a cofounder.

"Your letter," he replied solemnly, "informs me that you have grave misgivings about the Congregation. . . . You talk as if we are turning our back on the work God called you to establish and get going. You say this in a spirit of utter discouragement.

"Suppose for a moment that you pull out and then I lose courage too. If I gave up also, I wonder how the two of us would extricate ourselves from divine justice. And yet, for every reason you cite, I could adduce a hundred. Laboring under the superiorship, I'm carrying the ultimate responsibility for the whole work. I'm constantly encountering the terrific shock of the sorrows and trials that

Divine Providence sees fit to send this enterprise. . . . Moreover, I have to care for proposed missions as well as those already established. Then there are worries about the novitiate, the studies, and the various houses, . . . the order to be established, the rules to be polished up, the general consolidation of our position.

"In doing all this I am quite alone. There is only one of the confreres who is able to help me efficiently in setting up and maintaining good order here, taking care of correspondence, dealing with all sorts of people, selecting good candidates, and disposing of a host of other things that can be most annoying and time-consuming.

"Ever since God thrust me into this business, I haven't had a moment's consolation. My soul seems to have lost its receptivity for anything agreeable or consoling, but at the same time it has become highly sensitive to painful experiences. Divine Providence certainly hasn't spared me in this respect. Think how sad all this makes me and how oppressive it is not to have one moment throughout the day that I can devote to my soul's welfare. Yet you know how ardently and continually I have been inclined toward a life of retreat and solitude.

"I, with my great abhorrence and almost insurmountable repugnance for public relations, find myself thrust into the middle of things. I, who have difficulty even in talking to people, have to chatter away constantly. From morning till night I am tied up giving direction, despite the fact that I am so repelled by it that it utterly bores me. I have to be giving conferences all the time, and yet even introducing the subject for meditation disturbs me for three hours before it is due.

"It seems that everything in me rebels at my staying here. All the attractions of nature and grace pull me in the opposite direction. Every fiber in my body and every tendency of my soul draws me toward solitude. Nonetheless, I feel it would be criminal to entertain even the thought of it for an instant. God has bound me hand and foot to this crucifying but beloved work. I am quite convinced that, in order to obey the mighty Will that binds me, I must give up rest, satisfaction, and happiness, and, what is infinitely more important, my spiritual progress. The fact that at present I can't do a thing for the betterment of my soul fills me with regret.

"I beg God to forgive my maladjustment and submit with all my heart to the Divine Will that holds me so tight it nearly strangles me. I believe that I can honestly say I've never made a move to loosen the irons that God has clamped on me. After all, it's better for me to be the least one in my Heavenly Father's Kingdom and obediently work for the salvation of so many destitute souls than achieve the front rank by abandoning the pathway traced out for me by His adorable Will."

After this lengthy preamble, Francis now addressed himself to a systematic consideration of Le Vavasseur's charges. "You have declared war on me," he said, "but it is a tactical war and I will reciprocate. (Please note that I am saying this lightly and ignoring the sorrow that marked the beginning of this letter. If one doesn't put his trust in God and make up his mind to suffer even the most violent grief at God's hands, he can never become strong with the strength of God.)

"I think you're being terribly rough. I should imagine, however, that you're not nearly as rough with others as you are with me, else you would spoil everything and everybody by kicking up a row each time things didn't go according to your liking. Don't be so savage with people. Make an exception for me. You cut deeper than you think. . . .

"You want everything to be perfect right away. . . . Now look. I couldn't have been rigorous right from the start. The setup was too precarious. There were no strong foundations and my authority was much too weak. Judge by yourself and Father Tisserant. If I had followed your principles, I would have had to throw you out or keep you for two full years of training. (Remember the temptations you had?) Now do you think that would have been advisable? Wouldn't I have acted rashly? If I had adopted your rigid recommendations there would not be a stone left upon a stone. . . .

"You want the members of a community to be so perfect and renounced that we can yank them around like puppets. That might make a nice show, but it has never existed and never will exist in the Church. The Jesuits are certainly one of the most fervent societies in the Church, but if they listened to you they'd have to expel half their members.

"You want me to dismiss you. That would be committing a

grievous sin against God and against your own soul. You are vowed to God and the Most Holy Heart of Mary, your dear Mother. Every thought about breaking your bond is an illusion."[7]

All of this fell on deaf ears. Frederic had made up his mind. Libermann's gentle words fell harmlessly off the thick rampart of resentment and bitterness that he had built up. He replied in short grim sentences, reaffirming his decision to leave and demanding his superior's consent. This time Francis eliminated explanatory material and assumed a more practical tone.

"It is utterly impossible for me to comply with your request. I believe I would be unfaithful to God, for I don't think it is God's will for you to leave the Congregation and enter the Society of Jesus. It's hardly worthwhile discussing every point you raise because we wouldn't get anywhere that way. I'll content myself with one observation: you have a higher opinion of the Jesuits than you do of your own Society. I concur with you fully in that opinion. I'll tell you exactly how I feel about it. Without setting myself up as a judge on the fervor of religious groups now flourishing in the Church, I would certainly put the Society of Jesus in the first rank and I don't know of another that is equal to it. But that's not what determines a vocation. Nor does it insure great perfection. Otherwise, everybody would have to join the Jesuits. It often happens that a man can sanctify himself in an organization that is in itself less perfect than he could have in much more perfect situation. . . .

"Don't imagine I'm trying to hold you at all costs. That's not so. I'm completely resigned. It would break my heart, but I've gone through worse things and this won't be the last. Therefore, I'm not asking you to stay. I just won't give my consent. All I ask is, '*quod facis, fac citius*' (What thou dost, do quickly).

"Forgive me for using that quotation. I really didn't intend to make an odious comparison. The phrase flowed from my pen automatically and I don't want to start the letter all over again to eliminate it. Make up your mind and tell me what the decision is."[8]

By the time Le Vavasseur received this letter, grace was already at work. His excitement had abated; the bitterness had turned to sweetness and light. In his next letter his regret, his good inten-

[7] N. D. 8, 28 ff.
[8] N. D. 8, 363 ff.

tions, and his remorse were now as stormy as his recalcitrance had been. That same evening he began still another retreat to restore some balance to his seething emotions, and when the days of recollection had ended he penned an abject letter to Libermann. "The retreat has done me good," he averred. "It has completed what God began. At this moment I would undergo anything and be a simple gate-keeper at La Neuville rather than leave you. If you send me away I will lie down at your door like a dog. Please forgive me, I beg of you, for everything I said in those letters."[9]

Francis welcomed back the prodigal with great joy. "No doubt you feel terrible," he said soothingly. "You need a few words of comfort. Believe me when I say there's not a trace of rancor in my heart over what happened. On the contrary, I've been overjoyed." Then he immediately proceeded to propose enthusiastically that Le Vavasseur come back to La Neuville and help him with the general administration. Father Boulanger could replace Frederic in Reunion and then the two of them could share the burdens of the enterprise they had started years before. The happy letter ended on a wistful note: "I hope from now on peace will be yours at last."[10] The crisis was over and the sun was shining again.

The other original colleague, Eugene Tisserant, had gone off to Haiti, resolved to become a fearless reformer just when that island was in the throes of a political, social, and religious upheaval. Some of the local clergy, far from ideal themselves, feared this man who openly threatened their freedom, and the civil authorities, mistakenly identifying the Catholic Church with the Parisian control they had just thrown off, rejected him as the representative of a foreign power. Tisserant himself had absorbed some of Libermann's idealism and heroic fidelity, but he never achieved the tact, gentility, and easy tolerance with which Francis cushioned his reform movements. Eugene's unsteady personality nullified to a great extent his pathetic and violent outbursts against injustice and dishonesty wherever he encountered any delinquency. His tense striving for perfection and his addiction to certain contemporary ascetical practices caused himself and everyone else a lot of trouble.

---

[9] Alexander LeRoy, C.S.Sp., *Le T. R. P. Frédéric Le Vavasseur,* Paris, n.d., 95 (hereafter quoted as Va.).

[10] N. D. 9, 129, 131 ff., 135.

Finally, a rather limited point of view seriously handicapped him at every turn. Even Le Vavasseur, himself no paragon of diplomacy, confessed: "I am quite apprehensive about him. I very much fear that the affairs he'll have to handle require a different sort of brain than he has."[11]

The frequent meddling of this well-intentioned but narrow-minded friend caused Francis considerable anxiety. Once he wrote to Le Vavasseur about it: "Our good Father Tisserant has finally gotten over his black mood — the ill humor that has given me so much trouble. It was a trial and a visitation. But it's all gone now. At the moment we see eye to eye."[12]

The Haitian political situation worsened after a time and Tisserant, who had now become Prefect Apostolic of the island, was obliged to leave the country. During the years preceding his departure he had gained experience and achieved much greater maturity. Consequently, when Rome authorized Libermann to select a Prefect Apostolic for Guinea after Bishop Barron resigned, he nominated Tisserant. Eugene was at the home of some friends in France recuperating from a serious illness when the appointment arrived. He rushed off to the boat immediately.

After embarkation, the first few days out passed uneventfully. Then, off the coast of Morocco, a stiff breeze came up. It soon developed into a gale of hurricane proportions that savagely drove the ship aground on a sandbar. The rudders jammed and the sea poured in through a gaping hole in the ship's side. Tisserant knelt, a motionless embodiment of prayer, amid the turbulent mass of humanity on deck. All around him people were shouting, masts creaked and groaned, the wind howled fiendishly, and the waves kept thrashing at the stricken vessel. At last he rose and began to move quietly among the panic-stricken passengers and crew, an inspiring personification of peace and surrender. Even the captain, who blamed himself for the catastrophe, welcomed Tisserant's words of encouragement and consolation. Then he told everyone to kneel and make an act of contrition while he pronounced the final absolution. Subsequently, one of the survivors tearfully admitted: "Without Father Tisserant we would never have had the moral stamina to save ourselves."[13]

[11] N. D. 6, 533. [12] N. D. 6, 114. [13] N. D. 8, 102.

There was one Jewish man on the doomed ship. He came running up the deck screaming, "I don't want to die; I don't want to die!" Then he saw the quiet, self-assured figure of the handsome young priest and listened to the words of comfort he was addressing to those around him. Pushing his way forward, he begged for help. A short, serious talk about eternal values ensued. It ended in a baptism that brought calm and confidence to one more beleaguered soul.

Suddenly, with a tearing crash, the ship broke in two, and everyone who could fled to the bridge. The black December night closed in on them. An icy rain soaked them to the skin. Towering waves rose up and as each one fell with a mighty rush, more of those human dots who clung to broken spars were washed into the sea. There was nothing but a long agonized cry and then the night and the waves closed over them. Tisserant gave away his hat and overcoat and then braced himself against a mast, shivering in the icy tempest and continuing his work of encouragement.

At dawn the exhausted survivors saw the coastline less than half a mile away. The more daring among them threw themselves into the still turbulent surf. Eugene had done all he could at the scene of the shipwreck. His thoughts now turned to Guinea. He must try to save himself for that unhappy land where five of his confreres had already made the supreme sacrifice. Grasping a fragment of planking, he cast himself into the churning water, hoping to strike out for the Moroccan shore that looked so near. A massive wave rolled up before him, caught him on its crest, and pounded him furiously against the broken hull he had just left. Then another and another, till at last they tossed him aside, a limp and bloody form.

The survivors in the rigging watched through their tears the end of a man who had given them strength in this tragic hour, the only one of their number who showed no fear and who refused to think of himself for even a moment. He had perished a hero like his grandfather, General Bauvais.

It was the Feast of the Immaculate Conception. Back in Paris, Tisserant's mother was coming out of church with a group of her friends. They had just finished a novena to Our Lady, asking her intercession for Eugene.

The newspapers first carried a report of the disaster. Then surviving seamen added further details. Libermann was utterly crushed.

"Mine is a three-fold grief," he said. "I have lost an intimate friend and devoted co-worker of whom I was exceptionally fond. Then too, an important mission will be deprived of a man on whom I built my brightest hopes. Lastly, there is a family, to which I was closely attached, now plunged in sorrow and shock."

Almost immediately, however, the customary resignation and surrender flowed from his pen like an ancient Hebrew psalm. "Thou art the Master, we Thy poor servants. Thou hast seen fit to strike down our fairest hopes and tear our hearts asunder with profoundest grief. We assent to Thy Holy Will; we adore what we cannot comprehend, we offer Thee this sacrifice from the bottom of our hearts."

The one consoling feature of it all was the fact that Tisserant died like a hero. As Libermann observed, he had gone "down on the field of battle" and finished his career, "in a death that gave high honor to his God and salvation to his soul." "When I saw him in his recent illness, I feared that death might claim him then. It would have been regrettable for him and me and for yourself if he had departed this world, surprised by the grim reaper at a time of complete inactivity. Our good Mother staved off such an untimely and useless death. She saw to it that her client left his mortal remains on the battlefield. . . . From the moment they reported the shipwreck, I knew for certain that his zeal had found full scope in that solemn hour."[14]

[14] N. D. 8, 3, 23, 50 f.

CHAPTER TWENTY

THE DARK CONTINENT

Far from La Neuville, in the steaming jungles of Guinea, Bessieux and Gregory were grimly battling the lethal climate. Libermann's thoughts often turned to this sorely tried pair. "I assure you that my soul is plunged in grief when I think of you. We regard you as an inspiring vanguard of true confessors and hope that a marytr's reward is in store for you. Actually, I find it difficult to express everything that is in my heart. . . .

"My regard for you has increased a hundredfold. I am moved at the sight of your sufferings and yet cannot help blessing the God who has deigned to send them to you. I sympathize with you, yet I rejoice in your affliction. I am sad and depressed, yet at the same time I am full of joy and peace."[1] Through this series of paradoxes, he meant to indicate that so much suffering at the outset augured well for the ultimate success of the mission and enabled his men to grow in maturity and holiness. In the same vein he was later to say, "I fear for that work which is not marked with the sign of the cross."

He wanted his men to hold out in Africa, for he knew that they were the first Europeans to engage in the systematic evangelization of that country. Toward this end, God was moving him irresistibly. "You see," he pointed out, "I am not doing what I wish. Divine Providence runs our affairs in spite of me. Let me tell you, if I had followed my own bent, I would certainly have avoided taking on so much at one time. It scares me, but what can I do? I cannot oppose the Will of God that is positively forcing me.

[1] N. D. 6, 279 f.

"However, our poor natural caution has a very limited value. Maybe my fears will turn to gratitude. . . . Human reason thinks it imprudent to start everything simultaneously. God will help us accomplish what he drives me to undertake against my will."[2]

Bessieux and Gregory were two infinitesimally small specks in the vast stretches of that unknown continent, yet they represented the flower of Western Christianity. Their pitiful establishment housed the essence of European culture. It sheltered treasures more valuable by far than the assets of all the military forts and commercial posts combined. Francis was fully aware of this. That is why he wrote with almost prophetic earnestness: "Have courage. If you are under the impression that you didn't achieve anything up to now, I might counter with an estimate that you have done a thousand times more than the missionaries in Reunion. Experience is needed before we begin our conquest of Africa. We may be farther ahead than we think. Always remember that you are laying the foundations of a new and extremely far-flung Church."[3]

He chafed over his inability to mount a full-scale offensive. His mission was to kindle an apostolic enthusiasm in Europe — and he found himself becoming a constant indictment against a civilization that had repudiated the black race. He never had the satisfaction of seeing a Christian world reawakened to its missionary duty. He would not live to rejoice in the day when other orders, congregations, and even lay groups would march in to widen the breach that his lonely pioneers had made. "Look at me," he sighed, "with my desire to save millions of souls that will be forever lost. I have no help and no resources. I have only a handful of men and the means at our disposal are almost nil. There is not even one little corner of the earth which I can call with certainty a missionary starting point. . . . Honestly, I can't understand why I don't give up in utter discouragement over the tremendous difficulties and our limited resources. It is best explained as a special grace of Our Lord who desires the salvation of these poor people despite all obstacles. This alone encourages and strengthens me and makes me hope that our work and worry will some day be crowned with success. I feel confident that no other society in the Church would

---

[2] N. D. 6, 322.
[3] N. D. 6, 250.

want to assume that mission under the present conditions. What group would be willing to undertake such a dangerous job, where no post is certain, no true home to be found, no solid foundation, no spot where beginners might adjust themselves before encountering the dangers, and no center from which to direct missionary operations and maintain contact with Europe?"[4]

His was the role of a lonely pioneer who could not envision the impact on history that his heroic endeavors would have, for as yet there was no shadow on the distant horizon of those stalwart groups of men and women from Europe and America who in years to come would fill the ranks of orders, congregations, and lay institutes coming to Africa. In his day there was nothing but the crying need of those vast tropical regions and only a handful of men to answer the call. He was the first to sound the trumpet that mustered a world force that has since converged on the Dark Continent and made it glow with the light of Christ.

His anxiety to arouse the world in Africa's behalf kept him constantly on the lookout for opportunities to expand into countries other than France. His interest in Germany, Belgium, England, and Ireland has already been referred to. Now he wanted to educate a young Spaniard in his house because he confessed to being plagued by persistent concern for the 600,000 Negro slaves in the Spanish colonies. "Then there is Haiti too, and the English and Spanish colonies, Brazil and other countries, immense territories where there are more than 6,000,000 Negroes. . . . I am anxiously waiting for God's good time to get in touch with some fervent Spanish priests and start something in their country."[5]

The more keenly he realized the vast scope of his mission and the importance of his role in Church history, the more humble and apprehensive he became. He began to fear that his sins might handicap the work and thereby jeopardize the salvation of those millions who depended on its success. "The sins I commit," he lamented, "fall indirectly on every member of our beloved Congregation and on all its works, for 'God does not hear sinners' and yet I have to pray constantly for everything that concerns it."

As time went on, he was able to increase the task force in Guinea

[4] N. D. 7, 330.
[5] N. D. 7, 256.

little by little. As he did so, he kept emphasizing to each new recruit as well as to the veterans that the new type of apostolate demanded an intelligent marshaling of mental and physical forces. "I have a recommendation to make to you," he wrote Bessieux. "Do not kill your body. You are in an unhealthy territory. Avoid excessive privations. I am putting the confrere who is with you in charge of your bodily well-being. You must obey him in everything that pertains to your health. Read him this passage of your letter and don't add any commentary of your own.

"Keep an eye on your confreres and don't prescribe any mortifications for them. It is important to preserve your own life and that of the other missionaries for the benefit of the souls God wants to save. Then, if in spite of all precautions Divine Providence sees fit to take them out of this world, may God's will be done. For our part, we must conduct ourselves so as to avoid unfortunate accidents that would work to the detriment of souls."[6]

For the greater stability of the mission and as a deterrent to excessive government interference, Francis was convinced that bishops would be more effective than Prefects Apostolic. He sketched out an extensive memorandum embodying this and a number of other suggestions and then set out for Rome to discuss it with the Propaganda. It was to be a leisurely, roundabout trip with recruiting stops at various seminaries and a short visit with Samson in Strassburg. Father Blanpin, just back from the missions and suffering from a throat condition that had nearly destroyed his voice, was to be Libermann's companion.

After a tiresome stage run of two days and two nights, the two invalid travelers arrived at Samson's house. It was a wonderful reunion. First off, with typical considerateness for the family budget, Francis forbade his excited sister-in-law to prepare anything special for dinner. Then, despite his extreme fatigue, he turned his attention to all the nieces and nephews gathered wide-eyed around this beloved uncle who had sent all the jolly letters. They "almost forgot to eat, so intently did they watch and listen to their uncle, and they were ecstatic when he smiled at them, or hugged them, or gave them his blessing."[7]

[6] N. D. 8, 297 f.
[7] N. D. 8, 454.

It was during this visit also that Francis met Isaac, the half-brother who had never become a Catholic. They had a long and earnest conversation in German which, as far as Father Blanpin could make out, was not doing his superior any good. Had Blanpin been able to understand the gist of it, he would have heard Isaac berating this exhausted and weakened brother for having disgraced the family as an apostate and for having driven their father to an untimely grave.

As the diatribe grew more intense, Francis saw forgotten places and scenes rise up once more before his mind's eye. It seemed as though the old rabbi was standing there in front of him and that strange, intangible sense of guilt took possession of him again. Under the lash of Isaac's denunciation, the old sensitivity returned and the old wounds were laid open for still another time. He thought he had conquered all that, but no, the familiar clenching pain began to wrap its steel bands around his temples and the room began to swim. "God's will be done," he gasped and then fell heavily to the floor.

Doctor Samson and Isabel stood paralyzed for a moment as the convulsions gripped him, then they rushed to his aid. As soon as the crisis had passed, he lay there weak and lifeless but with an expression of indescribable peace suffusing his features. Very quietly he whispered that he was offering up this affliction for the conversion of Isaac and Sarah.

Poor Father Blanpin stayed there impotently wringing his hands through the whole episode. His confreres at home had charged him specifically with taking care of their beloved Father and now he had failed them utterly. "As a matter of fact," he wrote back, "I am very much afraid that I shall have to answer to the community for my stupidity in not taking better care of our Superior's material wants."[8] It was a great relief for him when Francis saved the situation by simply and unaffectedly asking what he should do to improve his health.

Then they left Strassburg and went on to the seminary of St. Dié, where the rector invited Libermann to address the seminarians. By this time the poor man had a burning fever compounded by headache and dizziness. Nonetheless, he complied with the request stoi-

[8] N. D. 8, 164.

cally. It was an opportunity he could not afford to pass up. "In spite of fever and the vertigo," he reported, "I spoke for more than a half hour to the assembly."[9]

After that they visited the town of Sainte-Marie-aux-Mines, where only half the population was Catholic. As the two exhausted priests in mud-stained cassocks carried their heavy carpetbags down the main street, a little crowd of urchins collected behind them, jeering and throwing stones. Blanpin was very much disturbed, but Francis dragged himself along, so happy in the chance to suffer something for his Master that he actually seemed to be in a jolly mood. Bystanders were struck by the serene emaciated face of the little priest who walked on so unconcerned amid the hail of stones. When angry housewives ran out with brooms to chase the little hoodlums, Francis called them back and kindly told them not to punish the boys.

When the trip continued by stagecoach, other passengers seemed to listen with special attention and forget the hardships of travel as Libermann launched into one of his cheerful conversations. One kind lady offered him food from her lunch basket and with his usual simplicity and good nature he accepted it gratefully. Wherever he could, he stopped to pay his respects to bishops and seminary rectors, taking advantage of each opportunity to establish good relations between them and his congregation. At Fourvières they learned that Pope Gregory XVI had died. At Lyons, they visited Pauline Jaricot, the girl who had founded the Society for the Propagation of the Faith. When they reached Avignon they were told that Pius IX had been elected to the papacy.

And so it went on. Francis was dead tired. Despite the cheerfulness and amiability that so fascinated fellow passengers and seminarians along the way, he was very near exhaustion. Moreover, he felt terribly homesick for the house at La Neuville. "I'll bet it's a long time," he wrote home, "since I've been as sad as I have been since I left."[10]

When they got to Marseilles, he felt much better. The warm climate did him so much good that the improvement was remarkable. He had a particular interest in the work being done by Father Perée and his two colleagues. These devoted priests had undertaken to

[9] N. D. 8, 174.
[10] N. D. 8, 177.

labor among the destitute characters of that seaport town and had achieved some success with the working class. Francis plied them with questions about methods and procedures, for wherever they were found, neglected souls always attracted his attention. His inquiries must have been fruitful, because he wrote back to La Neuville: "Tell Father Cacheleux that I hope I can bring him some data that will be helpful in dealing with the laborers at Amiens."[11]

For the first ten days in Rome, Francis was ill again but, despite the indisposition, he immediately began to compose his great proposal to the Propaganda. "I was so deeply involved in writing a memorandum of eighty-six immense folios," he said, "that I couldn't do anything else during that time." Through it all, the homesickness persisted. *"Heu mihi quia incolatus meus prolongatus est* [Woe to me, that my sojourning is prolonged, Ps. 119:5]," he sighed. " . . . When I left La Neuville, I thought I'd be back in two months."[12]

Because of the recent papal election, it took a while before the general administration of the Church returned to normal. The two pilgrims had to wait, therefore, until it was possible to conduct their affairs with the proper authorities. Since the delay made inroads on their already thin resources, Francis exploited his business acumen to save every franc he could. In those days, it was the recipient of a letter who paid the postage. Consequently, since Libermann's old classmate Bishop Luquet was in town doing business for the Propaganda, and since that agency was taking care of His Excellency's mailing expenses, Francis saw a chance to save money. He wrote back to La Neuville: "Always address your letters to Bishop Luquet. . . . The Propaganda pays for it. It is richer than we are. It certainly is better off than I am. I'm bankrupt."[13]

Toward the end of July, the document was ready. It had developed into a flaming defense of the neglected Negro race. "For many centuries," it argued, "legions of apostles sent out by the Mother of Churches . . . have sped to the ends of the earth with a divine zeal that the grace of Jesus Christ alone can stimulate. Yet at the same time millions of people languished at the very gates of Europe, perishing in ignorance and wretchedness and no one offered to rescue them. . . . On the other hand, we have watched the growth

[11] N. D. 8, 179. [12] N. D. 8, 194. [13] N. D. 8, 197.

of a spontaneous movement all over Europe that has been pointed toward aiding the black race and lifting it out of its degradation. We have observed commercial and philanthropic organizations becoming actively engaged in that endeavor, while the most powerful European governments have launched a program of colonial civilization with an investment of tremendous sums of money."[14]

After placing his subject in its proper historical perspective, Francis went on to show that here was a providential opportunity for the Church. Acknowledging the fact that many people regarded such a project as doomed to inevitable failure, he set forth a detailed procedure that would insure its success. First off, he maintained it was not a matter of baptizing great masses of natives as had been done years before. Instead, missionaries would have to "consolidate the fruits of their labors by giving to those Christian communities the stability of an organized Church."[15]

With a surprisingly modern outlook, he recommended as a prime objective the establishment of a hierarchy chosen from among these peoples. "It is certainly not enough," he insisted, "to strike out at random with the intention of converting pagans. From the very beginning we should aim at achieving more substantial results and have positive and specific ends in view. In order to do so, we will have to determine from the outset a system of procedures which in their total reach and bearing will serve to efficaciously plant our holy religion forever in the soil. For this we need a carefully premeditated plan and a very powerful hierarchical organization."[16]

To these general principles, Libermann then added practical conclusions regarding schools, teachers, catechists, professional men, and native priests. He even went so far as to propose that minor orders be conferred on catechists, although limiting their use of the clerical garb to times when they were exercising their ecclesiastical functions. "It is our plan and intention," he declared, "to devote particular care to the education of young people and to provide the most perfect civilization we are able to offer."[17] He was deeply convinced that his congregation's role must never be limited to the purely spiritual functions of a missionary. A permanent church, he knew, could never be established without educational work.

---

[14] N. D. 8, 223 f.
[15] N. D. 8, 235.
[16] N. D. 8, 242.
[17] N. D. 8, 275.

Libermann closed the memorandum with an immediate and practical proposal: that a Vicar Apostolic should be appointed for the Two Guineas to replace Bishop Barron. Then, two weeks after its delivery to the Propaganda, he went back to La Neuville and Father Blanpin went to Eaux Bonnes to find a cure for his illness.[18]

On the way home, Francis stopped at the "Blue Convent" of Castres. With pious curiosity, the nuns flocked to the parlor, eager to see this saintly man about whom they had heard so much. He stood there in the midst of them, smiling good-humoredly at their expressions of solicitous concern for his comfort. He had to agree with them that his travel-stained cassock had seen better days. Jolting about in stagecoaches and walking for miles on country roads had wrought havoc with both seams and fabric, but he had only one to his name and could not take it off for repairs until he got home. When he went on to indicate that he would not be averse to some emergency tailoring if any of the Sisters wished to render first-aid while he talked to them, several of the nuns flew to their needle and thread. The assembled community listened with rapt attention to his short discourse on the secret of maintaining interior peace and joy in the midst of suffering as two of the Sisters deftly moved around him on their knees, mending the torn and threadbare cassock. Long after, they spoke of the radiant happiness in his eyes, the quiet ease of his delicate figure, and the unearthly impression that years of pain and sorrow had given him a holy intimacy with the Light of God.

His return to La Neuville was a festive one. The community had missed his consoling presence for five long months and everyone rejoiced to see him home again. As the confreres came during the next few days to chat with their beloved superior, however, he grew more and more deeply concerned over the spirit of extreme asceticism that had crept into the house while he was gone. It was ever thus. His men were constantly returning to a harshly rigorous routine as soon as he was out of sight. "During my absence," he wrote, "Plantaz indulged in such fervor that he almost killed himself with

---

[18] Shortly after, he returned to Rome, his illness worse than ever. He was cured suddenly, November 7, 1846, while praying before the painting of the *Mater Admirabilis* in the Motherhouse of the Religious of the Sacred Heart at *Santa Trinità dei Monti*. Cf. N. D. 8, 457 ff.

mortifications. The man who took my place as superior was entirely too soft with him. He allowed him to do what he pleased and it almost cost him his life. He's all right now. He's recovered. But from now on, this sort of thing won't happen again. We will put some order into it."[19]

Yet it was to happen again, and in a most tragic fashion. Francis had proposed Father Truffet among others for the post of Vicar Apostolic of Guinea. Before entering the Holy Heart of Mary novitiate, Truffet had taught sacred eloquence for twelve years in a junior seminary. He was a recognized author who had won a prize in a literary competition and had engaged in extensive correspondence with the noted Italian writer, Silvio Pellico. As a refined littérateur and poet, he was poles apart from Libermann in bearing and expression. In fact, Francis himself said: "Truffet's character and manners are totally different from mine. . . . During all the time we've been together, we have always seen eye to eye on questions under discussion, but our way of saying things was always quite unalike."[20] Yet Libermann's greatness is evident in the fact that he never tried, under the pretext of inculcating simplicity or humility, to put the stamp of conformity on his highly distinctive novice. He took him as he was, respected the gifts with which God had endowed him, and concentrated on guiding him within the framework of his personality. Finally, he underscored his complete absence of petty prejudice by proposing the man for a bishopric.

Rome accepted the nomination while Truffet was still an unsuspecting novice at the end of his probationary period. His episcopal consecration took place on January 25, 1847, in the church of Our Lady of Victories. Then he and several young priests set out for Gorée to join the veterans there. His earlier experience as a sheltered seminary professor and his recent year as a novice served to combine a lamentable absence of practicality with an effervescent fervor that was to have dire consequences. Now that he had escaped from the influence of Libermann's restraining sense of balance, he lapsed back into the wild and romantic ideas of holiness which were then so prevalent. Though quite mature and intelligent in other respects, he had absorbed hardly any of Francis' flexibility and practical good sense.

[19] N. D. 8, 314.

[20] N. D. 9, 322.

No sooner had he arrived in Africa than he gathered all his men together in one residence and modeled its regime on the novitiate he had just left. Contact with the native population was to be limited. There was to be none at all with Europeans. Prayer and study, theological conferences three times a week, and a diet of millet soup, rice, and fish constituted the only routine he would hear of. The barbarous climate added a final touch of incarceration. Father Gravière had ruled out adding porches to the little house because such luxuries would spell the doom of religious poverty. Moreover, no air could circulate between the rooms because communicating doors had been vetoed by Father Arragon, who felt such apertures were a threat to holy silence. Father Warlop, the enthusiastic architect, had constructed the roof in a style that for some reason was meant to be oriental, though the only oriental characteristic about it was the gracious way in which it offered hospitable entry to every torrential downpour.

The household had enough money now and there was no famine in the land, yet the starvation menu was continued in the weird belief that a native diet was the only diet for missionaries. Outwardly, it appeared that everyone was happy in this wonderful simplicity of life and Father Arragon wrote to say that their culinary routine ought to be introduced in all missions. Others, like Father Warlop, had enough sense to see that monastic asceticism might go far toward cultivating the contemplative life in healthier climes but had little to recommend it for active missionaries in the tropics. He reported that some of the younger Fathers were so near starvation that they secretly devoured anything they could lay their hands on.

After six months of highly restricted activity and extremely limited caloric intake, everybody was ill. Bishop Truffet, himself among the victims, refused everything except a therapy of his own prescribing: sugar water and nothing more! He blindly maintained that an apostle should accept illness like everything else with supernatural resignation. Obstinately refusing to see a doctor, he grew so weak that eventually he could no longer say Mass. He would shuffle in to assist at the Holy Sacrifice and then lift his shaking hand at the end to give his blessing. Soon he was confined to bed, but even then he refused all special food and medicine. The confrere who attended him asked despairingly, "Father, do you really want to kill yourself? Don't you belong to the mission?" The dying prelate lifted his head from the pillow and replied, "Friend, never put your trust in humans. If I go away, Providence will look out for you."[21]

When the bishop finally consented to receive special care it was too late. Father Briot, passing through on his way from Gabon back to France, administered the last rites. Truffet died on November 23, 1847, after less than seven months in Africa, the victim of that regrettable extremism which his age confused with holiness. It was this sickly ideal of mortification, rigidity, and unrealistic simplicity, this mystical disdain for natural means that Libermann battled against with increasing earnestness and vigor, trying to save his congregation and his men from the dangerous inheritance of an age that was given to romanticism and heroics.

When the bishop was laid to rest, Father Arragon became acting superior. It looked very much as though the tragedy of Cape Palmas was about to repeat itself. Father Dréano and Durand required hospitalization. Others dragged on weakly. Still there was no change in diet or routine. Arragon refused to change a thing. Then Father Briot contracted dysentery and found it impossible to continue his journey home. When he requested some assistance, the acting superior observed that after all it was more perfect for him to die at his post. Briot, considerably more level-headed about such things, decided that it was a lot more reasonable to stay alive and do some work. He headed for the nearest ship and quickly recovered from his dysentery on the voyage back to France. Only then did Father Arragon dare to modify Bishop Truffet's routine so that the missionaries could now have enough to eat and an opportunity to leave the house for apostolic activity.

Trouble did not end there, however. Along with their distorted asceticism these men had other extreme views on matters of administration. They seem to have suffered from a sort of black race complex that led them to confine the congregation's work to the Negroes and preferably the Negroes of Africa. This unhealthy restriction of purpose Francis opposed stoutly to his dying day, but as in other areas, they failed to follow where he led. The Fathers in Africa absolutely refused to have anything to do with the other

[21] N. D. 10, 43.

Europeans there and, as a result of that strange mentality, they even disdained to inform the French authorities of Bishop Truffet's death.

A short time before, Father Arragon and his companions had started off on a rather imprudent expedition and fell into the hands of unfriendly natives. The military commandant of Gorée sent armed troops to the rescue. When the prisoners were brought back he politely suggested that they refrain from doing such things in the future. Since Arragon and a number of his confreres were citizens of the independent duchy of Savoy and not of France, he wrote the French authorities a rude and insulting letter that questioned their right to interfere and spurned any financial aid that the government might provide. This letter and the disaffected attitude of the Holy Heart of Mary missionaries became the subject of a report that went to the admiral of the French Atlantic fleet. From him, Communications carried it to the Parisian Colonial Ministry where they decided that all subsidies would cease at the end of the current budget period. It took careful diplomacy on Libermann's part to counteract the affront and its disastrous effects. Had state support been withdrawn, it would have meant the end of government-sponsored travel to and from the mission, free supplies of rice and bread, and gratuitous hospital care — a loss that would have amounted to 25,000 gold francs per year. The mission's shaky finances would never have recovered from the blow.

Bishop Truffet's death laid a double burden of grief on Libermann. The loss was heartbreaking enough, but the knowledge that it need not have occurred was even more depressing. "The most painful thing about this situation," he wrote dejectedly, "is the regret one feels at seeing such a tragedy occur through a rash way of doing things that flouted the most elementary rules. Undoubtedly it was the diet that caused this catastrophe." "I might have derived some edification and consolation from it if they hadn't been so horribly imprudent." He began to wonder if he would ever get his point across. "I confess," he sighed, "that I foresee many more accidents because our missionaries will never learn to be reasonable."[22]

Now he expressly forbade his African confreres to fast during

[22] N. D. 10, 35, 67, 78.

Lent and went on to report with evident satisfaction that everyone at La Neuville enjoyed good health and had a good appetite. Now too he emphasized even more strongly than ever that sanctity is not usually an acceptable substitute for natural human means. He spoke of "a certain lack of experience" on Bishop Truffet's part which, he stoutly maintained, could not be made up for by holiness and virtue. The next Vicar Apostolic would have to be more reliable and the whole thing would have to be better organized.

Francis gave the problem his fullest consideration and finally proposed not one but two bishops. The distance between Dakar and Gabon was too great for efficient ecclesiastical administration. A division of the territory into two vicariates seemed much more logical. Accordingly, he nominated Father Bessieux for the Two Guineas and Father Kobès as his coadjutor. Bessieux had grown in stature and experience since the early days of his own childish imprudence. The mission would be safe in his hands. Kobès, another Alsatian and a professor of theology, exhibited quite a flair for practical matters and organizing techniques. Rome objected to his age — he was only twenty-eight — but ultimately appointed both him and Bessieux. After their consecration, Libermann thoughtfully watched them depart for Africa. Was it safe for him to feel a sense of fulfillment now? He hoped so. His life thus far had never seemed successful. In fact, it almost looked as though whatever he touched was threatened with tragedy.

Humanly speaking, there was no reason for optimism, yet events seemed to be turning in his favor at last. Instead of doors closing in Rome and in Paris, high functionaries in the Church and the government respected his intelligent diplomacy and received him courteously. One might have expected people to shun his star-crossed organization, but vocations came so rapidly that he had to enlarge the novitiate three times in five years, while donations large and small flowed in from every side to support the rapidly expanding household. The Colonial Ministry granted him subsidies; the Nunciature in Paris gave him advice and support; the Propaganda conferred on him full powers to nominate Prefects Apostolic for the mission fields. Yet all of this timely cooperation materialized despite the fact that he never played down his failures or hid his reverses from the public eye. Moreover, the constant slander of his enemies even distorted and exaggerated his lack of success. One cannot help feeling, therefore, that God sent him into the world for a specific purpose and meant to see that purpose served even in the midst of human failure.

Now he began to send more and more priests and brothers out to join Bishops Bessieux and Kobès in a truly systematic program of evangelization. It was he who plotted the campaign, inspired and directed its development, launched bold new projects, and encouraged, consoled, and stimulated the young pioneers by his letters. Always faithful to his original concept of a modern, well-organized apostolate, he never permitted the venture to degenerate into a haphazard and unrealistic squandering of forces, bright with the luster of heroism but hopelessly inept in its fruitlessness. The young missionaries kept him abreast of every problem, every advance, and every stalemate, eager to pass on to him each detail so that his wisdom might be exploited for their benefit. On his part a stream of letters poured out to Africa — gems of guidance couched in his curiously forceful French and dashed off in a racing scrawl from his desk, from stagecoaches, or from a sickbed, where the migraine thundered in his head or searing pains tore at his abdomen.

Libermann was never to set foot in Africa. The breadth of his mission would never give him an opportunity to visit it. Since his activities embraced a complex and worldwide apostolate, other interests kept him from confining his attention to the Dark Continent long enough to travel there. It was only one portion of the heavy burden that God had placed upon his frail shoulders. Yet even with divided attention and only a part of his resources, he laid the foundations of modern African missiology so wisely and so well that a century later Pope Pius XII commended him for having "inspired and animated a new legion of apostles who . . . have written a glorious page in the history of the Church's missions."[23]

---

[23] B. G. 42, 245.

CHAPTER TWENTY-ONE

EUROPE

Despite many alterations and additions, the house of La Neuville was still too small. Even before Libermann's departure for Rome, the Council had considered the advisability of opening a new establishment nearer town so that the Fathers could more easily help in the parishes on a part-time basis and thereby increase the community's income. The situation became even more acute when Francis' recruiting trip began to show results. Father Lannurien wrote to Rome that they were so overcrowded in the old place that everyone was at his wits' ends trying to squeeze in the newcomers. Something just had to be done.

The Louvencourt Sisters offered their orphanage at Faubourg-Noyon near Amiens, but it was too small to accommodate Libermann's entire community. Then there was the ancient abbey at Notre Dame du Gard which the Cistercians had abandoned because the Amiens-Abbeville railroad had just cut a new right-of-way through the property and passing trains interfered with the monks' contemplative life. Since Francis was still in Rome when these opportunities arose, he left the decision up to Father Schwindenhammer and that enterprising young man bought both the abbey and the orphanage, using the proceeds of the La Neuville sale as part payment for the new properties.

Twenty-eight philosophers and theologians followed Father Schwindenhammer to Notre Dame du Gard. The nine novices, of whom six were priests, ensconced themselves at Faubourg-Noyon and Libermann made his headquarters there also. Father Lannurien stayed with him as his private secretary. It was a most satisfactory arrangement, for Francis had a high regard for and implicit trust in this gifted young man. For his part, the secretary had an excellent opportunity to gain a clear and deep insight into Libermann's ideas and intentions. His intimate acquaintance with his superior's plans and aspirations enabled him to render the Congregation an inestimable service when, after Libermann's death, his confreres asked him to write down for posterity the aims and objectives of the great man with whom it had been his privilege to associate so closely.

Although Francis had taken up residence at Faubourg-Noyon, he never neglected the young students in the old abbey of Notre Dame du Gard. When the schedule permitted, he had one of the Brothers hitch up and drive him over to the senior scholasticate at least once a week. His driver rejoiced in anticipation of a long chat with the venerated Father, but he soon found that Francis always avoided wasting time by bringing along someone who needed spiritual guidance or provided information on business matters.

Not content with adequate physical facilities, Libermann now turned his agile mind to an energetic organization of the curriculum. He insisted on academic standards of a high order, fully aware that both the education of his priests and the prestige of his establishments depended on a routine of solid study.

The case of Father Leo Le Vavasseur demonstrates this rather pointedly. From the very outset, Francis admitted him with the proviso that he would serve the Congregation at home. "I am not at all hesitant about accepting your young deacon," he wrote to the parents. "However, I have formally declared that I took him, not to send him to the missions, but to use him in Europe."[1] It was this young man, now ordained and a professor at Notre Dame du Gard, whom he selected to write a truly scientific handbook of the liturgy.

This was not to be a pedestrian work. It was meant to be a genuinely solid volume that would measure up to the demanding criteria he himself had laid down. With the same practicality he had displayed in missionary organization, he now turned editor, rejecting any thought of a book that would merely repeat what other liturgists

[1] N. D. 7, 305.

had written. It had to be an original documented study based directly on Roman sources.

"Here in France," he observed, "we need an elementary and complete treatise on the Roman liturgy. We are working on a practical study of that subject and one that is in conformity with the decrees of the Sacred Congregation of Rites. It is our hope that this work will be finished after several years of constant observation and research in the field." "Every statement must be justified by a note referring to the source from which it is derived . . . ; the rules must be drawn from sources that are both authentic and absolutely certain. . . . In cases where details are not expressly given but flow logically from prescriptions of the authorities, some indication must be given that they are set forth as our own conclusions."[2]

Libermann then proceeded to organize an informal brain trust which would insure a high degree of scientific objectivity by means of checks and balances. With growing enthusiasm he warmed to the subject: "I shall make Father Lannurien and Father Kobès examine every question carefully. They will verify quotations and test the veracity of conclusions that have been drawn from official texts. They will do the same for items that are not found explicitly stated in authentic works. After that, they will meet and go over the entire treatise together. In those conferences we shall [again] verify quotations and conclusions. Through this procedure, I hope we can produce something really solid. Even for points that are only slightly uncertain we shall consult the Holy See, i.e., the Sacred Congregation of Rites or one of its members. If we end up with a number of items that are not clear in our sources, and if these are left up to our own free choice, we shall then make some decision to achieve uniformity, following Italian authors by preference. Our treatise must then indicate the relative value of those rules, i.e., that they have been derived from a particular authority."[3]

Here as in the missions Libermann guided his men with quiet determination into a strictly objective approach to the special field of study at hand. His attitude toward this academic project was the same as his *modus agendi* in setting up an apostolic enterprise: search the field for sound factual data, proceed carefully on the

---

[2] N. D. 9, 199, 348.

[3] N. D. 9, 349.

basis of information derived, and then deploy men and resources to achieve the established goal. He despised anything unrealistic, superficial, and disorganized; refused to be satisfied with only mediocre results; planned for years ahead; parceled out the work to different individuals; and outlined precisely the phases and the methodology to be pursued.

In this way, Francis inspired the creation of a standard work that soon gained widespread renown. Previously, nearly all France had followed the Gallican Liturgy. Before long, however, one bishop after another adopted this new opus as the official manual of ceremonies of his diocese. Because Libermann had made such uncompromising demands for exactitude, Leo Le Vavasseur became a generally recognized authority among liturgists and attained such a degree of eminence that the luster of his name's prestige was subsequently shared by Fathers Haegy and Stercky, confreres who revised his work and kept it up to date as time went on. When the Archbishop of Bourges praised the treatise for its methods, clarity, exactness, precision, and scrupulous fidelity to scholarly accuracy, he may not have suspected it, but he was indirectly paying tribute to the wise superior who had made it possible by his discerning orientation of a young and gifted character.[4]

In much the same fashion, Libermann aroused the enthusiasm of his other professors also, urging them to approach their task with thoroughness, originality, and responsible objectivity. He himself indulged in direct research when he could, as is evidenced by his statement that he had "begun work on the Bullarium of the Propagation of the Faith in order to line up material for a course in Canon Law."[5]

Care of the destitute in Europe next claimed his attention. When he was still at La Neuville, he had organized a program for chimney sweeps, young boys who battled desperate poverty by going through cities and towns cleaning the interiors of chimneys on houses and commercial buildings. Francis saw to it that they were fed and instructed in the catechism. He liked nothing better than to be in the midst of these forlorn soot-covered unfortunates, cutting the

---

[4] *Manuel de liturgie et cérémonial selon le rit romain.* This book is now being prepared for its eighteenth edition by Henri Littner.

[5] N. D. 9, 350.

bread and personally distributing the portions. Then he would stay with them, chatting pleasantly while the food disappeared into those hungry little stomachs. After that he or a confrere would conduct the class in religion.

Mendicants and tramps quickly sensed his friendly solicitude. Once an old beggarwoman came to the door and asked to see the saintly Father Superior. "The mere sight of him makes me feel good right away," she said. Obviously, the Brother Porter could not find it in his heart to turn her away. She had her opportunity to see the venerable priest.

Gradually, Libermann went further. He began to admit to his Congregation men who felt no vocation for the foreign missions and he gave them his assurance, moreover, that they would be kept in Europe. One of these whom he steadily guided in this direction was the nephew of the bishop of Amiens, Father Clair. Another was a deacon from the diocese of Clermont. A third was Father Delaplace, who later founded the Sisters Servants of the Holy Heart of Mary. Then there was Schwindenhammer, his future successor as superior general. Nonetheless, when he seriously considered supplying chaplains for the French navy, a commitment that would have required thirty priests, he expressly stipulated: " . . . I would not want those who have a positive vocation for the missions to be used for this work."[6]

Mr. Germainville, a layman of the archdiocese of Bordeaux, had organized certain social activities in that highly commercial center. Libermann readily accepted responsibility for them. "You still want us to settle in Bordeaux," he wrote. "I would like to take over this little work as much as you want us to, in order to lay the foundations of an important enterprise that will spread far and wide. It could be the first establishment, the first attempt along a road that stretches ahead. I've wanted to do this for a long time and the desire has been intensifying ever since I returned from my trip last year. I would like to set up something that would benefit all the poorer classes. It would be extra-parochial; that is, it would lie outside the responsibility of parish priests for it is not included in their regular duties. This work would extend to working-men, sailors,

[6] N. D. 9, 323.

soldiers, prisoners, and even tramps. For that reason, I would like to establish centers in all the major sea-ports: Bordeaux, Toulon, Marseilles, Brest, etc. Such a work lies wholly and fully within the scope of the Congregation!"[7]

Such activities, he insisted, "are not contrary to the aims or the spirit expressed in the Rule. In the beginning, it is true, we did not think of them, but that does not prove that God didn't want them. It wasn't possible for us to think of them at that time. God impelled us to work for the Negroes, but even then we felt so keenly the need for broadening our objectives that the Rule speaks of destitute and poor souls in general."[8]

Then he really warmed to the prospect of engaging in social work. "I cling with all the energy of my soul," he declared, "to the work for laborers and disenfranchised people. That gives you some idea of my profound interest in the success of the Bordeaux project where we began. I regard that house as one of our most important endeavors. It is absolutely imperative that I do everything in my power to make it succeed."[9]

When others grew anxious about having enough men to staff all these works, Libermann quickly replied that special vocations for this type of apostolate would not be wanting if a clear distinction were made between those who wished to devote themselves to the ministry in Europe and those who had an inclination to work in foreign lands. He felt it was necessary to give each type an opportunity to promote the welfare of souls in the way that aptitude and attraction indicated. Once again, his unfailing respect for each man's personality came to the fore.

"It shall be an absolute rule with us," he stated, "that every cleric who wants to enter the novitiate with the formal plan and positive desire to go to the missions will not be used in Europe for this type of institution [i.e. social works]. These European houses will be staffed only by missionaries who cannot bear the climate of Africa or even by those who feel a sufficiently pronounced attraction for ministry in Europe. We will never, or hardly ever, admit a candidate with the proviso and promise that he will be kept in Europe. But if someone with that particular leaning presented him-

---

[7] N. D. 9, 151. [8] N. D. 9, 288. [9] N. D. 9, 274.

self we would *de facto* keep him there. If God wants us to do this work in Europe, I believe candidates for it will come, for that sort of activity is badly needed in France right now."[10]

He waxed really enthusiastic over the job to be done and felt sure that Providence was calling on his congregation at that precise moment of history to face the needs of centuries yet to come. Events had made the care of neglected souls more necessary than ever: abolitionists were moving toward the elimination of slavery in underdeveloped countries and the proletariat was in the throes of an emancipation movement at home. Libermann was keenly aware that a timely approach to these unfortunates in Europe and abroad could stave off a mass defection from the Church. "You see," he wrote, "how Divine Providence seems to declare itself in favor of your works which are more necessary than ever before. The working-class in France has lately acquired a position of major importance, and it is to be hoped that we shall have more freedom of action." "It looks right now as though Divine Providence wants us to inaugurate a program for the poor of France."[11]

As one phase of this work, Libermann advocated home missions. He hoped to start a new foundation in the Breton town of St. Brieuc and its "first aim would be to give missions in the country and even in the cities." He referred to it as "the house of diocesan missionaries." Its personnel problems did not seem to be insurmountable for, he said, "In the beginning we can use some of those who are slated for the foreign missions, and when the diocesan missionary work expands we can staff it with newcomers who right from the start showed no definite calling for the Negro missions. In a few years I believe we would find enough men in Brittany to join us for this purpose."[12]

Later, when his Congregation of the Holy Heart of Mary was merged into the venerable Society of the Holy Ghost and he became its Superior General, Libermann wrote in his formulation of the "Constitutive Articles" that Divine Providence had fixed the principal object of the Society's zeal as the most abandoned souls. In Article V, however, he added emphatically that it "will not

[10] N. D. 9, 290.
[11] N. D. 9, 130, 169.
[12] N. D. 10, 171, 177, 202.

abandon the needy souls of Europe; it will direct the zeal of its members to projects for the poor and abandoned who clamor for its help."[13] Subsequently, his successor in the generalate inserted a constitutional clause indicating that special attention would be given to the Negro race.

Francis had little patience with the divergent attempts and improvisations then being made in France for the assistance of the needy. Once again he sought to promote within the Church a new and realistic approach, a modern technique of organization whereby the problem could be efficiently attacked. As was the case in his program for Africa's evangelization and his pattern for academic excellence within his own group, we again see Libermann's insistence on concreteness, careful planning, and a judicious exploiting of up-to-date methods for the best possible adaptation of social work to the various categories of European people. He sought contact and cross fertilization of ideas with other social workers in the clergy and with the St. Vincent de Paul Society. He strove to foster an amalgamation of all the loose and scattered efforts of his contemporaries into a flexible but unified force for social reform. He drafted a proposal for a mighty new association of all welfare agencies, of all enterprises that were devoted to the care of orphans, needy students, laborers, the unemployed, prisoners, and servicemen, but the revolution of 1848 thwarted his plans.

A few years earlier he had actually written an essay in defense of the rights of illegitimate children, a question considerably more controversial in the nineteenth century than in our own. "No doubt you are amazed," he went on, "that I have delivered myself of such a lengthy dissertation on the subject, but I have been preoccupied with it for three years now. I feel awfully bad that such children are excluded from the religious life. Having no authority in these matters, I cannot do anything for them, but I fail to understand why up to now no one has tried to make available to these poor souls the joy that they need much more than other people. . . . Maybe God will inspire you with the desire to start something for this purpose. You may wish to discuss it with some devout and generous men in order to get such a project going. Once a work like that is started, it will be emulated in other dioceses."[14]

[13] N. D. 10, 451.

[14] N. D. 7, 211.

This wholehearted dedication to the destitute continued unabated despite the 1848 revolution and its aftermath. In this, as in the African campaign, he refused to retreat. By that time he had taken up residence in Paris as Superior General of the Spiritans and he wrote with evident satisfaction: "For some days now we have been opening the chapel to poor unemployed laborers. They are reduced to utter penury, with no food, no clothes, and no morale. Our Fathers instruct them and give them coupons for vegetables. Then too, we've organized a lottery for the distribution of articles that we have received such as shirts, trousers, socks . . . particularly blouses and shirts. The Fathers made an appeal to those who had not yet made their First Communion. A really impressive group registered for the catechism lessons which we are going to begin Saturday evening. Every Sunday they come to Mass and behave quite well. It's the finest work one can do for both society and religion. . . . This is a prodigious job and one that could actually restore peace to Paris and all of France, but it is especially pointed toward the salvation of souls."[15] Libermann's biographer, Father Briault, points to this as "the first origin of the social works, orphanages and reeducation centers that form part of the Congregation's tradition and mission. They were to survive beyond upheavals other than those of 1848," he says, "and are still in our hands today."[16]

In Lannurien's memorandum we read, "The Rules state that those who remain in Europe must also engage in the work of caring for souls. From the days of La Neuville on, we have busied ourselves with work for the poor, for example, the Savoyards and the orphan girls. Later, when we took over the Bordeaux house, it was decided that the Congregation would not confine itself to neglected souls in Africa or even to the missions generally, but that its scope should extend to all types of apostolic concern for abandoned people, i.e., to all necessitous operations for which there is a shortage of personnel, whether in Europe or overseas. This, then, clearly appears to have been the first objective of Father Libermann's mission and foundation."[17]

Father Schwinderhammer, Libermann's immediate successor, was particularly concerned about keeping intact the mission which Fran-

[15] N. D. 11, 48 f. [16] Briault 225. [17] Lann. 69.

cis had explained in great detail during a long series of intimate conversations. Moreover, Libermann had selected him personally as the man most qualified to carry on his work. He in turn had his views set down for posterity by Father Emonet, the next incumbent in the generalate, and from the Emonet documents we learn that Father Schwindenhammer reacted strongly to the "tendency to consider Africa as the whole Congregation or at least as its only work. This tendency has two very disastrous results":

> If we operate on that principle, it follows that all members should be sent to Africa. This is what they used to insist on in the most consistent and stubborn fashion and it was accomplished to some extent. What was the result? a) The Motherhouse and other works of the Congregation were deprived of the personnel they needed, although these men were inclined by nature and grace to [European] works. (I cannot help adding here and calling attention to the contradiction in the behavior of some of the confreres located in Africa. On the one hand, they accuse the Motherhouse because, as they say, it is composed exclusively of youngsters who are not particularly capable, and on the other, they hammer at the Motherhouse and try to force it to send off to the missions everyone in whom they suspect there might be some degree of experience and ability!) b) Out in Africa they have been asking us to send them even those who did not feel at home there for God did not call them to that type of work. The idea that all the members of our little Congregation were called for work in Africa has proven to be wrong and disastrous. The original idea of our Founder was different. The proof of it lies in what he himself has done. The most striking proof, of course, is the merger with the Holy Ghost Society.
>
> The policy of forcing men to go to the African missions when the Motherhouse did not want to send them and they themselves did not want to go, has not resulted in an increase of laborers for God; it has multiplied the number of dissatisfied and highly critical men.[18]

Schwindenhammer then went on to set down what he felt to be the best way of returning to Libermann's original aims. The first step was "not to send every member to Africa, but to make a choice. It is written: 'Thou shalt not tempt the Lord thy God!' We do just that when we send to Africa every member without distinction just because he possesses the qualities of mind and heart requisite for being a good member of the Congregation. In making our choice,

---

[18] Manuscript about Father Schwindenhammer, written by Fr. Emonet, 3 (hereafter quoted as Emonet).

we must start with inclination, health, temperament, and above all, character and virtue; yes, even the typical cast of that virtue."[19]

From all this it is obvious that Libermann's successors were determined to keep the Congregation faithful to his aims, no matter how great the pressure from special interest groups whose sectional enthusiasm blinded them to the general good. The extent of that fidelity finds ready demonstration in the breadth and variety of Spiritan activities all over the world.

The revolution of 1848 brought out the political scientist in Francis. For many years, the opposition party had clamored for a reform in the voting laws. King Charles X had been expelled by the revolution of 1830, and Louis-Philippe took over the government, first as Consul General, then as King. Guizot, his conservative prime minister, stubbornly refused to consider any change in matters of suffrage until the Parisians threw up barricades in the streets once more and inaugurated the short but violent February Revolution of 1848. Two days later, the King abdicated and a Second Republic led by socialists and republicans was proclaimed.

The fighting had broken out suddenly. The enraged populace invaded and seized the *Tuileries* and triumphantly hurled battered furniture through the windows. The National Guard fraternized with the people and together they disarmed all combat troops and drove them out of Paris. Railroad tracks were dismantled for long distances outside the city in order to forestall the advance of reinforcements. Through the heat of combat, however, it appears that religious houses went unscathed, for Francis wrote from Amiens: "The revolution is not directed against the clergy. . . . For our part, we are perfectly undisturbed. . . . My God, how much blood is being spilled in the streets of Paris! How many people are perishing in this atrocious mêlée!"[20]

Despite the tragic events in the capital, however, Libermann had to smile when he thought of his brother Felix there. The little bookbinder was given to adolescent boasting and to Francis' great amusement he used to brag shamelessly about how courageous he would be if anything happened. In reality he was timid as a mouse. "Intrepid Uncle Felix!" Libermann wrote. "I am positive that at

[19] Emonet 11.
[20] N. D. 10, 88.

the first sound of an alarm he grabbed his uniform, threw it on, perhaps inside out, being in such a hurry, then snatched up his gun with the deadly bayonet at its end, and with all the energy of his soul ran with his arms and his pack to hide under the bed. This, at least, is what I prophesied to him a week before the revolution broke out."[21]

In more serious moments, Francis pondered over political developments in the ancient Europe that he loved. Like Jeremias of old, or St. John Bosco addressing his warnings to Italian princes, Libermann set down his judgment on contemporary governments:

> I think this revolution is an act of justice that God has directed at the recently fallen dynasty, because it sought its own ends instead of the welfare of the people committed to it, because it sacrificed for its own advantage the interests of God and the Church that it knew quite well as an agency set up to procure the happiness of human beings. . . .
>
> This same act of justice is leveled at all the crowned heads of Europe. . . . I am fully convinced that the tide of the French revolution will reach them all and engulf a great number of them. The autocrat of Russia will also have his turn. . . .
>
> Should we grieve because pride is overthrown?
>
> The same act of divine justice is also striking at our great politicians. By their trickery and confounded craftiness they sacrificed God and humanity to their own aggrandizement. . . . Justice and equity existed in almost no government wherever their interests were involved, no matter how remotely. Is it not natural, then, that God's arm is raised against so many criminals who gave justice only to those they feared? They were strong with the weak and weak with the strong, even to the extent of sacrificing the weak to the strong ones they feared. . . .
>
> I must confess that, despite all this uncertainty about the future, I cannot help experiencing a profound feeling of gratitude to God because He has stepped in at last. He has blown on the pretentious great and with His breath He is toppling their pride and crushing it to bits.
>
> Another group of people who have been cast down by this hurricane is the civil aristocracy, the bureaucratic *pays légal,* who so arrogantly outraged the Church and refused it every shred of justice, trampled underfoot the welfare of the poor, sacrificed their souls and their country to miserable selfishness and special interests. The anger, or rather, the justice of God has swept aside all these haughty egotists. Great and small, they have been overthrown in France, and

[21] N. D. 10, 107.

> in all probability the same thing will sooner or later occur throughout Europe.
>
> I feel sure that the Republic will prosper if it is as faithful as the other governments have been unfaithful.[22]

Obviously, then, his progressiveness was not limited to systematic missiology, objective scholarship, and organized social work. It extended to politics as well. He even went so far as to rebuke his contemporaries among the clergy for clinging anxiously and stubbornly to attitudes inherited from a time that would never come again. "It has been the misfortune of the clergy in recent times that they hold to ideas out of the past. The world has progressed, the enemy has set up his batteries in line with the situation and the spirit of the age, but we have lagged behind. We must keep abreast of the times. With complete fidelity to the Gospel we must do good and combat evil according to the state and the temper of the period in which we live. We must attack the ramparts of the enemy wherever they happen to be set up and not give him a chance to entrench himself and consolidate his position while we are off seeking for him in places where he is no longer to be found. Clinging to olden times and retaining thought patterns that ruled a previous era will destroy the efficacy of our endeavors and enable the enemy to establish a stronghold in the new order. Let us then frankly and simply embrace the new order and breathe into it the spirit of the Gospel. We will thereby sanctify the world and the world will be on our side."[23]

The next morning Libermann did something that shocked a lot of people. He gathered together those of his confreres who were eligible to vote and marched them down to register. He accepted the right of suffrage for which the people of Paris had paid a bloody price on the barricades. "I understand very well," he said, "that elections are not ecclesiastical affairs, and yet we must keep in mind that we no longer live in the political situation of the past."

In an era of monarchist clerics, this was a superb example of his perfect adjustment. If only the contemporary clergy had heeded his advice, the terrible persecutions around the turn of the century could have been forestalled.

---

[22] N. D. 10, 146 ff.

[23] N. D. 10, 151.

CHAPTER TWENTY-TWO

THE EMERGING PATTERN

Francis Libermann's enterprise was growing in breadth and effectiveness, spreading the message of hope among destitute souls both in Europe and in distant lands. His emissaries ranged far and wide to seek out the neglected of the earth and lift them from their degradation. At home they were stemming the tide of misery by their social works; in Africa they were carrying onward the torch of faith among tribes that stumbled in the dark misery of paganism; in the islands they were healing broken souls that had fallen among the robbers of the spirit. Everywhere, the world's wretchedness and suffering were a little less devastating because he and his men had passed that way. The whole thing gave meaning to the waves of suffering and loneliness that had pursued him from his earliest years. History marked him plainly as the patron of all who are sick, forlorn, and needy.

While his burning desire to lay a soothing hand upon all the raw wounds of humanity was given expression in these ever expanding activities, another deep and mysterious urge had not yet found its outlet. From the first years at Stanislas College he had been haunted by an unshakable zeal to work for the betterment of the priesthood. Even as a seminarian fresh from the baptismal font he was thrust into the forefront of a guidance movement that made him the adviser of his fellow students at St. Sulpice and at Issy. Older and wiser heads had seen fit to recommend him as novice master for the Eudist priests at Rennes, though he himself was not yet ordained at the time. The visionary figure of Christ had placed in his hands the treasures of divine grace for distribution among the clergy. In Strassburg, at the very beginning of his foundation, he had resolved to include the training of German priests among its works, but Father de Brandt balked that move by providing a house in what Libermann disappointedly called the "interior of France."

This long-standing and repeatedly thwarted desire was at last about to be fulfilled. The Congregation of the Holy Heart of Mary had served its purpose as the vehicle whereby his missionary and social aims might find expression. It was now to be dissolved into the Society of the Holy Ghost, there to blend its riches with the golden tradition of education that the Holy Ghost Fathers had stored up in the eighteenth century.

A young Breton noble, Claude Francis Poullart des Places, founded the Society of the Holy Ghost in Paris on May 27, 1703. A former lawyer from a family of considerable means, he spent his income on the poor, first caring for the little Savoyard chimney sweeps as Libermann was later to do also, and then supporting impoverished students for the priesthood. This latter activity developed into such a major project that he soon rented a house and established a community of seminarians while he was still one of them himself — another biographical similarity that Libermann shared with him. Soon the group was formalized as a seminary and Claude gathered about him a number of "directors" or faculty members who, together with him, formed the nucleus of the Society.

These Spiritans, as they came to be called, grew in numbers and renown throughout the eighteenth century. Their purpose was to educate young men for the priesthood and they fulfilled it admirably. An ever widening stream of their graduates went off to religious institutes, French dioceses, foreign missions, and colonial parishes. Some of them joined the Society to swell the ranks of the professors whose reputation for learning and holiness was spreading so rapidly.

Although Claude died in 1709, his institute went on to write glorious pages in the history of the Church. Royal recognition and approval came three decades later. The Archbishop of Paris granted it ecclesiastical approbation in 1734 and took the seminary under his immediate jurisdiction. Other members of the hierarchy, impressed by its products, began to regard it as an interdiocesan training center. When increasing academic prestige brought requests to staff other seminaries, the Spiritans took over at Verdun and at Cardinal de Bissy's famous seminary of Meaux.

The Jansenists, particularly influential at that time, recognized these specialists in ecclesiastical education as their archenemies. They often mentioned them in the same breath with the equally detested Jesuits and pursued them with hatred and calumny wherever they went.

Finally, after almost a century of glorious educational achievement, the Society was struck by the full fury of the French Revolution. Its professors were forced out of their seminaries; its immense motherhouse and central seminary building in Paris was confiscated by the State, the institute itself was dissolved and its members dispersed. Father Bertout, a man of indomitable strength and perseverance, managed to retrieve something from the wreckage when the Terror was over. He succeeded at least in restoring its ancient legal rights and privileges, but the devastation had been too great to permit a quick recovery of all its former glory. The thread of continuity had nearly been severed. Moreover, the constant interference of capricious and sometimes inimical civil authorities still kept it weak with recurrent persecutions.

In the context of this melancholy situation, one can more readily understand the apprehensiveness of Spiritan Superiors General like Fourdinier and Leguay as they watched the growing influence of Libermann's Congregation of the Holy Heart of Mary. True, their basic aims were different — one was engaged primarily in the spiritual and academic training of priests and the other concentrated on missionary and social works — but their paths crossed overseas, because the Spiritans were responsible for staffing the French colonies with their graduates and their own members. The "Libermannists" looked like a serious threat to the beleaguered Holy Ghost Fathers, inasmuch as their every move, innocent though it was, seemed to be redolent of intrigue and cross-purpose operations.

Then Spiritan affairs deteriorated still further. Montalembert made a vigorous speech in Parliament, during the course of which he exposed abuses among the colonial clergy. It was a highly exaggerated diatribe, but it had the effect of shifting blame to the Holy

Ghost Fathers for a condition which the government itself had hindered them from correcting. When a new Colonial Minister threw down the gauntlet over the slavery question, Father Leguay saw the writing on the wall and resigned.

This new minister, Mr. Schoelcher, was a fanatical democrat, an ardent abolitionist who somehow convinced himself that Father Leguay and his Spiritans were opposing him in his progressive colonial policies. He recalled Leguay's appointees from overseas and replaced them by men who had previously been summoned back to France for bad conduct and who now presented themselves as victims of the Spiritan's anti-Negro attitude. Affairs worsened to a point where the Society of the Holy Ghost lived under constant threat of suppression by the irascible Mr. Schoelcher. At last it appeared that only Father Monnet could save the situation.

Monnet's chief value at this juncture lay in the fact that Schoelcher regarded him as a heroic defender of the Colonial Ministry's new policy. Actually, his heroism in this regard was a matter of pure coincidence. An excellent and thoroughly zealous missionary, he had received harsh treatment at the hands of slaveholders in Reunion because they interpreted his great interest in the Negroes' spiritual welfare as part of an abolitionist design. Consequently, when they forced his return to France, Mr. Schoelcher looked on him as a martyr for the cause. The Spiritans unhesitatingly drafted him as their only hope in the Generalate and he was promptly elected to succeed Father Leguay.

In the frantic scramble to trim their sails to the prevailing government winds, however, the Holy Ghost Fathers had overlooked an important aspect of the candidate's temperament: he had little talent or liking for administration. As a missionary, he could point to an enviable record of achievement, but at home he was lost amid the myriad details that engulf every major executive. Moreover, Schoelcher gave him no positive help. Suppression was staved off for the moment, but government support of the seminary was cut drastically. Colonial appointments were made over his head and high-handed interference met him at every turn.

Though personally well disposed toward Libermann (at one time he had actually wanted to join the Holy Heart of Mary Society), he began to share the apprehensions of his confreres who felt that some sort of treachery might be afoot. In his anxiety, he wrote to Francis and betrayed his concern in the course of the letter. An immediate and friendly reply did its best to allay his fears. "I told him among other things," Francis said, "that I not only wanted to be on good terms with the priests of the Holy Ghost, but that for some time now I have experienced a desire to see the two Congregations amalgamated. That sentence set Father Monnet on fire. The second day after I sent my letter, he was with us at Notre Dame du Gard, asking that we earnestly tackle the question of a union. I desire nothing better."[1]

Most members of the Holy Ghost Society recognized that such an amalgamation would add to their number an important contingent of well-trained young priests. Francis saw in it a way of achieving for his work that stability and security which could only come from official recognition which would have been so hard to obtain directly. Both sides welcomed the prospect of ending the eternal bickering over jurisdictional rights and responsibilities in the Colonies.

The most significant feature of the proposed merger for our purposes here, however, lies in the fact that it finally gave meaningful reality to Libermann's constant preoccupation with the problem of developing leaders in the Church. This was an interest that antedated his love for the missions. As has already been noted, the ceaseless drive to train good priests had thrust him into premature activities in the various seminaries where he stayed and the prospect of reforming the German clergy had beckoned so strongly that it nearly led him to give a new dimension to the young missionary society of the Holy Heart into which Tisserant and Le Vavasseur had drawn him.

More than anything else, however, this persistent interest in the academic and ascetical needs of the Church demonstrated its depth and seriousness by continuing unabated throughout the demanding years of the African venture. Its thread paralleled his intense missionary activity, running through an unbelievable mass of correspondence with seminary rectors, professors, and students. They, together with many privileged souls in the world, soon discovered that this controversial priest had a special faculty for

[1] N. D. 10, 218.

shaping their lives in a new and wonderful way. His sublime yet practical doctrine had no reference to the immediate needs of those African converts, Amiens and Bordeaux laborers, street urchins, and servicemen with whom his society was then dealing. It would have been impossible for them to profit by his spiritual letters, his essays on human psychology, or his lofty Commentary on the Gospel of St. John. All such creative work was directed toward the leading members of Christ's Mystical Body rather than to abandoned souls.

The strange, mystical conviction that God wanted him to engage in training other Christs finally made sense in the light of the proposed merger with the Spiritans. He thanked God that, in plunging into the academic tradition of the Holy Ghost Society, his little group would not have to sacrifice its own objectives, for the Spiritans had long since begun to send their own men into apostolic endeavors overseas as well. Providence had prepared each one for the other and the parts fitted together in a most harmonious whole.

Such a breadth of activity would provide that flexibility for which he had striven so vigorously these past few years. It would ease the burdens of administration to have a greater variety of work toward which candidates of diverse backgrounds and inclinations might be directed. Each should realize his full potential through wise and efficient placement. To one so respectful of the individual human personality and so desirous of its proper adjustment as Libermann was, this constituted an ideal situation.

The main historic objective of the Spiritans had been to educate personnel for anything that the Church found difficult to staff. No rigidity, no narrow limitations, no preconceived barriers. It was all so very much like the principles he had been advocating that Francis bowed his head in a whispered prayer of thanksgiving. Now the pattern of Providence grew clear. Now it was evident why God had driven him on, restlessly seeking and never quite finding exactly what he wanted.

At the start of the negotiations, Libermann experienced some anxiety over the possibility that his distorted reputation might somehow jeopardize the amalgamation. "I believe," he wrote, "that these Fathers are well disposed and anxious for what is best, but they have heard so many tall tales about me that they are full of fear and distrust."[2]

It was true. The men at Holy Ghost Seminary approached the affair on tiptoe, expecting the worst from the conniving, intriguing figure who was still a dark mystery to them. They assigned Father Loewenbruck, their most polished and able diplomat, to carry on all further discussions. He was highly in favor of the merger and had been one of its strongest advocates at home, all the more so now because his confidence in Father Monnet's leadership was diminishing rapidly. "I perceived rather quickly," he stated, "that he did not in any way possess the qualities needed for stimulating, sustaining, and fostering the progress of the failing Congregation of the Holy Ghost."[3]

Loewenbruck's diplomacy had to be exercised at home as well as abroad. He would bring his confreres to a point where they were adjusted to the idea and then, as soon as he left the house, Father Gaultier would swing Monnet in the opposite direction. "Every time I came home," Loewenbruck complained, "I had to start and rebuild what had been demolished during my enforced absence, even though it might have been only for a few days or even a few hours."[4] Gaultier's fears were based on years of association with Fourdinier and Leguay, both avowed enemies of Francis.

The negotiations proceeded with swaying fortunes. Monnet, a jovial giant with a heart of gold, familiarly called "the drum major" in ecclesiastical circles, blew hot and cold over the project in direct response to alternating demonstrations of good and bad humor on the part of that *bête-noire,* Mr. Schoelcher. When things went smoothly at the Colonial Office, he would have none of the proposed merger; when storm clouds gathered, he scurried back to the protective cover of the forthcoming amalgamation. All the while, Loewenbruck moved relentlessly forward, weaving together the most divergent points of view and advancing the cause by dint of prodigious activity.

Both sides soon came to the conclusion that Monnet was not the man for the Superiorship. From the very start it was agreed even among the Spiritans that only Francis could successfully guide the

[2] N. D. 10, 297. [3] N. D. 10, 416. [4] *Ibid.*

institute's destinies through the hazards of governmental caprice and internal stress. But what to do with Monnet? Archbishop Affre had just appointed him one of the Vicars-General of the diocese and His Grace, already no lover of Libermann, would resent it mightily if it appeared that his appointee had been shouldered out of the Spiritan superiorship to make room for such a "dangerous" character.

Quite confidentially, Francis mentioned to Loewenbruck that the Propaganda was searching for a Vicar Apostolic for Madagascar and that Monnet would be an ideal choice for the post because he had already proved himself a superb missionary. If Rome could be induced to entertain the nomination, much good would flow from the arrangement: the cause of religion in Madagascar would benefit, the Archbishop of Paris would be pleased, and the way would be left for Libermann's election as Superior General. Everyone applauded the idea when it was broached in open meeting and it was decided that both principals should go to Rome, Francis to propose Father Monnet as Vicar Apostolic of Madagascar and Monnet to advocate the union and to propose Francis as the new Spiritan General. Just then another revolution erupted and, since the two superiors had to remain at their posts, Father Loewenbruck went off to the Eternal City representing both parties.

He returned to Paris on August 2, the bearer of glad tidings. Verbal approval had been given and the Propaganda promised to confirm the merger, as well as Monnet's episcopal election, in writing after the next formal meeting of the Sacred Congregation. Much to Loewenbruck's annoyance, however, he found that his superior's fears had once more been aroused in the interim.

"Charmed and elated at my great success," he wrote, "I rushed to bring the good news back to Paris. But what a disappointment was waiting for me when I got there! I soon found out that, during my absence, two of our disaffected confreres had brought about in him such a change of heart that he no longer desired what he had so positively wanted — or at least had agreed to and authorized before I left for Rome. Consequently, I had to get busy to bring him around again and hold him there.

"I had the satisfaction of succeeding in this, thanks to the hope I could hold out that he would soon get his official appointment as Bishop and Vicar Apostolic of Madagascar. As a matter of fact, the documents arrived about a month after my return from Rome. From then on, there was no more tergiversation on his part nor even any attempt to put obstacles in the way of it."[5]

Finally, on August 24, 1848, both parties met at the Holy Ghost Seminary, signed the agreement and, on Father Monnet's motion, unanimously elected Libermann as the new Superior General. The merger was now a fact. One month later, September 26, the Roman documents arrived. They said in part: "It is now your task to bring the union of the two Congregations to a conclusion in such a way that henceforth the Congregation of the Immaculate Heart of Mary ceases to exist and its members and associates are aggregated to the Congregation of the Holy Ghost, thereby becoming its members and associates, sharing the same rights and privileges and being subject to the same disciplinary rules."[6]

After Monnet's nomination as bishop, Libermann went to Rome to obtain pontifical approbation of his own election as Superior General. Then he returned and submitted a petition to the Holy See whereby he asked the Propaganda to ratify such changes as Father Loewenbruck had failed to bring about in the hectic speed of his previous negotiations. These had to do with the practice of poverty, suppression of Leguay's "second order," and a change in the name of the institute.

On this latter point, comparatively little needed to be done. Both Poullart des Places and Libermann had a special devotion to the Holy Spirit and the Immaculate Mother of God. That is why Claude dedicated his seminary to the Holy Ghost under the invocation of Mary conceived without sin and Francis, having consecrated his foundation to the Holy Heart of Mary, had constantly preached the close relationship of the Blessed Virgin and the Third Person of the Trinity. This dual patronage was a natural outgrowth of tradition on both sides and the new title was easily formalized as "The Congregation of the Holy Ghost, under the Protection of the Immaculate Heart of Mary." It constituted a fitting climax to the long negotiations.

All was not sweetness and light, however. Much to his regret,

[5] N. D. 10, 417.
[6] N. D. 10, 375 ff.

Libermann had not been able to wait for return mail from his distant missionaries — not even from Father Le Vavasseur in far-off Reunion. "It is impossible for me," he sighed, "to await answers from our confreres before finishing this work if we don't want to threaten its success. To insist on waiting for replies would remove all hope of achieving the union. I feel I have to rely on the Congregation's confidence that I will interpret as best I can the intent and the view-point of all members and then act accordingly." "I have already consulted the Bishop of Amiens, the Jesuit Provincial, the Sulpician Superior, and Father Desgenettes."[7]

When the final version of the union became known, however, it stunned the Holy Heart of Mary men. Father Kobès met the postman at the door when the papal rescript arrived. He tore open the seal, read the contents and then, brandishing the document wildly, he rushed into the conference hall where Francis was lecturing to the novices. "Treason," he shouted. "We have been betrayed!" He was not alone in this reaction. Even Father Lannurien regarded it as a "betrayal of the whole past." Opposition to the whole idea had been brewing for quite some time at Notre Dame du Gard, but the Libermannists had at least expected an *ex aequo* union of the two societies. Instead, Rome had simply suppressed the Congregation of the Holy Heart of Mary and directed its members to join the Spiritans.

Francis knew that he was testing his confreres' loyalty to the breaking point, but he doggedly forged ahead, driven by the same mysterious power that urged him onward at every decisive crisis in his life. Subsequently, with the better perspective that only passing time bestows, Father Lannurien analyzed the dilemma more sympathetically:

> The union of the Congregation of the Holy Heart with the Society of the Holy Ghost was a great event in the active life of Father Libermann, *qua* founder.
>
> There are only two possible alternatives: either this event, this merger, lay outside the scope of Father Libermann's divine mission or it was part of that mission.
>
> In the first case, he repudiated his mission, for he had, as it were, frustrated the function God had committed to his care and dealt a

[7] N. D. 10, 224, 341.

mortal blow to his work and his Congregation. Humanly speaking, it would not be difficult to adduce reasons compelling enough to justify us in arriving at such a damning conclusion.

However, there are very strong reasons, too, seen in the inner light of Faith, which suggest the opposite view, *viz.*, that this union was truly in accord with God's plan.

These are the reasons:

1. The providential circumstances that surrounded the events. It was certainly quite natural that distrust and rivalry should have existed between the two congregations. These actually were present.

2. The manner in which our Father behaved under those circumstances. We remember how he went ahead despite the preferences, desires, and feelings of nearly all, or perhaps all confreres. They submitted to this merger solely because of their high regard for Father Libermann. He did this against his own wishes and in spite of his clear foreknowledge of the burdens, the problems, and the accusations — both to his face and behind his back — which would result from his action.

3. The effects of the merger, *viz.*, the reformation of the Seminary [of the Holy Ghost], which is such an important agency for the church in the Colonies; the establishment of a Colonial Hierarchy, which was due so much to Libermann's efforts; the greatly increased influence we achieved with the government offices, and the beneficial results flowing therefrom. This too formed part of God's designs and I trust we shall appreciate it even more fully in the future.

Nonetheless, because these things lie beyond the confines of Father Libermann's first purpose, and on the other hand, because this merger would necessarily entail something of a destruction of his first work even if we limit ourselves to the above mentioned results, I feel I must conclude that God intended some other permanent supernatural objective to be attained through the union.

I believe that this objective, which Libermann's congregation was called to pursue over and above the apostolate in which members were already engaged, consists in training diocesan priests who would be imbued with the same spirit of zeal and devotion, prepared to care for souls in truly apostolic fashion and especially to preach the gospel to the working-class, to the poor, who have been left to their own devices all too long and are currently being thrust into such an important social role that they are now subject to clever exploitation and manipulation by evil forces.

It should be observed at this point that the founder of a religious society usually enjoys, over and above other graces, . . . a special one that enables him to advance the aims of his work and his institute.

Now if God had called Father Libermann for no other purpose than to found a missionary congregation for Negroes and other neglected souls, it would be hard to see why He gave him that extraordinary faculty for giving spiritual direction to those who wished to lead an interior life.

Actually, it seems to me, one could be a saint and even the founder of a congregation without receiving such a tremendous measure of that sublime grace, that influence over souls, and that delicate sense of guidance which, if I am not mistaken, no other saints share to such a high degree.

Therefore, both that significant event, the merger with the Holy Ghost Congregation (which was so fraught with danger for us), and the special type of grace that was accorded Father Libermann, appear to me to be a clear indication of the second objective of his foundation and his mission, *viz.*, that God destined his children for the education and training of spiritual and devoted priests.

For this reason, I do not in any way regard it as chance or accident but rather that result of the founder's grace and a sign of our vocation that the first new foundation of the Congregation after the Venerable Father's death was the establishment of a Seminary and that in the most important city in the world, at the very center of the Church.[8]

Subsequent developments in Spiritan history have confirmed Father Lannurien's analysis. They demonstrate that it was not an unfortunate accident or a distorted interpretation of God's will that prompted Libermann to shoulder the educational mission of Poullart des Places. Instead of operating to the detriment of more immediately apostolic functions like foreign missionary work and social endeavors, absorption of the ancient academic tradition of the Holy Ghost Fathers seems to have given a mighty impetus to the growth of other endeavors. The record in Africa alone shows with abundant clarity that missions sponsored by institutes with a strong educational tradition showed a much greater concern for endowing the African Church with a well-trained elite that is capable of exercising leadership in an atmosphere of growing autonomy. Indeed, Libermann had sensed the importance of mission schools from the very outset and this merger with a professorial society, far from deflecting his aim, gave it an even stronger orientation toward a well-planned intellectual approach in every type of work.

A second and vitally important result of the merger was the healthy polarity which resulted from it. Anyone who has studied

[8] Lann. 73 ff.

the growth and development of the older but still extant orders in the Church will see at once that some measure of polarity inevitably made its appearance in the course of their history. All others consumed themselves and faded into obscurity after a few centuries in which they feverishly pursued the rigidly limited objective of their founders and then, since they were not able to formulate an adequate response to contemporary needs, their very existence lost its significance for a new age and they languished and died. Only those institutes survived whose scope was broad enough to let them ride with the tide of events and adjust to the changing emphases of passing eras.

Libermann had seen this problem from the beginning and strove constantly to meet it head-on. He refused to be shackled to the old French Colonies when Tisserant and Le Vavasseur could think of nothing else; he withstood vigorously the limited view of his early African missionaries when they rebelled at any diversion of personnel from the mission fields of Guinea; and when a faulty interpretation of the Rule threatened to eliminate houses in Europe, he countered by observing that, if such were the case, it was "important that the constitution of the Congregation be changed." Then he went on to further clarify his position. "The Rule says that we must not undertake the instruction of young people. However, conditions indicate that we will probably be obliged to do so."[9] Four years later, these chafing restraints vanished when he and his confreres entered the Congregation of the Holy Ghost. Only then did his great soul have room to soar untrammeled in marshaling new shock troops for the Church.

The full pattern of his life had emerged at last.

---

[9] N. D. 6, 121.

CHAPTER TWENTY-THREE

THE REFORMER

In December of 1848 Father Libermann moved into the Superior General's quarters at old Holy Ghost Seminary in Paris. With due ceremony, he was escorted to the administrative suite and left to his own devices. For a long moment, he stood there in the doorway, smiling and shaking his head in amused wonderment at the scene before him. Slowly and carefully picking his way across the polished red tiles, he suddenly came face to face with his own modest, tired countenance staring out at him from a monumental mirror that hung above the black marble mantelpiece. In front of it, a highly ornate clock with built-in flower vases and other complicated features sat enthroned in regal majesty. Two stately urns kept silent guard over it and these in turn were flanked by a pair of enormous seven-branch candlesticks of richly gilded bronze that stood thirty inches high.

In terms of mid-nineteenth century décor, there was nothing particularly lavish about these appointments, but the more Spartan atmosphere of La Neuville and Notre Dame du Gard made these new quarters seem palatial by comparison. As he turned from the mantel, he was confronted by a round marble table that stood in the middle of the room, its proud severity softened somewhat by a deep red coverlet embroidered with flowers of even darker hue. He continued the inspection with widening eyes. Along a wall a luxurious sofa with two soft pillows beckoned to him invitingly to relax for a change. After all, he was now the Superior General of the ancient and illustrious Society of the Holy Ghost. Moreover, the silent invitation of the magnificent sofa was loudly reaffirmed by eight heavily-upholstered armchairs of royal velvet. How could such a tired, emaciated little man resist these blandishments?

The gingerly promenade through this strange new world continued. With the naïve astonishment of an unsophisticated tourist in an art museum, he inspected a stupendous mahogany writing desk and a smaller mahogany table that was its companion piece, both of them crowned with the inevitable marble top and the table further ornamented by a large ivory crucifix. From the shadowy walls, six original canvasses peered disdainfully at him from their carved and golden frames. Closer inspection revealed ten less pretentious but equally disdainful paintings that shone like so many lesser stars among their mighty fellows, doing their best to fill up every void in the dusky firmament.

Francis suddenly became conscious of the utter stillness in this forbidding museum. It brought on a rush of nostalgic memories that took him back momentarily to the quiet hours he had spent so long ago in Patriarca's garret. There the street noises of Rome had failed to filter back through the narrow alley and up the long flights of stairs; here the bustle of Paris was imperiously shut out by a double set of curtains, white and yellow, which adorned every window. The contrast and its implications were inescapable.

Continuing his tour, the new Superior General ventured into the adjoining bedroom. There his astonished glance was met by "an immense mahogany bedstead of ultra modern design, a marble-topped mahogany night stand, and a matching commode surmounted by a marble wash-table." The imposing nature of this latter item appealed to his sense of humor. He went back to the sitting room smiling sardonically and asking himself: "Now . . . with all that, do I still have the right to call myself a member of the Congregation and teach poverty and self-denial?"

Obviously, something would have to be done, but Francis was far too much of a gentleman to engage in an abrupt iconoclasm right now. "In order to show some respect for the ideas of other people and not give the impression that I disapprove of the past, I don't want to act hastily in this business," he said. Nonetheless, there were a few of these museum pieces he just could not live with, so he threw open the door and asked a passing confrere to relieve him of those massive candelabra. "I couldn't stand the sight of them," he confessed. "I transferred them to the sacristy immediately." Shortly thereafter he succeeded in divesting himself of the luxurious toilet facility and reported gleefully: "I have managed to get rid of it, replacing it by a similar 'machine' that is older and has a crack in the marble top."

While he freshened up before the weather-beaten washstand he continued mapping out his campaign to disperse his new possessions. An acquittal was granted the armchairs. "I have to be fair," he conceded. "The upholstery is quite old and ugly, so I think I'm justified in keeping them. But I'll get rid of the paintings in short order and cover up the mirror with some sort of religious picture. I want to get installed with as much simplicity as the circumstances warrant. I shall do nothing without my confreres' agreement, except for the paintings which I shall send packing as soon as I can." Yet he wanted to spare the feelings of his predecessor. "It was Bishop Monnet," he recalled, "who was so naïve as to get all these nice things for me. I don't want to hurt him by proceeding too rapidly."[1]

If the physical assets provided by Bishop Monnet were strange to Libermann, the situation which he left in the house was even more extraordinary. An air of restlessness prevailed in those ancient halls. Uninvited guests ran in and out of the seminary at will. They were, for the most part, returnees from overseas France who found it convenient to take up lodgings there while they were in Paris. These passing priests came with their complaints, their prejudices, and their strongly held opinions, ready to buttonhole anyone available and harangue him at length about government policies, political affairs, ecclesiastical superiors, the slavery question, and a host of other inflammatory topics. The cloistered students, eager for news of the outside world, formed a most appreciative audience for even the wildest orators among them and then proceeded to take sides vigorously on every controversial question proposed. This, together with the cholera epidemic and the continuing air of revolution in Paris, effectively nullified the seminary's program of academic and religious training.

Only a firm hand at the helm could have kept any semblance of order in such troublous times, yet Father Leguay's hectic tenure of

[1] N. D. 10, 354 f.

office had been characterized by long and frequent recruiting trips and incessant visits to unfriendly government bureaus, and Father Monnet's short tour of duty involved only a provisional sort of direction, for in the beginning he was content to exercise a modicum of benevolent supervision from the inner recesses of his suite and toward the end he spent his time vacillating between involvement in the merger and rejection of it.

Other members of the professorial staff contributed little in the way of strong and helpful guidance. Father Warnet was frail and sickly. He had to limit his out-of-class activities to the direction of a few neighboring convents. Father Gaultier, burdened with work and ruled out of most disciplinary questions because he was confessor for a great many of the seminarians, did what he could within those limitations. Loewenbruck, a renowned preacher and expert public relations man, spent more time on the road than at home. Neurotic Father Hardy had no function at all for, with ill-concealed anxiety for his health, he carefully abstained from anything resembling work.

Once the merger was an accomplished fact, the students adopted a wait-and-see attitude. Some found it difficult to conceal their antipathy toward the convert Jew about whose person and conduct strange rumors were circulating both in France and in the colonies. They vaguely suspected this friendly, weak, and apparently defenseless man would not tolerate the disorder that reigned in their midst, but they confidently felt that his retiring and simple character was no match for their ingenuity. Francis sized them up quickly. "When we arrived at the Seminary," he wrote, "we found a great number of badly disposed seminarians. The house was not properly regulated; its direction had been neglected. The seminarians who were ill-disposed feared a reform."[2]

Libermann set down an unequivocal policy. "You will readily understand," he stated, "that we will not consent to be manufacturers of priests: we won't permit things to remain in this state." A little later, he wrote to the Colonial Minister: "May I have Your Excellency's permission to express my deep regret at the misfortunes that are constantly befalling the colonial clergy. They point up the fearful responsibility we have assumed in taking over the seminary

[2] N. D. 12, 142.

whose function it is to provide the colonies with priests. We shall redouble our efforts to bring about a reform and inculcate that spirit of fervor and piety which is required for the dangerous apostolate in the colonies."[3]

True to form, however, he moved with great prudence. "I found the seminary in disorder when I got there and, although I regard the *status quo* as indefensible, I have introduced few changes during the first year. Despite the mildness of my conduct and reforms of little consequence, a clique assembled to oppose my efforts. But God came to my rescue. The Government cut off half of the scholarships and we were not permitted to keep more than thirty. I took advantage of that opportunity to dismiss fifteen, but since that was only three months after my arrival, I did not know them well enough to make a real choice. Some of those I kept gave me a lot of added trouble at the end of vacation."[4]

There was some improvement after that, but Francis had only begun. He spent as much time as he could with the seminarians and accorded them free access to his room where he gave them leave to speak freely about their problems and air their grievances. Imperceptibly, his conferences began to exercise their wonderful influence in creating a new atmosphere of zeal and fervor in the long-neglected seminary. The happy development, however, was cruelly cut short by a new misfortune.

The cholera epidemic returned in full force, raging with particular fury just around the seminary. In short order, it spread to the little villages around the house of Notre Dame du Gard as well. Father Libermann feared to think of the devastation if this plague should invade his two major seminaries and the motherhouse. He quickly recalled that the Mother of God had saved them before. She would do it again. In full faith he committed his sons to her and placed her statue in the seminary hall, designating our Lady as guardian of the house. The cholera went its murderous way but it stopped short at the seminary gates and never affected Francis or his confreres even though they engaged in widespread visiting of the sick.

Francis himself, however, was visited by another affliction that

[3] N. D. 12, 124. 137.
[4] N. D. 12, 123 f.

baffled the doctors. A high fever and violent abdominal pains repeatedly sent him to bed, but even then he continued to work, writing letters and reports with a trembling hand or forcing his tortured brain through a detailed maze of material concerning Spiritan affairs. Now and again he sank back exhausted on the pillow, waiting a few moments till his breathing became less labored. Then he would lean forward again and drive his pen relentlessly across the page. When it was all over he could rest and rest eternally; now he must go on, building a renewed Society that would defy the ages.

In the midst of it all came the crushing news that Felix had been stricken with cholera. Kindly, jovial Felix, who had welcomed him so warmly years ago when he was wandering through the streets of Paris in an agony of doubt, who visited him so faithfully when he lay white and helpless after an epileptic attack — Felix was dying. With tear-dimmed eyes he commended his brother to God and focused his thoughts on the scattered family in whose bosom he had lived as a child. The old pain began its persistent gnawing once more as he followed in his mind's eyes the varied careers of his brothers and sisters, allowing each one to draw him closer and closer to the tragic old bearded face of his father. No! He must tear himself loose from the horrible fascination that it held for him. This was no time to permit the seizures of bygone days to lay hold of his exhausted body.

At noon that day, on the arm of Father Morel, Francis sadly and slowly shuffled through the narrow streets that seemed more than usually dejected in the aura of death that hung over them. With difficulty he reached the *rue Mazarin* and entered the little book-binder's shop. Felix was lying in the back, already so wasted by cholera that he could scarcely utter a word, his ashen face bearing the unmistakable signs of approaching death. Francis stared at him in bewilderment and for a moment that gray mask melted into another dead face, the face of one who had loved him deeply yet died in loneliness, cursing and disowning him.

"My poor father," he groaned. An involuntary tremor shook him. With that fearful warning, he slammed shut the gate that led to dangerous memories and turned his attention to other things. Like a frightened animal, his heart fled to the God of his fathers, the Yahweh of Abraham, Isaac, and Jacob. Then he left the bedside to console the family.

When the community saw him slowly climbing the broad staircase of the motherhouse step by step, leaning heavily on Father Morel's arm, and when they learned how badly shaken he had been at the sight of his dying brother, there was general alarm. Everyone pressed around him, begging him to go off to the country where the air was pure. He must not die. He must think of them.

That night he tossed feverishly and sleeplessly as the hours inched their way toward a troubled dawn. Over and over again he repeated his special prayer of surrender to God, that prayer which had saved him so often from despair. When morning came at last, he summoned all his remaining strength and prepared to leave the house. He would go away as his confreres had requested, but first he must visit Felix once more.

When he and Father Morel got to the *rue Mazarin,* Felix was in the death struggle. The eyes were already growing dim, but a flicker of grateful recognition passed over them momentarily. As it faded, Francis reeled under a wave of that awful loneliness to which Jews are particularly susceptible. Henceforth, there would be no one in this great impersonal city who could share with him the intimate memories of that little house in Saverne, the expressive Hebraic turns of phrase, the stories of their childhood, the terrifying affection of the old rabbi amid his sacred scrolls, the loving refuge in the background whose name was Leah. No one now would understand that other world from which the two of them had been so violently torn, that mystery which had brought them so tragically close in that last hour.

An approaching carriage clattered its way over the cobblestones. Perhaps it was just another one of those dreary hearses that moved back and forth across Paris, monotonously picking up and depositing their gruesome cargoes. But no; it was Father Boulanger who had come to take him to the country. Boulanger was a man from that strange otherworld which he and Felix had entered long ago. Its people were kind and good, but they would never understand what Felix did. They would never fully penetrate the lonely core of his being. The ancient chasm would never be entirely bridged.

Francis pressed the clammy, trembling hand of his dying brother, then reached out to grope for the door that he could not see through the mist of his tears. The carriage door slammed shut on a part of his life. The separation was accomplished. A whip cracked, the horses leaped forward, and they were off. As the rattling wheels carried him away through the empty streets, he settled back into a dark corner of the carriage and the silent tears flowed freely.

Father Boulanger took him to some friends in Angers. He was so weak and feverish that they put him right to bed. It was then he heard that Felix was dead. Repeatedly he pulled himself up to write a letter to his sister-in-law, but every time he fell back helplessly on the pillow. Finally, after four attempts, he managed to prop himself up and write: "My good and dear sister, Three times I started to write and three times the fever kept me from doing so. Today I hope I shall succeed. I find this greatly consoling in the midst of the sorrow that God has seen fit to afflict us with. I always felt that I was very fond of my beloved brother, but it was only through this sad situation in which God has placed us that I came to know how deeply attached to him I really was. I have been able to realize, then, through what I experienced myself, how much your poor heart must have suffered. Poor sister! I can hardly think of you without tears coming to my eyes. I find it particularly regrettable that I have to leave you and the childen alone in this hour of sorrow and bereavement and that I cannot even give you much comfort by letter. Good Lord, what you must have gone through!"[5]

On Pentecost Eve, Father Libermann's concern for the situation in the capital made him decide to go back to the seminary. Just before his departure the intestinal spasms came on again, but he insisted on leaving nonetheless. Things were too ominous to justify his continued absence from the motherhouse. "The day before I left Tours," he reported, "I was seized with stomach cramps, but they disappeared by morning. Under any circumstances, I felt it was my duty to go to Paris because of the unrest that had been engendered by the dissolution of the National Assembly. I feared an uprising and wanted to be home in case something happened. I got to Paris at nine that night and the next afternoon I had to go to bed for a ten-day siege of the colic."[6]

[5] N. D. 11, 121.

[6] N. D. 11, 126.

His condition deteriorated to such an extent that he could not even read the incoming mail. When an important letter came from Bishop Bessieux and Bishop Kobès, his secretary read their painful contents to him slowly and deliberately. Now and then a particularly cutting phrase caused a twinge of suffering to pass over his tired and sunken features. It was the old story, and he could do so little about it. Both prelates, consumed with zeal for their immense territories, were demanding more men from Europe and, if need be, from the colonial islands. In case he refused to send reinforcements, they would look elsewhere for their man power. Behind their indignation lay an implied reproach that Francis was keeping too many men at home and sending too many others to the more civilized colonies. These bishops could think of nothing but missions to pagans. They had no sympathy whatsoever for the breadth and variety of his views and their lack of comprehension at this late stage of his career pained him deeply. As the secretary finished reading, Francis could not help wondering if his apostolate was doomed to failure because his sons refused to understand it.

The community began to fear for his life. Someone was with him now at all times. The seminarian who functioned as night nurse hovered over him solicitously, preparing a large mustard plaster to be placed on his stomach. When the fiery nature of this medication began to have an unbearable effect on his already weakened intestines, Francis quietly observed that this was the wrong therapy; the doctor had prescribed a linseed poultice. Since the seminarian was so very positive that a mustard plaster was exactly what Father François had directed him to apply, Libermann made no further protest. The young man lost confidence, however, when the ensuing martyrdom brought his superior close to fainting. He went to awaken Father François and the secretary rushed to the sickroom.

"When I got there," he later reported, "tears sprang to my eyes. I wanted to grumble and scold about it but with a hint of a smile at my angry looks he said, 'Hold on; I did warn him.' With that, my bad humor vanished. I pulled off the mustard plaster and did my best to assuage the pain it was causing."[7]

Just at that time Paris was sweltering under a tropical heat wave and the cholera was at its height. Victims were falling everywhere

[7] N. D. 11, 592.

like stalks of corn before the reaper. Since anyone who was ill or debilitated seemed more susceptible to the infection, they packed Francis out of Paris as soon as he was well enough to be moved and sent him to Normandy where Father Leo Le Vavasseur's family cared for him during his convalescence. He felt better as soon as he got there and so, without sparing himself at all, he plunged into his enormous correspondence. Before anything else, a reply had to be sent to Bishops Bessieux and Kobès. In it, he limited himself to a general admonition, promising to go more deeply into the matter when he returned home stronger and in better health.

"You say in your latest letter," he wrote, "that you have the grace of state. This was read to me when my illness was at its worst. I was in danger of death and said to myself: 'Let's see. How would I judge the dispositions that dictated those letters if I had to appear before God?' I grew convinced that those letters were not written under the influence of grace. . . . You are bishops and I am only a poor man, but I know to whom I'm speaking and you know me well enough to allow me to speak fearlessly to you. Let me tell you, then, that you are proceeding too quickly. There is too much stiffness and haste in your gait. The Spirit of God doesn't operate that way. If you do not adopt a gentler, wiser, and more moderate approach, I feel sure you will set back the success of your Mission and on occasion do irreparable damage to it."[8]

With the progressive improvement of his health, he decided to go South to speed up his recovery and engage in promotion work at the same time. However, on June 20 those terrible cramps gripped him again while he was in Bayeux. There was nothing for it but to beg for hospitality at the Sulpician seminary in that city. They received him affectionately and immediately put him to bed. Then the illness really became serious. Racked by constant fits of vomiting, tortured by fiendish intestinal pains, and suffering especially from what seems to have been a liver involvement, he lay helplessly on his couch in a strange house.

It was then that his tired mind turned to thoughts of Father Frederic Le Vavasseur. Throughout those long years of disappointment, he still continued to believe in that man. Frederic was a saintly priest, generous to a fault, on fire with zeal, and completely

[8] N. D. 11, 129 ff.

unsparing in his own regard. Might not this friend of the first hour be induced to overcome his violent temper, divest himself of the old narrow-mindedness, and grow into a tactful balanced man of broad vision? Those letters from Bishops Bessieux and Kobès were a case in point. It would indeed be difficult to find a man who would not sacrifice the over-all mission of the Congregation for his own limited view.

Accordingly, a letter was dispatched to Frederic. "God gave you," it said, "the first inspiration for our work. It seems clear to me that He means for you to uphold that work. My physical weakness leads me to believe that I cannot live much longer. We need you. . . . During my illness I went through some pretty painful moments. I feel the need of a good talk with you. I was in danger, or thought so at least. What a comfort it would have been to have you with me. I admit I was depressed at seeing myself about to die with no leader to take over the Congregation."[9]

Father François came to take him home. Nearly six weeks had gone by since his departure from Paris and now he came back looking "like a dying man." Since he could not retain any food, the house physician brought in three great specialists for consultation. Meanwhile, Father Briot ignored the objections of his confreres and engaged Dr. Benech, a naturopath. Benech ordered all kinds of meat for the poor patient and insisted that it be consumed even when it brought on prodigious vomiting. Francis obeyed unquestioningly and, even though the diet was sheer torture, he finally succeeded in keeping something down. Feeling slightly improved, he went off to Strassburg to recuperate until mid-September.

When he returned, he wrote again to Frederic Le Vavasseur: "I've been back since the first of October, and the work is more overwhelming than ever. . . . I ought to be careful; unfortunately I can't do so. I am overtaxing my strength and I don't think I can manage to shoulder this enormous burden much longer. However, winter suits me better. I hope I can carry on."[10]

It was a broad and obvious hint that Frederic should hurry home and its message was repeated more emphatically in another letter not long after: "It is really necessary that you be with me,

[9] N. D. 11, 133 ff.
[10] N. D. 11, 208.

especially since the Congregation's works are expanding. If I were to have a relapse, there wouldn't be any suitable replacement. No one could take my place adequately, even though I'm just a poor fellow. I don't manage famously, that much is well known and certain, but my age, the sequence of events to date, the impetus that has been given to the work, and my title as superior, keep things rolling in spite of obstacles. Yet others do not enjoy these advantages and they lack practical experience. I can detect this lack of experience in every one without exception. How can they replace me? They all have some limitation. You alone seem to be the one that God has picked out for this job. At all events, it would be good for you to be here in case I die. Don't let this disturb you; my sickness hasn't left me with any serious aftereffects. It may return, but it's not a fatal sort of illness. There is probably reason to suspect some inflammation of the liver, but it isn't dangerous."[11]

When Father Libermann spoke of "keeping things rolling in spite of obstacles" he reached the nadir of understatement. His troubles at the seminary were at their height. During his long absence, disorders, complaints, and intrigues of all types infected the student body. Tall stories were carried to the archdiocesan chancery and the government offices. Stranger yet, they were welcomed and believed. A sufficiently strong contingent of his old enemies still beamed at every chance to discredit him. Now they found a ready ally in a highly neurotic member of his own household: Father Hardy, the man who spent all his time secretly fomenting rebellion among the seminarians while maintaining an air of exemplary piety in himself. The opposition that had been smoldering for some time broke out openly in October, 1849. Five newly ordained priests refused their commissions for Guiana and threatened to make public their accusations against the Congregation. Francis succeeded in bringing them back to reason. When they had left, he called in three of their fellow revolutionists who were not yet ordained and gently but firmly dismissed them. But the plotting did not end there.

The scene changed to the archdiocesan chancery. It was petitioned to drive the "Libermannists" out of old Holy Ghost Seminary and put the direction of it under a Vicar-General. Since Father Hardy aspired to that position himself, he now redoubled his clan-

[11] N. D. 11, 324 f.

destine activities among the disaffected seminarians. At Christmas, he spread the watchword: "Right will triumph within two months. Be patient. They will be expelled." Then, when the allotted time had passed and nothing happened, his battle cry became: "By Easter they will all be gone."

Francis watched it all with his customary patience. "During the past year," he wrote at this time, "I have had to put up with a lot from the seminarians. My protracted illness did no end of harm. At the beginning of this year I still had a good many problems, in fact they were immense, but I solved them by firmness, kindliness and patience.

"Father Hardy is causing a good deal of annoyance to all of our confreres. He's at odds with everybody. He has tried to ruin the house — at least he wanted to. I never could and never wanted to fathom all his activities and plans. . . . It's quite definite that he fostered the seminarians' spirit of unrest and insubordination. . . . He upheld their conviction that we would be expelled from here and sent back to Notre Dame du Gard."[12]

Those problems that Francis felt he had solved by patience and kindness were still there. They had merely gone underground. Following Hardy's direction, the plotters carefully avoided any overt act that might give Father Libermann reason to dismiss them. They replaced the tactics of open warfare by a more refined guerrilla-type operation and proceeded with their carefully planned program of subversion. First they sent a secret memo to the Colonial Minister, falsely accusing Francis of feeding and educating the Congregation's own scholastics at the expense of the government. When, by pure coincidence and with no knowledge of the report, Father Libermann sent his religious back to Notre Dame du Gard shortly thereafter, the colonial seminarians jubilantly interpreted the move as a victory for their cause. Next, seven students signed a paper that accused Francis of listing for government support certain seminarians who were paying their own way. After that, when Father Gaultier tried to stem the tide of revolt, they said he was violating the seal of confession and that he was using the Ministry's funds to build up his library.

[12] N. D. 11, 319 f.

The insurgents now became really vicious. A formal charge of simony was prepared against both Libermann and Monnet. It intimated that they had bought and sold the seminary and its superiorship for an episcopal miter. Then they reported that Francis had recently sent thirty thousand francs to the Mission in Guinea, even though the Society of the Propagation of the Faith had given the motherhouse only ten thousand for that purpose. The white paper proceeded to indict him for embezzlement, stating that he had stolen the remaining twenty thousand from state funds. The source of all their distorted information was, of course, the ubiquitous Father Hardy.

As one of them subsequently wrote to Francis about his dismissal: "I daresay in everything that happened we were only secondary wheels. We blindly obeyed a director who we mistakenly thought was worthy of our respect. Yes, it was Father Hardy alone who, with his high signs and cryptic expressions kept the minds of everyone without exception in a state of violent hatred against the directors of Holy Ghost Seminary. For instance, he repeated a thousand times: 'I guarantee you, they will be thrown out. Keep going as you have been and I'll take responsibility for everything. The merger was illicit. The blessing of God cannot be with those men.' "[13]

Poor Father Hardy! He steadily became more daring and his neurosis grew more apparent, especially since his conspicuous piety kept pace with his advancing treachery. He dragged Father Warnet and Father Gaultier into court to contest Father Fourdinier's will and the harrowing experience of sitting in the courtroom like a common criminal was too much for Father Warnet. He left the house.

Far from remorseful over the tragedy he had wrought, Father Hardy turned it to his own advantage. He spread the rumor that sick old Warnet had been cruelly dismissed by Libermann, but the victim protested against this distortion of the facts. "You seem to say in your letter and lend credence to the rumor that I was excluded from the Seminary of the Holy Ghost in a way that was unjust and contrary to my rights, in other words, against my will. My dear friend, I see in the slanderous account that was given you, the tail

[13] N. D. 12, 668 f.

of a completely infernal intrigue against the merger of the two congregations and particularly against the Fathers of the Holy Heart of Mary. . . .

"My friend, it was that fellow Hardy who was the first cause of my departure. . . . He made me very ill and I found it necessary to take a long rest. Do not believe, then, as has been insinuated to you, that I ever had any complaints against Father Libermann and his colleagues. On the contrary, they have been full of kindness and considerateness for me. I have lived with them and been a thousand times happier with them than with Father Fourdinier, for he didn't have the gentleness and helpfulness of those Fathers."[14]

Throughout this incredible persecution, Francis maintained an attitude of perfect gentility toward Father Hardy and the recalcitrant seminarians. His forebearance amazed Le Vavasseur. That volatile Creole wrote afterward: "One of the circumstances of his life in which his self-control and humility seemed incomprehensible to me was the Hardy affair. Not one word ever betrayed the slightest impatience on his part. . . . It seems that during all the time between his arrival at the seminary . . . and my return to France, his equanimity and humility in the face of such irritations by the seminarians . . . was admirable and so was his attitude toward the man who was at the bottom of these disturbances, Father Hardy."[15]

Frederic was back from Reunion now and he had no intention of putting up with this nonsense. One day he burst into Libermann's room and found Hardy standing in front of the superior's desk, gesticulating wildly and nagging the tired little man who was patiently waiting to get back to the mountains of work that lay before him. The flood of complaints and nasty innuendoes continued to pour out in a bitter harangue. As it proceeded, Le Vavasseur's blood pressure rose ominously. "I held my peace for a while," he reported later, "and did not want to say a thing because I was turning up inside and I knew if I opened my mouth, Father Hardy would hear a lot more than he had ever heard from anyone else."

Unaware of his danger, Hardy stepped up the pace of his wild tirade. Frederic looked unbelievingly at the quiet man who sat there gazing so sympathetically at his tormentor. True enough, he had said

[14] N. D. 12, 644 f.
[15] N. D. 13, 633 ff.

once that we should love Jesus in crude and rough people like a fruit in its shell. Yet the furrows that slander and pain had graven on this suffering face and the slight quivering of the poor man's lips were more than anyone could bear. "I started off like an erupting volcano," Le Vavasseur said. "The good Father here is duped by you, but I, I won't be. Let me tell you that I am on to your designs and your intentions. If they aren't evil because your twisted mind makes you think they are good, they are dangerous and unjust." It was the opening cannonade, a preface to the merciless lashing that Frederic felt should have been administered long before.

When he paused for breath, he looked to Francis for some sign of approval, some recognition of the fact that a just rage had its place in the scheme of things. Hardy was shaken by the unexpected outburst. He was off-balance. Now was the time to move in for the kill. "But no!" Le Vavasseur sighed. "[Father Libermann] did not take advantage of what I had said. He continued to talk humbly and gently and didn't share my anger in the least. After listening to me overwhelm Hardy, he showed even greater gentleness and kindness toward him."[16]

Finally, the situation became unbearable. Francis had been reluctant to remove Father Hardy from the seminary for fear of causing difficulties with the Archbishop and giving his enemies another pretext for further attacks. However, the Council met during vacation and decided to send the troublemaker to Notre Dame du Gard or to the colonies. Hardy refused to budge. Dismissal proceedings were then instituted and he was canonically expelled. Using the pension they had settled on him, Father Hardy took up lodgings at Marie Thérèse Hospital. From there he continued to plague Libermann with lawsuits, accusations, and intrigues.

When he heard that Bishop La Carrière of Guadeloupe had come in and was staying at the motherhouse, Father Hardy rushed over to enlist his aid but the prelate was not at home just then. At nine the next morning, oblivious to everything but his venomous thoughts, the poor unfortunate hurried across the *rue Lhomond* again. He did not see the ponderous water cart bearing down on him. Its wheels crushed his abdomen.

Bishop La Carrière, whose room was just above the main en-

[16] N. D. 13, 634.

trance, threw open his window when he heard the agonized scream. On the street below he saw a priest lying in a pool of blood. After imparting a hasty absolution, he watched them carry the limp and broken form into one of the parlors. Then Le Vavasseur asked Father Bouix, another guest, to go down and give the dying man a chance to make his confession. By noon, Father Carbon came to administer the last sacraments. From then on, they did all in their power to alleviate his sufferings and make him comfortable. He died the following day, surrounded by the former confreres he had fought so bitterly.

Francis was away in Alsace when the tragedy occurred. After he returned to Paris, Dr. Samson wrote to ask for details on the accident but the reply discloses no gloating, no morbid interest in the downfall of the archenemy. "At Notre Dame du Gard I learned the news of Father Hardy's misfortune. He was run over by an immense water wagon right in front of the seminary entrance. An account of it appeared in the newspapers."[17]

After this, the internal reform gradually became a reality. The weeding-out process continued. Yet even the expelled seminarians received a full measure of Libermann's devotion and love. Those who appeared to have a vocation to the priesthood found in him a powerful ally in their efforts to be accepted elsewhere. The rest he helped get adjusted to life in the world. One of them, a difficult character who crowned a long career of recalcitrance with an insulting communication to Father Briot, received the following notice of dismissal:

> Your letter to Father Briot grieved me deeply. You know how much I like you and wish you well. . . . I regret that I have to give you this sad news. I fully realize the grief I will cause you and feel bad about it myself. Submit to God's holy will. If He has not called you to the priestly state you need not regard our decision as an evil. If you became a priest without a vocation, you would be afflicted with sorrow and trouble all your life. You would lose your own soul and drag others down with you.
>
> Don't be angry because we have taken this step. You may be sure we hold no animosity against you personally. Even though your letter to Father Briot contained improper words, we are not and will not be vexed with you on that account. We have simply weighed the

[17] N. D. 13, 27.

> case objectively and compared it with what we had observed in your character. As a result, we concluded that you do not and never will have the requisite qualities for receiving the divine and holy priesthood.
>
> If I can be of any service, my dear friend, in helping you plan your future, please don't hesitate to call on me. . . . Let me know what you come up with and be assured that I shall do everything in my power to be of assistance.[18]

Through a series of inspiring conferences, Francis now instilled new ideals in the student body. They began to sense in his words the stirrings of a new life, the life of a saint. Every sentence added another dimension to the loftiness of the sacerdotal career. Every phrase was a burning testimony that they could not ignore. One found it hard to be indifferent before that dedicated priest on the rostrum whose spiritualized face and slender, gesturing hands reinforced the wonderful glow that came into his eyes when he spoke of the goodness of God and the overwhelming gift of grace. Traces of pain were there, etched indelibly by lines that only suffering can draw, but the dominant expression was one of serenity that sometimes took on overtones of ecstasy. At such moments, even the most rebellious held their breath. The hall grew quiet as a tomb. And at the end of the conference, everyone silently moved off toward the chapel.

Outside, things were not so quiet. Archbishop Affre had now been succeeded by Archbishop Dominique Sibour. Like his predecessor, he resented the fact that Leguay's revision of the Spiritan constitutions withdrew the institute from his jurisdiction and made it directly responsible to the Congregation of the Propaganda Fide in Rome. Sibour decided that Francis would have to write a letter to the Holy See, requesting a restoration of the old arrangement and making the whole thing appear completely spontaneous on his part. When none of Libermann's drafts proved satisfactory, the Archbishop sent him a ready-made letter and insisted that he sign it. Francis ultimately acceded to this request and then promptly dispatched a communication of his own to the Propaganda, explaining therein how he had signed the first under duress. He ended by recommending that the Eminent Fathers might find it easiest to do

---

[18] N. D. 12, 671 f.

nothing at all in this case. That is exactly what they did.

Meanwhile, a priest in the colonies died and bequeathed two thousand francs to the Spiritans. French law demanded that such bequests be presented for government approval by the bishop of the diocese in which the beneficiary was located. Archbishop Sibour refused to play his part and thereby deprived the Spiritans of the inheritance. Even then, Francis refused to capitulate. "I have become indifferent to these official and unofficial angers. The Good Lord can do with us as He pleases. We cannot yield to such thunders. Before all else we must maintain the good spirit of the Congregation. No temporal loss can be allowed even slightly to outweigh the spiritual peril. If we give in, then good-bye to the firm principles with which God has been good enough to endow us."[19]

While this unhappy controversy dragged on, Francis busied himself with another reform, this time far from the ancient seminary. In his earlier years, when he lacked an intimate knowledge of the situation, he had lent some credence to the exaggerated reports of abuses among the colonial clergy. In fact, he set down some very uncomplimentary observations about the situation. Later on, when he had access to the complete record, he modified his judgment considerably and reported: "The majority of the colonial clergy is just as good as the majority of the French clergy. The clergy of Brittany are generally held in high esteem. Nevertheless, most of these priests, if they had been transferred to the colonies, would not have done better than those who are there."[20] Nonetheless, conditions were far from ideal and misconceptions had already begun to make matters worse.

"You cannot imagine," he wrote, "the trouble which Satan has stirred up against us. Rumors are circulating in the colonies to the effect that we want to replace the parochial clergy by members of our own Congregation. Other lies about us have gained currency too." "A multitude of intrigues surrounds us and those intrigues do a lot of harm. They nullify the little bit of good I have achieved in the critical situation that presently obtains in the colonies."[21]

In point of fact, he had not the slightest desire to take over the colonies with his own men. That was contrary to his *modus agendi*. Instead, he preferred to approach the problem through his old

[19] N. D. 13, 279. [20] N. D. 13, 322 f. [21] N. D. 12, 69; 11, 247.

method of research, analysis, organization, and recommendation, just as he had done for Africa and for the social work program. This time, his study uncovered three major problems: (1) the government's policy of obstructionism which had hampered Holy Ghost Seminary in the prosecution of its task; (2) the practice of accepting for colonial ministry priests who had no connection with Holy Ghost Seminary and then holding the Spiritans responsible for them; (3) the lack of an insular hierarchy with sufficient authority to maintain discipline.

Francis addressed himself to the formulation of an exact and clear report that would set forth these difficulties and propose solutions for them. One morning, the astonished Colonial Minister found on his desk a detailed memorandum that began — of all things! — with statistical data. He had expected anything from prefatory prayers to the recommendation of holy water, but here was a cold, matter-of-fact inventory. Such things were still quite unusual in an age that doted on high-flown rhetoric and emotional zeal. Indeed, the renowned Foreign Missions Seminary in Paris still greeted with enthusiastic cheers every announcement that another missionary in the Far East had been martyred. According to the criteria of the day, a violent death was to be preferred to a long, heroic life of work, and fiery zeal to studied organization.

Libermann's statistical tables demonstrated better than the most impassioned plea how few priests there were in the colonies. Then he proceeded to several carefully reasoned deductions from his factual data: the ratio of clergy to laity could be improved only through additional government scholarships at Holy Ghost Seminary; the elimination of undesirable characters could be managed best by appointing to the colonies only those priests who had undergone at least one year's training by the Spiritans; real stability and disciplined organization would never be achieved in overseas France until regular bishops replaced the Prefects Apostolic who, at that time, did not even enjoy the external badge of a Monsignor's purple. With these three recommendations, Francis drew his report to a close.

He did not stop there, however. No sooner had the memorandum been submitted than he embarked on a program of activity which in our day could only be described as lobbying. Libermann the intellectual had done his work; Libermann the diplomat now went into action. He visited members of parliament and won them over to his cause. When the Minister of the Colonies proved difficult, he met with the Minister's wife, charmed her by his presentation of the problem, and elicited her full cooperation. After that the troublesome bureaucrat was putty in his hands.

Before long, the government doubled its scholarship grant to Holy Ghost Seminary. Then the Propaganda ruled that henceforth the ecclesiastical superiors in the colonies should accept no priest unless he had spent some time at the ancient seminary. Finally, on May 3, 1850, the Legislative Assembly voted to accept *in principle* the proposal that the colonial prefectures be raised to the status of dioceses. Libermann's three major objectives had been realized.

The decree erecting the new dioceses met with a number of obstacles, however. Approbation had to come from the Holy See. When it finally arrived, the Ministry of Religious Affairs engaged in delaying tactics for five long months. Meanwhile the government began to sense uneasily that it had to some degree voted itself out of control of the colonial churches. In the interim, Francis did not lapse into inactivity. Working with the Ministry, he saw to it that a list of qualified candidates was drawn up for the forthcoming episcopal sees and by this time he had won such a high degree of the Minister's respect that all but one of his eight recommendations were accepted. Incidentally, that one exception was the only prelate who subsequently proved ill-suited for the task.

When the decree was finally executed and the bishops were appointed by Rome, Libermann was standing by, ready with another detailed memoir to give them a deeper knowledge and understanding of their respective circumscriptions. He had even hoped to have them convene at the seminary for a general discussion before their departure, but they were so immersed in preparing to leave France that a mutually convenient time could not be set for it. Consequently, he committed his material to paper and gave it to them. It emerged as an extensive document, twelve chapters long, full of hardheaded advice about the bishops' future dealings with civil authorities.

By this time, the Ministry of Religious Affairs had been so impressed by his abilities that it delegated a purely governmental function to him. He was asked to compose the first draft of the presidential decree and the ministerial ordinance, both of which were to be promulgated on this occasion.

Father Le Vavasseur recalled the triumph later. "You cannot imagine," he wrote, "the number of difficulties great and small that he succeeded in brushing aside, surmounting, or dodging, in that important business which would have failed so completely without him. His prudence, his tact, and his influence were really indispensable when it came to winning their approval, forcing concessions from them that they were loathe to make, or stripping the Minister (without pressuring or offending him) of his government-authorized privileges in ecclesiastical affairs. The bureaus not only agreed with him; they ended up by admiring the delicacy, quick-wittedness, and completely even disposition which he showed in business transactions and in contacts with people."[22]

The most noteworthy feature about all this was the fact that Francis Libermann, the saintly, practical gentleman, was able to succeed where so many of his predecessors had failed. He achieved it, not through violence and force, but through prayer, factual analysis, precise presentation, politeness, and tact. The rare combination of piety, information, and diplomacy proved invincible.

---

[22] Briault 304.

CHAPTER TWENTY-FOUR

THE NEW APOSTLE TYPE

In the midst of his prodigious activity, Father Libermann never lost sight of his first love: the guidance of priests. Some twenty of the archdiocesan clergy gathered about him and formed the Association of St. John. Its purpose was to stimulate personal holiness among the members and broaden their knowledge of pastoral theology. They met every Monday at the seminary and Father Lannurien kept a record of the assemblies. Between January 3, 1849, and April 30, 1850, for instance, forty-seven such gatherings took place. Francis always directed the discussions as chairman unless illness or business prevented him from doing so.

The agenda normally included a prepared introductory talk by one of the members, in which some phase of the practical ministry was presented. General discussion from the floor then followed and during this part of the session they would listen with close attention when Father Libermann expressed himself, for he always seemed to offer surprisingly fresh approaches to the problems with which these Parisian priests were wrestling in that difficult postrevolutionary era. He drew a clear and captivating picture of the way their lives should unfold to the full stature of Christ and it must have been a touching experience to hear the soft voice of this frail little man as it floated down the long conference table. Everyone present knew his story. They knew that he had lifted himself by God's grace out of the depths of a horrible nervous affliction and that he had extricated himself from a network of prejudices that surrounded his race, his person, his activities, and his doctrine.

More than once he astonished them when, with utter calm

and peacefulness, he demolished ideas that had lost their value in the changing scene. That old benevolent smile with which he met the irritated condemnations of high and mighty opponents, seemed to lend him an air of impregnability. He fearlessly expounded new ideas as if he were totally unaware of the tumult they had generated down through the years. One could not help thinking that here was a man of distinction, an aristocrat of the mind, a refined and original thinker. His was the gentle, unconscious superiority proper to the God-centered who somehow share in a divine overview that covers centuries and peoples. They cannot but smile in mild astonishment at the storms of excitement they engender in some quarters when they are simply fulfilling God's plan.

In these weekly sessions, Francis poured out a wealth of that wisdom which he had stored up in the course of an intense and laborious life. Like a precious tapestry, his concepts had blended into a striking design that took shape from a thousand interwoven skeins of grace, suffering, and personal dealings with countless men. Under the influence of God's guiding hand, his genius became encrusted with the constant drip of individual experiences until at last his wisdom resembled in its variegated beauty one of those subterranean caverns where the splendid towers and crystal galleries grow in serried glory out of nature's tears.

Somehow it all conspired to give him a clear idea of what the apostle of future centuries should be. The concept builds up, element by element, throughout his gigantic correspondence, in his essays, and in his deeds. It originates in the generally accepted premise that a man achieves his full and ideal stature when he realizes in himself as completely as possible the role God assigned him from all eternity. The divine intelligence has, so to speak, a specific idea about each one of us. That idea is always unique, applicable only to us. Personality development, therefore, is simply a matter of respectfully actualizing the divine plan in so far as it affects us individually. In harmony with our very personal being, God had appointed each of us a task that no one else can rightly assume. He has assigned every man his irreplaceable role in history and the more perfectly we unfold the potential that God has placed at the root of our being, the better we serve the ends of Providence.

On this basis, Father Libermann insists that we begin by gratefully accepting as a treasure from God's hands the nature we have received. "The nature you possess is a gift of God, a beautiful gift, but that gift costs its owner dearly because it entails deep and piercing pain. Nonetheless, if a soul's vigor is strengthened by God's grace, it gains immensely by such suffering. It perfects the gifts He has accorded it and attains to that high vision, that mobility of sentiment which forms great souls, souls that are eminently Christian."[1]

Accepting one's nature involves accepting its shortcomings too. "You will not be able," he told one of his clients, "to change your nature. It is extremely sensitive and impressionable. Besides, it is inclined to extraordinary violence and ardor. That's a cross you will have to bear. It is engraved in the core of your being. Basically, it is not a handicap in serving God, provided you put up with it quietly and don't give in to discouragement."[2]

"You do have a difficult character, a troublesome temperament," he frankly admitted to another. "Don't get it into your head that you absolutely have to get rid of it. Convince yourself rather that God intends you to live with that enemy. . . . What can you do? Your nature is very bad, but you must live in peace and humble submission to God as far as that's concerned. . . . Don't be unhappy with your lot. Your natural imperfection is compensated for by great interior graces that you aren't aware of, graces that get results in spite of the bad features of your character. . . . That is why you are quite wrong in thinking that the feelings of remorse you refer to are reproaches that Our Lord is addressing to you. No, my dear fellow, Jesus doesn't speak to your soul so harshly. He loves you too much for that. . . . Don't talk to me about breaking your character. . . . You don't break iron; you soften it in the fire. Don't be in such a rush to shake off your fault. Don't long for it too vehemently . . . that would do you more harm than good. . . . Don't take things so much to heart. Forget yourself and quit all this self-analysis. All these troubles will then disappear gradually."[3]

"The only thing we have to do is be faithful in following God's guidance and giving Him a free hand with us. To get distressed and anxious over putting into effect the good desires He supplies would

[1] N. D. 12, 107. [2] N. D. 7, 8. [3] N. D. 7, 35 ff.

only spoil the work of His grace in us and start us going backward in the path of perfection. Let's not try to be perfect all at once. Rather, let us quietly, peacefully, and sincerely do just what He asks of us. If He wants to bring our little ship along somewhat more slowly than we would like, let's submit obediently."[4]

The key to it all, Francis kept insisting, lay in strengthening and elevating nature, not forcing or breaking it. One can be conscious of his deficiencies and react to the knowledge with true humility, but he should never succumb to feelings of inferiority that paralyze a man's self-actuation and rob him of his resiliency. On this score he observed, "It seems to me that it is utterly necessary to lift the spirits of good people who are too conscious of character weaknesses. They have to be buoyed up, made to understand and feel that they are free, made to sense the beauty of that freedom and equality which they share with all God's children. The idea of inferiority should be rooted out of their minds, for it further weakens their natural aptitude and lowers them in their own estimation. That's very bad."

When we have adjusted to our nature as it is and are no longer oppressed by anxieties about the faults that stem from it, we are then in a position to develop more freely and fully the gifts with which God endowed us. When directing others, "try especially hard to develop their character. Bring out the good in it; take advantage of it to train them, perfecting what is good, correcting what is faulty, and stimulating whatever activity and energy they may possess."[5]

As an aid toward the natural flowering of personality, Father Libermann recommended healthy competition. "In your studies," he said, "never be satisfied with the place you hold. If you are at the bottom, try to get up there with those who are in the middle. If you are in the middle, don't be a coward and say 'that's good enough for me.' Work up a real ambition to be among the first. If you are in the upper third, you would be a coward also if you didn't bend every effort to come out on top."[6] His whole idea was to achieve full realization of each one's capabilities.

Moreover, the complete development of each man's potential in the service of God demanded good care of one's bodily welfare.

---

[4] N. D. 10, 121. [5] N. D. 9, 359 f. [6] N. D. 10, 7.

Francis knew from his own experience that personal accomplishment suffers when the body languishes. The immature asceticism of his early missionaries had further confirmed it. He developed a whimsical formula of the three H's: health, head, and holiness, and the order is significant. He sent twenty-four tons of supplies with the first contingent that went to Africa and, although his warnings fell on deaf ears for a long time, he repeatedly urged his confreres to recognize the importance of diet and hygienic practices.

The final aim of all this preoccupation with the uninhibited flowering of individual potentialities was Libermann's desire to see each man arrive at a mature, self-actuating mode of existence. He knew that only the mature, fully developed personality can surrender himself to apostolic activity without losing himself in it. The kind of independence he advocated in no way militated against religious life or the spirit of the vows. With full respect for independent thinking, he wrote to one of his priests: "The fact that you differ from your superior in your opinions and give expression to such ideas had nothing to do with obedience." As a matter of fact, he envisioned an ideal type of individuality and independence as the crown and culmination of the spiritual life.

"At the start," he maintained, "we are still in the period of emotion and sensitivity, we are still in the infantile stage. Then we feel we have to be led by the hand. That is imperfection. Later, when these feelings disappear and we have nothing left but pure faith, we have really arrived at man's estate."[7]

He regarded problems and difficulties as important factors in the process of maturation. "Those difficulties," he pointed out, "are given to you for the formation and seasoning of your character. . . . That is why the problems and annoyances that overwhelm you just now are actually a treasure from which you must derive the maturity that will be required by the position which Divine Providence has in mind for you. Every position involves its own dangers and difficulties."[8]

The most essential element in this unfolding into the mature independence of a fully realized potential is divine grace. The perfect development of a baptized man into final self-actualization

[7] N. D. 6, 102.
[8] N. D. 12, 106.

demands and presupposes its constant influence. Moreover, since the natural endowments of character and personality flow from the same Eternal Fountainhead as does supernatural grace, these two sources of action, far from excluding each other, are mutually complementary and psychologically resonant. Father Libermann continually emphasized the unity that is so characteristic of nature purified and elevated by grace. "God gives grace," he said, "diversifying it according to the character, the mind, the natural temperament of each man. Hence everyone has his own pathway, his own direction to follow in going to God."[9]

"Our Lord, from whom the priestly spirit flows, develops it by means of grace that is specially adapted to the varying temperaments of different priests. Grace does not destroy characters. It uses the good qualities of each one, turning them to the sanctification of each soul and to the Church's general welfare. Moreover, you have to take into account the particular destination God has for each of His servants. According to His plan, one is called to preach, another to help the poor, a third to devote himself to children. . . . This variety of vocations requires a corresponding variety of graces. Consequently, under the influence of grace we take on the special form God wants us to have and which He has destined for us from all eternity."[10]

Respect for the individual personality or, as he says it, God's unique idea for each man, constitutes the touchstone of Libermann's spirituality. Surrender to God's specific design of life for ourselves and our fellowmen is the be-all and end-all of his asceticism. Personal contact of the soul with God is the means of discovering God's will. Abnegation or mortification is nothing more than quietly removing anything that obstructs or beclouds our vision of the way of life that Providence has mapped out for us.

Francis feared nothing so much as thwarting personal grace or handicapping another's life orientation by the external imposition of alien patterns. That is why he frowned on a multitude of petty devotions or involvement in numerous ascetical practices. He felt that a busy holiness would distract men away from the core of existence, hinder the deep personal encounter with God, and repress

[9] N. D. 11, 546.
[10] N. D. 11, 523.

the essentially personal element of religion. He insisted that one interiorly divorce himself from mundane attachments so that he might enjoy that freedom which is the mark of a true, untethered personality. Then, without engaging in a pragmatic and mechanical training in the separate virtues, he recommends remaining in the presence of God in whom all that is best in every man lies hidden as in its source. The rest follows automatically.

In his constant agitation, modern man easily loses his inner freedom. Hyperactive, tense, and anxious, he is all too often at the mercy of momentary but overwhelming impressions. Most of the time he lives passively instead of actively, being influenced rather than influencing. Hence Libermann's continuing emphasis on calmness, moderation, serenity, and equanimity, in order to extricate the personality from that raging flow of fleeting impressions which do their best to suck him down into the vortex of anxiety and neurosis. Once disengaged from the hectic stimuli of external stresses and strains, a man can live a life that is actuated by those deeper levels of his being where God reveals Himself through the inclinations and desires that His own hand has engraved there. Here too, the truly free man will at last grow responsive to the grace whereby his Creator strengthens and ennobles his good dispositions and suffuses them with divinity.

The existence and the flowering of such a personality is the "manifestation in time" of that unique idea of the individual which God had from all eternity. True holiness, then, consists in an ever greater realization of what the Creator expected of His creature before time was. Father Libermann was so intent on achieving this in himself and others that he even discouraged the indiscriminate reading of spiritual books. He foresaw the harm that could be done if this highly individual unfolding of the soul were to be distorted by an attempt to imitate another's equally individual experiences and aspirations. Instead, he preferred to listen to the Word of God as it speaks from Holy Scripture and from one's own detached and docile heart.

It has long been recognized that a fundamental disorder in the human make-up handicaps the natural and supernatural growth that Libermann advocated. Without benefit of contemporary terminology, he calls this disorganization "our evil nature" and sometimes simply "nature." His warnings against it are constant and forceful, but in such instances he is referring, not to the natural complex which he regards as "a precious gift of God," but to that contrary factor which theologians call the "wound" of original sin.

His frequent use of the phrase, "God is everything; man is nothing," clearly indicates his conviction that whatever makes a man to be what he is, his whole capacity in the natural and supernatural order, is truly a gift and a mandate of the Creator. Our plan of life is not of our own choosing. It is God's idea. The path of our existence is a fascinating exploration in which God's eternal and unique plan for us slowly emerges before our fascinated attention.

Libermann summarizes this process of being true to one's self by using the word "simplicity." It is a concept that has nothing to do with uncouth or gauche behavior, want of intelligence, lack of refinement, or disdain for culture. Francis envisioned simplicity as a courageous and genuine faithfulness to what is really authentic in us, to what is in accord with God's plan for us. Thus, for example, when Thomas Aquinas wrote his great *Summa* it was an act of sublime simplicity, for that mode of thinking and writing was an authentic expression of his gifted mind. Had he forced himself to write out of character in an entertaining and popular way, he would have been wanting in simplicity.

Everything that goes counter to personal honesty and consistency denotes a lack of such simplicity. Paradoxically, there may be instances when a man may have to be so simple that he seems proud, for the mediocre minds around him often confuse this virtue with a leveling process, a lack of originality, an absence of culture. Throughout his life, Father Libermann himself was accused of inordinate ambition, when in reality he was nothing more or less than heroically faithful to his vocation. A lesser man might have counterfeited simplicity by escaping into the security of a nice little *"petit bourgeois"* life, but Francis never wanted to be "safe" at the expense of his integrity.

With considerable logic he argued that if a man had to respect his own endowments, others had to respect them too. If abilities and special graces had marked him out for a definite function in the scheme of things, no one should forcibly change that orientation. "We must accord to everyone the freedom to follow his own ideas and to do good in his own way. We should encourage him along those lines. This method will produce the best results, for we then have the person doing all that is good in his own manner. Perhaps he might have accomplished more if he had followed other ideas, but we cannot change that. He happens not to have those ideas. . . . When we allow everyone to act according to his own concepts, his own character, his own cast of mind, and the entire pattern of his being, a great deal of good will be achieved. Many will make mistakes and act imprudently, but experience will come with time and everyone will perfect himself in line with his own nature. . . . Accord everyone the freedom to live in a way that suits his nature. God made him that way. His intentions are good. Encourage them and they will all do good in the way they are inspired to do from above."[11]

"When people are put in a position that is not equal to their talents, they are in an unhealthy situation. Now, things never go well for a man who is unsuitably placed, for, finding himself under constraint, he will constantly be tempted to better himself. Besides, this method will end up doing great harm to his soul. He will indulge in eternal daydreams of ambition which in turn will cause him constant remorse of conscience. Moreover, he will do his job in an unsatisfactory way."[12]

Since the well-prepared and well-adjusted apostle must take his place, not in an abstract world but in a very real, intricate, and contemporary environment that may be wholly or partially foreign to his background and training, one of his most important character-traits must be flexibility. Father Libermann listed "an open mind" among conditions for admission to the Congregation, and complained for instance that Father Gravière, though a pious man, was "very narrow-minded." Once he wrote with his usual frankness: "You tell me that you need training. I'm aware of that! You lack experience with the way things work in the world. The human heart is the same in all countries; men's emotions do not change but their temperament differs considerably. In every era there is a particular *Zeitgeist* that exercises an enormous influence on indi-

[11] N. D. 8, 111 f.
[12] N. D. 6, 120 f.

viduals as well as on the masses. Like all seminarians and young priests, you have had your spiritual instruction from ancient authors. They provided you with basic principles for the Christian and sacerdotal life and they even taught you to know what lies at the bottom of the human heart. People haven't changed substantially since the time of Louis XIV, but the mentality of the age is different. For that reason, a wise application of those principles involves a different approach."[13]

"If you look at the way Our Lord taught, you will find that He always chose the method that was best adapted to the mentality of His hearers, and even to the character of each person He was instructing. Today new needs are felt everywhere. Every priest, without abandoning his assigned position, must study those needs, probe society's wounds, and grasp every opportunity offered by his position to provide remedies or alleviations for those wounds and needs."[14]

This can be dangerous, of course. The modern apostle cannot afford to be overwhelmed by the number and variety of problems that clamor for solution. Moreover, the danger grows in direct ratio to the increasing complexity of contemporary society. One must clearly order and structure the surrounding realities of life before he can control them. Consequently, Father Libermann demands a balanced judgment as the necessary counterpart of open-mindedness, lest too great receptivity leave us thralls of the "dominion of impressions."

"Never let yourself," he counseled, "be carried away by an idea. Make up your mind only when the enthusiasm and excitement have passed. Even that is not enough. Always beware of ideas that present themselves with such wild attractiveness that they take your mind by storm, arouse your imagination, fire you up, and excite you. You may be sure that every time you are not master of your thinking processes, you are either off the beam, or tending to exaggerate, or lost in a speculation that is hardly ever feasible."[15]

"Never listen to the first thought that comes to your mind. Let it mature before you put faith in it, especially if it was an idea that seized you violently and stirred you up to some degree. Beware

[13] N. D. 9, 181 f. [14] N. D. 11, 536. [15] N. D. 12, 319.

of such ideas and guard against being carried away by them. Put off doing anything as long as possible until you are completely calm. Then quietly analyze all the pros and cons.

"When you want to weigh something, if you throw it on the scale carelessly, it swings the indicator over to that side even though it is only half as heavy as the counter-weights. This is due to the violence with which you cast it on the scale. What do you do then? Why, you stop the indicator and wait till equilibrium has been restored. Then, when the balance is at rest, you gently release the needle and find out which side is heavier.

"Every time some new idea strikes you, it swings the balance in its favor even though the contrary reasons may be six times weightier. That's because the violence unbalances your judgment. . . . What should you do then? Stop the needle. Hold it for a while to keep it from going one way or the other until the agitation is over. Then calmly examine the pros and cons and the greater weight will be on the side marked by the indicator. . . . Little by little, try to moderate the impulsiveness that new ideas arouse."[16]

This done, the orderly structuring of reality and its ultimate control by the modern apostle can proceed apace. Possessed of a balanced judgment and fully informed through his open-minded approach, he is then in a position to engage in Libermann's third step: realistic planning. This is one of the foundation stones of apostolic success. Francis resolutely opposed it to the impulsive and emotional methods that were so widely employed in his day. "We should avoid forming vague and general ideas of things," he urged. "If we want to know them precisely, we have to consider them practically." "Don't picture things in your imagination. Observe them calmly, consider them practically. . . . In so far as you can, act in important matters only when you see clearly. . . . Leave nothing to chance, look ahead as far as you can. Then, when you have taken every precaution, put all your trust in God alone." "We should not go adventuring, banking on the breaks of the game."[17]

"You must . . . impress on yourselves that you are building not merely for the present but for the future. For every ten souls that you might save by a hasty and poorly organized procedure, you may lose a hundred thousand others. . . . If you are guilty of a serious

[16] N. D. 7, 423.

[17] N. D. 7, 82, 192 f., 287.

mistake in administration and organization, the damage resulting from it could be incalculable."[18]

Africa was a case in point. Some three hundred years before, scores of zealous and determined missionaries had gone out from Europe and baptized thousands of natives, yet by the nineteenth century hardly a trace remained of the tremendous work they had done. It was only when Libermann came along with his analysis and plans and memoranda that a self-perpetuating church was established in Negro Africa. He saw that action without thought is like a flower severed from its parent stem. Feverish activity and the passionate engagement of the most powerful forces is but a blow in the dark unless directed by an observant and reflective mind. The best-equipped army is powerless without tactical and intelligence staffs. That is why Father Libermann burst out with "For the love of God and the Blessed Virgin, don't be just a missionary. Be a leader as well. Get to know men and things. Look to the future as much as to the present situation."[19]

Even in the trivialities of life he kept this practical outlook. When Father Collin became overwrought because he had to wear long pants instead of the usual knee-length *culottes,* Francis wrote back: "I don't see any problem here. You say it's not our style, but the Rule doesn't prescribe our style of dress and we cannot adopt any one in particular. In Guinea, for instance, they wear straw hats. . . . Father Tisserant wore long trousers in San Domingo. . . . If God sees fit to enable me to send you the confrere I have in mind, I'll put long pants on him."[20]

Having assured the maturity, open-mindedness, balance, and practicality of the apostolic character itself, Francis then turned to the question of its relations with others. The new apostle's first encounter will be with others in the same field. If he reacts with suspicion and unconscious jealousy to the initiative and success of a colleague, he can do immeasurable harm to the Church, for he may dry up a fountain from which many souls might otherwise have drunk. On the other hand, when he helps his fellow worker develop in ability and grace, applauding his achievements and sympathizing with his reverses, he does more for God and man than he ever could have done alone.

[18] N. D. 9, 193. [19] N. D. 9, 589. [20] N. D. 9, 90.

"They will rejoice," Libermann wrote in the Rule, "at the good which God brings about through their confreres. They will not be depressed because of lesser achievements on their own part. They must always keep their intentions very pure. They ought to seek only the honor of God and desire it ardently. They will be just as much pleased . . . when that glory comes to God through their fellows as when it results out of their own endeavors. They must be satisfied and submit graciously to the Divine Will when they see that they are not so favored with natural and supernatural gifts and that their efforts are not so productive as those of their confreres."[21]

Patience with the shortcomings of others is another cardinal feature of the new apostle. Father Libermann regarded it as essential that we "always avoid seeking for and insisting on ideal perfection. It is worthwhile to keep in mind how things really should be to insure perfect success, it is necessary to know what should be done and how it might best be done, but it is even more important to know how to be flexible, how to adjust and accommodate ourselves to the people, things and circumstances we work with. . . . You are not sufficiently tolerant of the peculiarities, shortcomings, and mannerisms of others," he told Father Lossedat. "Admittedly, I have more influence over our confreres than you do. Now, what is my most effective approach in guiding others? It's this: I tolerate all the faults that I know I can't succeed in eliminating and put up with manners that are sometimes downright unbecoming and boorish. . . . For example, if you were to try and force Father Arragon to conduct himself in a sedate, polite and friendly fashion, you would be pursuing a will-o-the-wisp. You would stand a better chance of stopping the sun in its course. But if you treat him kindly and let him act according to his character and the way he is built . . . you will certainly bring out the good in him."[22]

This principle of tolerance for the imperfections of others was a natural consequence of his reluctance to force things. "Beware of that imagination which makes you demand perfection in human beings, in organizations, and in things in general," he counseled. "We are right in wanting to see everything done perfectly and wanting to bend every effort with calmness, moderation, and wis-

---

[21] N. D. 9, 538.
[22] N. D. 8, 112 f.

dom to bring men and things close to that ideal. But we may as well make up our minds that we will encounter imperfection wherever we encounter human beings. Let us try to achieve the maximum, but let's not break anything in the process. Otherwise, we lose twenty times more than we gain and in the end, if we're honest, we'll soon realize that we are rather far from being perfect ourselves because we demand such absolute perfection of others. I have observed that the really great saints always acted in the way I have recommended. Only the 'petty' saints, the ones who haven't gone very far along the road of piety, act contrariwise. . . . This sort of energy has another defect. It has a penchant for methods and remedies that are radical. Now, radicalism is good and even necessary in the realm of Dogma, but it is detestable and destructive of all good when it comes to the administration and supervision of sacred things."[23]

"Live in peace with the outside world. Be genuine in your dealings with poor Frenchmen who have no religion. Pity them but don't be angry with them. Excuse them when they oppose you. . . . Be particularly careful to overcome the embarrassment you may feel when you are in the company of men of the world whose habits of thought and judgment are different from yours, who look askance at you, or perhaps despise you. . . . Such embarrassment engenders a sort of stiffness, a kind of shyness that gives one the air of being ill-humored and stand-offish. . . . That type of attitude makes a very bad impression on them and estranges them from our holy religion. . . . In general, you ought to like all men, no matter how they may feel about religious principles or about you.

"If we are able to force consciences to be pure, wills to be good, and minds to be truthful, it is evident that we should do so. Charity would make it our duty. But there is no one in this world who can even slightly force the consciences, wills, or minds of his fellow-men. God didn't want to do it. Why should we?"[24]

This respect for individuality, this reluctance to hurt a fellow human being, this disinclination to force anyone to act contrary to his temperament demand a refined and accurate knowledge of the human personality. Father Libermann knew this. He urged

[23] N. D. 12, 319 f.
[24] N. D. 9, 248 f.

the modern apostle to develop a sound psychological insight and even his Rule prescribed a high degree of empathy on the part of his confreres: "They ought to adjust their speech and their behavior to the emotional make-up and the interests of the people with whom they deal. This emotional make-up and these interests cannot always be known by calculated conclusions, arrived at by reasoning. It takes a certain tact to do so, and this tact is normally acquired through a general and practical knowledge of the recesses of the human heart, of character differences, and of interest specialties. These things are picked up by observing the people you meet and paying attention to the sentiments and dispositions they display."[25]

For the guidance of souls, Francis laid down four major steps: (1) Examine the penitent's inner self, his character, his temperament; (2) find out his position in life; (3) study his character and temperament in relation to his position in life; (4) then quietly try to find out what God intends for this particular soul. That he followed the procedure himself is evident from what he wrote to his nephew, Xavier: "I have observed you closely for a long time. While you were with me, I did my very best to follow closely what went on within you, and as far as a man can be certain, I am certain that I know the mental and moral mechanism of your soul."[26]

The crowning touch in the new apostle's character is a consistent attitude of sympathy and courtesy. A passage reminiscent of Newman's famous sketch of a true gentleman gives Father Libermann's thinking on the point: "Speak little, but do not be taciturn. Always be good-humored and satisfied. . . . A multiplicity of words drains your spirit like water and gives self-love a chance to grow unhampered. . . . You ought to adjust your conversation to the taste and background of the people with whom you are speaking. . . . Don't be a know-it-all. . . . Don't parade your knowledge. Even when people obviously don't know what they are talking about, treat them gently. Don't pass judgment on or despise anyone because of his ignorance. Refrain from correcting misstatements all the time unless the glory of God requires it."[27]

He was particularly adamant about maintaining an air of refinement in letter writing. Even Bishop Kobès was gently criticized

[25] N. D. 10, 545. [26] N. D. 13, 130. [27] N. D. 6, 450 f.

for his shortcomings in this respect: "The expressions you use in your letters are occasionally too direct, too stiff, and too positive. Your epistolary style should always give evidence of mildness, moderation, and calmness. It should breathe that air of modesty and deference which the saints knew how to impart to their writings.[28]

When he was too ill to write his own letters, he drew up sketches of replies and then asked Father Le Vavasseur to compose the final version. The text that resulted never seemed to satisfy him. "Our way of writing," said Le Vavasseur, "was as different as our characters and temperaments. We were in constant disagreement over every phrase. . . . [His] letters were so mild, so kind, so pious, so charitable and delicate, so genuine, that no matter what I wrote I couldn't come near what he wanted. Sometimes I had to rewrite a letter three or four times. He never allowed any word or thought to slip in that might hurt or displease anyone in any way. No matter how fully he might have been justified in replying in like manner, he never allowed me to say anything that was foreign to his extraordinary kindness, delicacy, politeness, and humility. . . . In the government offices, they got to know his careful, friendly, cordial, and refined style, and when he allowed me to express something in my own way, they immediately noticed that the letter was not of his writing."[29]

Father Libermann carried this delicacy over into other phases of life: personal cleanliness, dress, deportment, and housekeeping. Nonetheless, he encountered great difficulties in inducing his confreres to accept the ideal he proposed. The early missionaries, influenced by the romantic age in which they lived, thought of themselves as Rangers in the service of the Church. The popular concept of such men involved something wild and careless in their clothing, their speech, and their outward appearance generally, and Francis nearly despaired of eradicating it. "As regards shortcomings in good manners, urbanity in dealing with people, and the personal hygiene of missionaries, I see no way of training them in such things. This is a question of tact, good sense, and character. Neither you, nor I, nor anyone else who manages well in this area can boast of superior instruction in it. On the contrary, others have

[28] N. D. 11, 197.
[29] N. D. 13, 630 f.

had much more contact with the world. They have had a careful upbringing, were born into excellent families, and yet they are none the better for all that. Consequently, it is a matter of tact and character."[30]

Even in business affairs, this same general refinement must come to the fore. Father Le Vavasseur bears witness to the fact that the adviser kept his own rule. "One of the things that contributed most to his success in any transaction was his delicate courtesy. His judgment was excellent and he was vividly, keenly, delicately sensitive. When he had to act, he mentally exchanged places with the people concerned and tried to imagine how he would feel if someone treated him as he intended to deal with them. He often said to me when I was composing a letter: 'How is it that you don't feel the effect that word is going to have?' Or again, 'When you're dealing with people, do your best to find out in what particular way each one should be handled. If you treat everybody identically alike, you will never succeed. Try to feel within yourself what impression your actions or words will make on others.'"[31]

Diplomacy and delicacy can, of course, in their endeavors to spare others whenever possible, brand the man who practices them as dishonest and insincere. The cultured heart rarely escapes being criticized by lesser minds who think that life should be rough and tough. Le Vavasseur admits that Father Libermann had his share of trouble in this regard. "I have heard people reproaching him for seeming duplicity. I myself often told him that he wasn't sufficiently frank, but when we examined the situation carefully and especially when we had a chance to listen to him frequently, we easily saw how false that accusation was. His phenomenal prudence, self-control, and goodheartedness in managing his business always led him to choose the way that was least painful, least liable to hurt the people concerned. Because he always eschewed anything that might grieve or offend people, anything that smacked of harshness, he sometimes appeared to lack frankness and directness, but fundamentally he was far removed from even a hint of duplicity or craftiness."[32]

An apostle who has found his proper position in the world, who

[30] N. D. 13, 118. [31] N. D. 13, 639 f. [32] N. D. 13, 641.

employs realistic, practical, and systematic methods in his work, and who treats others with respect and consideration must be a courageous person, indeed. Keeping his mind open for constant changes and rising needs in the society where he lives and labors will necessitate unending decisions and commitments on his part. Father Libermann offered no panaceas. "All the works that have been undertaken and carried through in the Church have had . . . difficulties. . . . Yet those difficulties did not scare off the apostolic men who initiated the projects, nor did they prevent them from going ahead with constancy as well as success. It has always been the way of Providence to manifest Itself in the midst of obstacles and the happiest results have normally lain beyond the greatest handicaps.

"It follows that we would actually be departing from the usual order of Divine Providence . . . if we insisted on undertaking something only when we had an absolute guarantee of its success and an assurance that every difficulty would be eliminated."[33] This is what Father Libermann had in mind when he wrote in his Rule: "They must be careful to avoid timidity, excessive precaution, lethargy and other faults that stem from false prudence. . . . We must courageously make a decision . . . and then follow through on it energetically."[34]

His portrait of the new apostle, then, is one of a man who develops that great gift of God, his own personality, as broadly and richly as he can — not by repressing his nature and throttling his aptitudes, but by unfolding his individuality with the help of grace. He is receptive and attentive to the ever changing situation around him, always keeping his mental and emotional balance lest mere impressions and feelings dominate him. He is realistic, precise, and practical. He plans his projects carefully and with full psychological understanding of men and situations. Always a gentleman, he cultivates courtesy, politeness, personal neatness. He is full of good will and tolerance toward others, yet courageous in facing the hardest tasks. The ideal that Father Libermann holds up is a timeless one, valid for all ages and climes. It grows out of the pages

[33] N. D. 8, 92.
[34] N. D. 10, 546.

of the New Testament where, without prejudice to His Godhead, the Second Person of the Blessed Trinity walked among men and loved to call Himself "the Son of Man." The new apostle can only humbly follow Him, patterning his actions after the sublime humanity of Christ and partaking of His divinity through the miracle of grace — "another Christ" in the fullest sense of the term.

CHAPTER TWENTY-FIVE

THE GENERAL

Father Libermann was a century ahead of his time. In an era when men's minds swung between the two extremes of positivistic rationalism and emotional romanticism, he walked like a stranger down the middle path of intuition tempered by practicality. The positivistic rationalists mistook his intuitive approach for anti-intellectualism, though in reality his unfettered mind soared above their hidebound formalism; the emotional romanticists failed to comprehend his hardheaded insistence on businesslike methods, because it was totally foreign to the mentality of the age. Like every original thinker, he met with scant understanding and less sympathy from his contemporaries.

Henri Bergson, himself a Jew, who gave his "moral adherence" to Catholicism at the end of his life, describes the situation quite aptly.

> True mystics simply open their souls to the oncoming wave. Sure of themselves, because they feel within them something better than themselves, they prove to be great men of action, to the surprise of those for whom mysticism is nothing but visions and raptures and ecstasies. That which they have allowed to flow into them is a stream flowing down and seeking through them to reach their fellow-men; the necessity to spread around them what they have received affects them like an onslaught of love. A love which each of them stamps with his own personality.[1]

Bergson goes on to discuss the mystic's "exceptional, deep-rooted, mental healthiness, which is readily recognizable. It is

[1] Henri Bergson, *The Two Sources of Morality and Religion,* Garden City, 1956, p. 99. Quoted by permission of Henry Holt and Company.

expressed," he observes, "in the bent for action, the faculty of adapting and readapting oneself to circumstances, in firmness combined with suppleness, in the prophetic discernment of what is possible and what is not, in the spirit of simplicity, which triumphs over complications, in a word, in supreme good sense."[2] He then points out that, once God acts through the soul in full and final union,

> . . . there is a superabundance of life. There is boundless impetus. There is an irresistible impulse which hurls it into vast enterprises. A calm exaltation of all its faculties makes it see things on a vast scale only, in spite of its own weakness, produce only what can be mightily wrought. Above all, it sees things simply, and this simplicity, which is equally striking in the words it uses and the conduct it follows, guides it through complications which it apparently does not even perceive. An innate knowledge, or rather an acquired ignorance, suggests to it straightaway the step to be taken, the decisive act, the unanswerable word. Yet effort remains indispensable, endurance and perseverance likewise.[3]

Francis Libermann verified all this. The simple directness of his inner life, nourished as it was at the pure fountains of Holy Writ, tradition, and authoritative teaching, led him to reject accidental forms that had grown stale and meaningless with the passage of time. This pilgrim from Judaism immediately saw the relation between divine values and modern needs. He seemed to give answers to questions that had scarcely been formulated and solutions to problems that had barely been perceived.

The old forms and archaic methods would still hang on for many years to come, but at last, a century later, the sincere minds of the world now hear in his voice a note that is strangely attuned to their own modern outlook. In him they find an evangelical simplicity, a renewed asceticism that outlaws rigidity, a loving and cultured attitude toward contemporaries who suffer from neuroses, confusion, and sin. The lonely, the neglected, and the abandoned of this earth for whom Francis had such an abundance of sympathy fill the contemporary scene at every level of society. Solitary, unbalanced, anxious, and neurotic, they face the ever present threat to personal existence which modern living constitutes for so many

---

[2] Bergson 228.
[3] Bergson 32.

men from the city tramp to the captain of industry. Precisely because Libermann suffered so keenly and so long from nervous disorders — tensions, anxiety, loneliness, suicidal tendencies — and overcame them so gloriously, he speaks their language and stands as a beacon of hope.

Nor is that all. He went on to demonstrate that the achievement of inner equilibrium opens the way to leadership qualities of the highest character as long as it is attained not by crushing but by harmoniously ordering the dynamic elements of one's nature. His own display of leadership in founding the Holy Heart of Mary Congregation was amazing enough, but it showed up in truly phenomenal fashion when it came time to surrender the very existence of his institute and shepherd his confreres into the Society of the Holy Ghost. Though zealous and fervent, his associates bitterly opposed the move because it looked like an abandonment of everything he and they had striven for. Their opposition became so highly charged with emotion that a man of lesser stature might have either yielded to pressure or disdained their limited visions. Libermann did neither. He calmly worked toward the fulfillment of his plans and still made full use of the modest abilities of less gifted colleagues.

But most of all, his leadership lay in magnificent self-control. It is described and advocated over and over again in his writings by the use of the word *"douceur"* — a term which, in its highly elastic applicability, defies translation. This *"douceur,"* resulting as it does from harmony within the personality, excludes harshness, tension, compulsion, and rigidity toward oneself and others. It moderates all hysterical agitation, relieves nervous anxiety, controls aggressiveness and hostility. It is the fruit of quiet self-possession that has been gained through daily growth in self-understanding through the light of grace. Far from generating a superficial make-believe conviction that all is sweetness and light, it rests firmly on an awareness of self and of outside reality. Francis Libermann gave evidence of its value in all the aspects of his life.

Though only forty-six years old when he assumed the generalate of the Spiritans, he was revered as a patriarch by everyone from the renowned old Father Gaultier to the youngest novice. The scholastics at Notre Dame du Gard were in high spirits when he stayed with them. Everyone felt there was a special spot for him in the heart of this man who always had a friendly word for each person he met. At Holy Mass they forgot their missals at the sight of his ecstatic face, at recreation they basked in the quiet happiness that seemed to radiate from him, and in the intimacy of his room they poured out their troubles to a willing listener and effective helper.

All of this easy good nature flourished in the midst of unbelievable amounts of work. Immediately after the merger, he added Constitutions to the Rules of the Holy Ghost Society, organized the colonial dioceses, reformed the ancient seminary, composed lengthy tracts on a multiplicity of subjects, carried on a superhuman correspondence, and still found time to handle the routine of administration and supervision.

The composition and redaction of a Rule for Lay Brothers was another labor of love that he engaged in. He regarded the Brothers as precious assets of the Congregation who not only freed the priests for the sacred ministry by devoting themselves to the material welfare of the community but helped directly in that ministry by teaching in schools and technical centers. His affection for them was so great that they never heard him utter a harsh or impatient word. When he was reading or praying in the garden, he stopped incessantly as the Brothers passed by, opening a door for this one, preventing a minor mishap for that one, and giving a passing bit of advice to a third. On occasion he would show them how to scrub and polish floors, how to make a bed, or how to handle a broom, and he was happiest of all when arranging for their courses in mechanical drawing and the various trades.

These multiple occupations bore down mercilessly on his frail shoulders. "During the last three months," he wrote, "I have worked harder than I have done in my whole life." "If you could just spend one day in my office, you wouldn't be angry with me any more. You would be sorry for the poor galley-slave who drags his chains about as well as he can during the day and who sleeps like a groundhog at night." "The establishment of the colonial dioceses has involved so much work for me since the beginning of last year that I cannot understand how I was able to do it, for I was in a state of exhaustion after my illness. . . . Add to that a seminary that was in sad shape and needed reform."[4]

As time went on, he found it impossible to write long letters to his numerous correspondents. Consequently, he decided to supplement short personal replies by general instructions that would benefit all his priests simultaneously. It was a wise move, but sickness and death overtook him before many of these major essays were completed.

The ready and patient attention he devoted to everyone's personal problems became a serious drain on his time and energy. A superior in the Congregation became annoyed because Francis listened so kindly to the complaints of one of his men. Libermann quickly set him straight: "I exercise particular care with confreres who are imperfect, difficult, or grappling with problems. I talk to them with an easy, mild, and considerate air. This seems to bother you . . . but I find it absolutely imperative to listen to those who have complaints. If I refused to pay any heed to their grievances, I would be closing my heart to all confreres who are in trouble. Their condition would get worse and I would be unable to provide the remedy they needed for their ills."[5]

His boundless charity went beyond the limits of Congregation business. When, for instance, the Jesuit Fathers lacked official recognition by the French Government and hence were unable to negotiate directly with the Ministries, Libermann helped them realize their desire to take over the mission of Madagascar and its neighboring islands. He initiated the affair at the proper governmental level and then carried it through with his usual expert diplomacy. Father Maillard, the Jesuit Provincial, subsequently wrote to the Madagascar Prefect: "Father Libermann is a saint, a real saint. I saw him in Paris when the question concerning you and your important mission came up. He took all the steps and did everything that would be expected of the most devoted and sincere friend. In fact, he could not have done better. Father Libermann is the *vir rectus et simplex* par excellence, the *vir sine dolo* above all."[6]

Among the numerous cares that filled up his days were the priests of every sort and description who came to see him. Their

[4] N. D. 12, 15, 12; 13, 14. [5] N. D. 13, 332 f. [6] N. D. 12, 690.

difficulties and problems rivaled in variety their background and characters, yet he received every one with sincere kindness whether they were at odds with their bishops, public sinners, or outright apostates. Even the notorious Abbé Châtel, founder of the "French Church," came at the end of his life for solace and encouragement. Gone were the days of his pride and glory. Reduced now to misery and wretchedness, he turned to the pious priest whose all-embracing love was known on all sides. Francis received him with typical considerateness. Instead of humiliating him with direct alms, he gave him some copying to do and paid him generously for it. Later, when it was learned that the old man used part of the money to spread his schismatic ideas, Father Libermann had to withdraw his benefactions.

Not all were "shepherds in the mist," however. "As long as our Venerable Father stayed at the Motherhouse," we read, "it was a center where priests who were eminent in scholarship, talent, and virtue loved to meet."[7] The learned Benedictine, Dom Pitra, who subsequently became a cardinal, had a regular room there. Then there were the Abbé Blanc, an ecclesiastical historian; Abbé Bouix, famous for his studies in Canon Law; Abbé Rohrbacher, another renowned writer of Church history; Abbé Martinel, celebrated for his apologetic and political books; Abbé Gaume, well known for his catechetical works and an epoch-making indictment of contemporary education; and, perhaps the most illustrious of all, J. P. Migne, who marshaled an army of collaborators and published an ecclesiastical library of eleven hundred quarto volumes, one third of which was devoted to the now famous collections of Greek and Latin Patrology which every priest encounters in his course of study. Years later, Migne was among the many eminent persons who petitioned the Holy See to initiate the process for Libermann's canonization.

Learned prelates like Bishop Gousset and Bishop Parisis loved to stay at the exciting old place on the *rue Lhomond* where, under Francis' direction, intellectual life once more sparkled through the ancient halls. Dom Cabrol described the vibrant atmosphere in these words: "Here was a scientific and literary group where everyone spoke freely about things that pertained to the Church, where every-

[7] N. D. 13, 597.

one contributed not only his own personal views but the results of his research as well. . . . Sometimes a veritable debate took place among the members of this scholarly areopagus."[8]

Father Gaultier, Libermann's First Assistant, was particularly well fitted to aid and abet this rebirth of the Spiritans' educational mission which the new General had stimulated. Making full use of the well-stocked old motherhouse library, he placed himself at the service of learned visitors, supplied them with precious data for their research, and inspired them with original approaches and views. His influence showed itself especially in the editorial work of Voigt's *Theology* and the *Graduale* of Rheims and Cambrai.

Conscious of the leadership responsibilities which the Society of the Holy Ghost had assumed long years before, Father Libermann made sure that the seminary contributed its share to the restoration of Gregorian Chant. He laid hold of the first editions, and then, in an effort to arouse interest in Paris and in France generally, he had his seminarians carefully trained in the ancient liturgical modes at a time when such a thing was still a much-debated novelty. "This year," he reported with satisfaction, "we shall have a special solemn celebration, for we shall use a Gregorian Chant that is said to be authentically compiled from manuscripts of the ninth and eleventh centuries. It is an experiment that we are undertaking in order to give impetus to the promotion of pure Gregorian Chant in Paris and in the Provinces. We have just finished a practice session. The Bishop of Langres came for the sole purpose of being at the practice. He was delighted with the way it went."[9]

Some of these men became permanent guests. Father Rohrbacher, for example, found the atmosphere of the motherhouse so conducive to quiet research that he asked permission to stay there for the rest of his life. One of his last desires was to be buried next to Father Libermann. When Father Bouix published his *Concile Provincial,* Archbishop Sibour grew indignant over its propapal orientation and relieved him of his office with only five francs in his pocket. Francis courageously took him in, even though he could ill afford to incur any more of the Archbishop's displeasure himself.

Before long, the Spiritan General received a summons to appear

[8] N. D. 12, 598 f.
[9] N. D. 11, 281.

at the archiepiscopal residence. Father Bouix left a personal account of the audience: "When he came home, Libermann described the conversation with that quiet serenity which even the most painful events could not affect. The prelate had reproached him with these words: 'You are harboring in your seminary priests who are at odds with their bishops. There's Father Rohrbacher, for instance.' Then the Venerable Father added for my benefit: 'I believe you were uppermost in the Archbishop's thoughts, but no doubt he didn't dare to name you. Moreover, I can assure you, I didn't say one word about you.' Father Libermann then answered regarding Rohrbacher: 'I did not know that he was at odds with his bishop, but Your Grace can trust me to set things straight with that prelate.' Then I offered to leave the Seminary if my presence there would do harm to his congregation, but he told me to remain. That question could be considered later on."[10]

Another group of dynamic people who sought inspiration and strength at the Spiritan motherhouse were the founders of new religious societies and charitable organizations. Blessed Mother Javouhey, foundress of the Sisters of St. Joseph, regarded Father Libermann not only as her own spiritual guide but as the trusted adviser in all that pertained to her congregation. Miss Clara was another who called on his experience and wisdom in behalf of her little foundation for the support of missionary work. Francis wrote to Schwindenhammer about her: "She will have to sweat blood and tears if she wants to achieve even a meager success. She'll have to live like a bird on a twig, with no security for the present or the future."[11] Mother de Bonnault d'Houet, foundress of the Faithful Companions of Jesus, testified later that "when he had spoken, one felt that everything had been said." Father Le Prévost, who started the Brothers of St. Vincent, declared, "I never left him without carrying with me some new light of the spiritual life and a more ardent desire to serve God."[12] Mother de Villeneuve, foundress of the Blue Sisters of Castres, depended on him heavily, as has already been noted, for the good administration of her institute.

Through it all, Libermann's frail constitution kept rebelling against the energetic spirit that drove it at such a murderous pace. "From now on," he wrote to his missionaries, "I can proudly call myself

[10] N. D. 13, 600 f. [11] N. D. 13, 180. [12] Briault 385.

as much an African as you — perhaps more so. I have had all the African illnesses. Around six or seven years ago I had dysentery. Last summer I began with a pernicious fever and ended with inflammation of the liver." He complained to Bishop Kobès of "a certain bodily lassitude that almost never leaves me and makes it impossible for me to walk for a half hour without getting a fever." The nervous headaches were so severe that Father Bouix "particularly admired the serenity of his patience in the midst of horrible neuralgias."[13]

Even then, however, his delicate sense of humor persisted. Father Briot, the community bursar, was given to pessimistic observations about the precarious financial condition of the house. On one occasion, when the predictions of bankruptcy were particularly terrifying, Francis observed mischievously: "I think nevertheless that those lamentations are bursars' lamentations, and I think that we should let them have a few." Just then a confrere sent some bills to the Jeremiac bursar and Libermann wrote to him: "You gave Father Briot some bad moments sending him your bills. They were like a shower of bullets." With equally sly humor he remarked that the office of "The Propagation of the Faith gives no indication that it is making any progress in generosity. The figure for Guinea this year is the same as last."[14]

Once he had a problem to discuss with the old war-horse, General Dufite. The General's dislike for interviews was matched only by his lack of enthusiasm for Parisian winters. That is why Libermann said, "I wanted to see the brave General Dufite and chase him out of his shell. Unfortunately, I couldn't find the shell. Undoubtedly he's a courageous man in the heat of battle, but he doesn't seem to be equally brave in the cold of winter."[15]

A subsequent letter describes in very human fashion how he visited some old friends. "They brought me directly to Mrs. Goltschmid. She was delighted to see me again. . . . Right off the bat the table was loaded with pastry, then more pastry, and still more pastry, biscuits, and attractive desserts of every description, yet my stomach would gladly have traded them all for a good piece of steak. Nonetheless, I figured I'd better make my supper out of it since I saw nothing else on the horizon but some more of these

[13] N. D. 13, 11, 101, 600. [14] N. D. 12, 32, 462. [15] N. D. 12, 31.

little things. Consequently, I got down to the job vigorously and I must say I had a rather good appetite. Then, lo and behold, along came Mrs. Laske and told us it was time for us to go to supper at her place! In spite of myself, I had to cut a poor figure at that feast, because I had been taken quite by surprise."[16]

This light vein of banter ran through his life to the end, even though the weight of his responsibilities grew heavier by the day. The problem of choosing his successor as Superior General thrust itself upon him ever more insistently. While he knew very well that God would attain His ends despite man, for the ancient Orders had taken years and sometimes centuries to reach the full span of their orientation, nonetheless his practical common sense made it clear that the designs of Providence should not be handicapped by a total absence of human planning. He had restored and revived the Spiritans and it was now his task to transmit to his heirs a clear concept of their hundred and fifty year old tradition, a tradition that was enriched and vivified rather than curtailed and modified by the saving polarity which he and his men had more strikingly emphasized.

A feeling of uneasiness came over him whenever he reflected on the opposition he had met with both in and out of the Congregation. Could he find someone who shared his outlook and had the courage to remain faithful to the steps he had taken under God's inspiration? So many that he thought of were concerned solely with their own little territory, their own type of work, the needs of their own apostolate, that they lost sight of the Congregation's over-all mission.

He had recalled Frederic Le Vavasseur from Reunion in the hope of training him according to his spirit and purpose, yet there were times when he despaired of ever succeeding in this. The greatest setback occurred when he sent Frederic on a recruiting trip through France, hoping thereby to attract vocations for both the Colonial Seminary and the Spiritan scholasticate. One week after Le Vavasseur's departure, a letter came back. Francis opened it with an optimistic smile, eager to learn how his potential successor had fared. The smile soon faded, however. Frederic had not changed. He learned in his travels that the Colonial Seminary was still in disfavor in the Provinces and his enthusiasm instantly dis-

[16] N. D. 13, 28.

solved. Now he took up the theme of Bishops Bessieux and Kobès, arguing that the Seminary should be closed, the colonial missions abandoned, and all resources concentrated on Africa! He was virtually spurning the task that God had assigned to them.

Libermann's dream fell to pieces once again. The last hope of his life began to vanish. It was a bitter experience to see how readily his sons could turn their backs on God's plan for the Congregation, how keen was their dislike for the drudgery of seminary administration, how quickly they cast off the historic educational responsibilities of the Spiritans in favor of the more recent and more glamorous enterprise in Africa. Would they never learn that the essence of success lay, not in spectacular courage or glamorous interest, but in seeking what God wanted, what God had determined to be the historic mission of this Society?

He sat down dejectedly to answer Frederic's letter. It was true, he admitted, that the educational task in the Seminary was demanding and unrewarding. It was equally true that work in civilized countries involved less freedom, independence, and satisfaction than the more fascinating African endeavor. But did those trials justify an attempt to slough off the Spiritan's traditional objective? His own experience with the ways of God had taught a different lesson.

"Until now," he remarked, "we have stayed in the path of Providence and God alone has been our guide. I was never able to bring to fulfillment a plan that I had conceived on my own. Nonetheless, I have consistently succeeded — as if by magic, though surrounded by problems and annoyances — in every enterprise that was thrust upon us by Providence. That is why it would do us more than others untold harm if we were to leave that roadway and substitute our own ideas for it, no matter how fervent and generous those ideas might be.

"You propose that we disband the Seminary, go back to Notre Dame du Gard and abandon the islands. I feel sure that that would be one of the most grievous faults, one of the gravest insults that our poor little Congregation could inflict upon God. In fact, I believe that such a program would ruin us completely because it would make us deserve to be abandoned by God; it would compromise us quite seriously in the eyes of men; and it might even cause trouble and dissension in our own ranks.

"I believe that we cannot leave the Seminary nor the islands without being seriously unfaithful to the Divine Will. It is God, Divine Providence, who has put us in the Seminary and sent us to Reunion and Mauritius. We have no right to grumble against His orders or say that we have done enough to obey His good and holy Providence."[17]

"The work at the Seminary is hard, very hard, and we are extremely poor and weak. But does that justify us in giving up? By no means! Even if we were to be crushed under the weight of that work, we should be ready to be buried in the ruins. . . . To abandon this operation is like watching the house of God burning and refusing to come to the rescue.

"Very likely, I have never been so buoyed up as I was by your presence, and the only reason for that was because I could say to myself that henceforth I would have someone in whom my hopes for the future could repose, one who would direct God's work wisely, energetically, and out of the experience he had gathered. That is precisely why I get so discouraged when I see how your mind rushes violently off toward the abyss.

"I recognize that you have an unshakeable will to do good and do it perfectly, but it is the will of a fervent seminarian who has no practical idea of the things of God and who, thinking he's devoting himself to the love and affairs of God, gives his turbulent nature free rein. So, at odd moments when I'm thinking of that, I wonder what will happen to the Congregation if Father Le Vavasseur is made its superior as I so ardently wish? If he acts then as he acts now, the poor Congregation will be in the throes of death two months after I am gone."[18]

There was no doubt about it. Le Vavasseur was hopelessly lacking in balance and self-control. When it was too late he came to recognize it himself. "My wild ardor, my activity, my haste, my natural boldness clashed with his prudence, his wise deliberateness, his patient considerateness. On such occasions I was always guilty of outbursts that would have made an angel lose patience. I often attacked him, blamed him. I returned to the attack a thousand times, I vexed and tormented him, not with the intention of hurting him, but because of the stubbornness with which I clung to my ideas."[19]

[17] N. D. 12, 199 f. [18] N. D. 12, 316 f. [19] N. D. 13, 627 f.

In a moment of remorse he asked Francis to make him obey like a child in even the smallest details, not even letting him think for himself. The proposal horrified Libermann. It was totally in conflict with the abiding respect he always showed to other personalities. Frederic persisted, but to no avail, and before long he was victimized once more by the old temptation to make Francis impolite just once, to see him lose his gentlemanly composure, to finally create a breach in his consistent respect for others. But he failed in that too.

Meanwhile, Father Libermann's roving eye still scanned the field for a potential successor. Ignatius Schwindenhammer looked promising. Though barely thirty years old, he had already creditably discharged a mission to Rome, directed the novitiate, and functioned as a superior of the scholasticate at Notre Dame du Gard. Now he was a member of the General Council. True, he was not the kind of man to find favor in the eyes of all the confreres. His methodical mind and somewhat rigid personality made others regard him as too cold, too intellectual, too inclined to formal organization. Some of these traits he shared with his superior, but Libermann had blended them exquisitely with a sensitive consideration for others and a warm friendliness for everyone with whom he came in contact. One could hope that grace might also soften and veil the harsher elements of this youngster's character so that some degree of warmth and sympathy might begin to radiate from it. Francis set about kindling the fire.

It was high time. He could feel his bodily forces weakening rapidly. As the dying leader of a young group (few were over forty), he felt that it was his duty to insure the Spiritans' fidelity to God's intentions regarding them. The evangelization of Africa no longer caused anxiety. It was progressing as satisfactorily as could be expected at that time. Its drama and heroism fascinated young minds and kept them looking forward to it eagerly. The non-African enterprises he had defended with holy stubbornness. Less romantic and more subject to misinterpretation, they would require a stanch defender if the ancient Spiritan commitments were to be honored. He must make sure of that.

How well he did so is evident from the Proceedings of the First General Chapter (Oct. 3, 1853), which took place only one year after his death: "The Superior reported on five new foundations that are being undertaken in accord with the decision of the General Council. He demonstrated the utility and potential of such establishments. He also made it clear to us that such endeavors are entirely within the scope of the aims and objectives of the Congregation. These are the five foundations: a French Seminary in Rome, a Junior Seminary in Martinique, a Junior Seminary in Guadeloupe, direction of the 'Lammenais Brothers' and of a small college in Brittany, and a small community near Notre Dame des Victoires (Paris)."[20]

Like a prophet in Israel, Libermann had striven manfully to keep aloft the vision of God's will amid the hurly-burly of deviating human tendencies. He had set his face against the strivings of men and shut his ears against the siren call of natural attraction. No one could cause his mighty heart and agile mind to swerve from the path that God had marked so clearly for him even when his confreres failed to see the way. That he built wisely and well only history would prove. From the vantage point of a century's perspective, one can see how fully he was vindicated by the passing years.

---

[20] Archives, p. 19.

CHAPTER TWENTY-SIX

CIRCLES OF LIGHT

In November, 1851, there was a significant break in Libermann's health. He could no longer work during the hours that followed his midday meal, for the process of digestion was accompanied by excruciating pain. He would lapse into a state of torpor that was close to unconsciousness. Although the house physician bent every effort to alleviate his discomfort, none of the medicines he prescribed seemed to have any effect. The organic disturbance refused to respond to therapy.

Meanwhile, political unrest gripped the capital once more. The president of the Republic, a nephew of Napoleon, dreamed of restoring the empire. The elected representatives of the people opposed his moves to revise the Constitution and abolish general suffrage, but on the night of December 1, he used the army to execute a *coup d'état*. After his forces had occupied the more important sectors of Paris, he imprisoned or exiled all political opponents, crushed all centers of resistance, and eventually proclaimed himself Napoleon III, Emperor of France.

Brother Thomas of the motherhouse staff was running errands in the morning and brought back disturbing accounts of what had happened during that first fateful night. Then Dom Pitra came. He had read the broadsides posted in the boulevards and the news he brought was even more disconcerting. Father Libermann began to fear another popular insurrection and worried about his sons at Notre Dame du Gard where there were no protecting troops to save them if a new revolution broke out.

At nine in the morning, he called John the cook and Brother

Thomas to his room and asked them to go out for more information. John was to circulate in the neighborhood of City Hall and Brother Thomas around the Place de la Concorde. When they returned at noon, their report was far from reassuring. No serious uprising had as yet occurred, but the whole town was a powder keg. Francis decided to go to the scholasticate that very afternoon. "You who are here," he said, "have the army and the police to help you. But at Notre Dame du Gard they are alone. I don't know how they would manage if something should happen."[1] At seven that evening, a cab took him to the station. He brought twenty-five hundred francs with him for use in the event of trouble at the senior seminary.

The whole scholasticate was overjoyed at this unexpected visit. His very presence created an atmosphere of peace and happiness within the abbey's old gray walls. But not for long. The desperate state of his health became immediately apparent. He spent most of the time in bed. Then, toward the end of December, when it was clear that no immediate danger threatened the seminary, he returned to the motherhouse. Pale and emaciated, he slowly negotiated the stairs and asked Brother Thomas to transfer his bed from the sleeping room to the office. The fireplace there would at least provide some heat for him and his many visitors. Then he wrote: "I am going to bed. When shall I manage to get up again? Things are pretty bad."[2]

They were indeed. He was deathly sick and a pall of sadness settled over the ancient building. The tread of many feet on stairways and in corridors grew perceptibly softer, while voices young and old were carefully hushed. Francis himself lay on his bed undergoing a veritable martyrdom. The autopsy was later to show a liver so shriveled, hard, and twisted that the attending physicians felt he must have suffered horribly for many years. Meanwhile, the sorrowing confreres probed their ingenuity to assuage his pain. They engaged the best doctors of Paris, but to no avail.

On January 7, Father Le Vavasseur wrote to Samson in Strassburg: "We are desolate. Our good Father is suffering so much. He finds it almost impossible to get any nourishment. In reply to your

[1] N. D. 13, 667.
[2] Briault 418.

letter, [he] says that he loves you, that he will love you more and more, and as a compensation and reward for this he merely asks you to believe it."[3] Disturbed by the news, Samson decided to go to Paris. Jacob was dying and he once more became little Jaegel, the delicate youngster who needed an older brother's protection. It was to be a sad and final farewell.

Father Le Vavasseur and Brother Thomas now kept constant watch at the bedside. "Please ask the Blessed Virgin," Frederic wrote, "to take me instead of our beloved Father. And since I don't represent one-hundredth of his worth, let her send me a hundred times more misery and suffering."[4] Through it all, Francis lay there quietly, still polite and obliging, still friendly and interested in everybody, just as he had been all his life. Everyone looked for excuses to be near him to carry away some last memory, some word of consolation, some final inspiration. He remained intimately united with God, yet completely unostentatious in his piety. The old simplicity asserted itself in the critical hour as it had done throughout the years gone by. He did not ask to live nor did he beg to die. With quiet courage he accepted reality as Providence unfolded it.

The attending physicians now held long consultations. They disagreed in their diagnoses and prescribed all sorts of remedies, some harmless and some downright horrible. Le Vavasseur urged rebellion: "Refuse to do what they tell you if you think they are mistaken," he would say. But Francis invariably demurred at that. "Let us obey. Then we shall not have to reproach ourselves."[5]

His sufferings were compounded by a deep concern that all this attention was costing the Congregation too much money. As Superior General, he knew its financial condition intimately and the picture was not good. Just that year, Father Gaultier, the First Assistant, had pointed out that the 20,254 francs and 65 centimes in the treasury would not cover all their indebtedness. "I fear we may end up like the Benedictines," he had said. "They banked on the future and on Divine Providence, but if the Pope and the French bishops hadn't come to the rescue, their Congregation would have failed. . . . We are taking too many chances."[6]

By now he had to remain flat on his back. Every movement racked

[3] N. D. 13, 648.
[4] N. D. 13, 650.
[5] N. D. 13, 642.
[6] N. D. 13, 558.

him with pain. At the sight of so much suffering in the man who had already suffered all his life for them, the Fathers tucked around him the softest pillows they could lay their hands on. It did no good. Everything now ground into this body that had grown hypersensitive in the process of dissolution. They brought in a specially adjustable bed in which he could be moved without being lifted, but Francis only worried all the more about the cost of such lavish care.

On January 26, Frederic went downstairs with the doctor and asked him for a frank appraisal of the patient's chances. The answer was not reassuring. Death might be expected at any time. Le Vavasseur dejectedly returned to the sickroom and slowly approached the bed. When he saw the large luminous eyes looking at him questioningly, he girded himself for the difficult task and said: "Dear Father, the Good Lord is calling you. You are going to be leaving us. Dr. Cayol feels that the end is not far away." The reaction was typically Libermannesque. No shadow of uneasiness crossed his features. "God be praised," he said softly. "Now take care of my soul." Frederic then asked if he wanted the Last Rites that evening, but he answered: "Do you think things are so bad that we can't wait until tomorrow?"[7] Later that night he called Father Briot to hear his confession and then meditated on the great hour that was approaching. When he received the last sacraments on the following morning there was no dramatic display of external piety — only quiet recollection and full surrender to the divine plan. He set about dying with the same matter-of-fact simplicity with which he had accepted all difficult assignments from the hand of God throughout life.

Father Schwindenhammer, superior of Notre Dame du Gard, now came in to stay at the motherhouse. From there he wrote almost daily bulletins to his community. In the course of one of them, he told his confreres how he had asked the dying superior for a message that he might send back to the scholasticate. " 'Tell them,' [Father Libermann] said, 'to pray to the Good Lord and put their trust in God alone. . . . Tell them to submit readily to His holy Will no matter what it may be. Say that I haven't forgotten them, that I shall never forget them.' "[8]

---

[7] N. D. 13, 644.
[8] N. D. 13, 654.

On January 29 Francis was appreciably weaker. He could hardly speak and his sunken face was completely jaundiced even to the whites of his eyes. Consumed by a burning thirst from which there was no relief, he occasionally lapsed into unconsciousness. The ominous developments made Father Le Vavasseur increasingly restless. He saw the end approaching and the succession problem still remained unsolved. Although Francis had singled him out on more than one occasion, it was evident that later developments had shaken his faith and raised serious doubts about the feasibility of that arrangement. Frederic himself now recognized how ill-fitted he was for such a delicate task. But suppose the good Father should die and people would mistakenly come to regard Le Vavasseur as the natural heir? What a terrible situation that would be!

In a quiet moment after the anointing, Frederic had broached the subject, but Francis brushed it aside then. "My dear friend," he whispered, "now you're asking me something very delicate and very difficult." Later, when the anxious Creole returned to the question, Father Libermann had asked for two days' time to think it over. Now it was the morning of January 29. Both Schwindenhammer and Le Vavasseur were alone with him and Frederic saw his opportunity. Once more he raised the issue.

"Tell me what you two think about it," Libermann suggested. Father Schwindenhammer began to list Le Vavasseur's qualifications for the position — his collaboration from the very beginning, his background, his experience in Reunion — but Frederic cut in decisively and said that only Father Schwindenhammer could be the logical choice. The tortured patient listened through it all and then turned to Schwindenhammer. "I fear," he said, "you are the one who will have to sacrifice yourself."

The young man was much upset by this announcement. He proceeded to cite a thousand and one reasons why he was unsuited and Father Le Vavasseur was qualified, but in the midst of it, Frederic bent over the wasted figure on the bed and said, "Isn't it true, dear Father, that I can control myself once or twice, but the third time I completely lose my head?" "That is to be feared," Francis admitted tactfully. "Well now, let's take no chances," Frederic exclaimed. "It's decided then. Nothing in all the world will make me accept the superiorship." But Schwindenhammer's repartee was quick and to the point. "If you can refuse, so can I," he observed. Then once more the drawn white face turned to the young Alsatian and the failing voice rasped: "You cannot refuse."[9]

The next day Father Schwindenhammer wrote to his community: "Our beloved Father is steadily growing weaker and weaker. Now he can hardly speak to us in a whisper. He is nearly always in a semi-comatose condition. All seem to be losing the confidence they had up to now. We shouldn't try to hide the fact: it will take a miracle to make him recover now.

"Let us beg for that miracle. I don't think it would be presumptuous. We are justified in making such a request because we still need our good Father so badly.

"Therefore, let us redouble our prayers at Notre Dame du Gard. I place the greatest trust in the prayers of our community there. Let each one offer himself as a victim in place of our beloved Father.

"This morning I offered my own person to Our Lord through the hands of Our Lady of Victories, and I did it most willingly. However, more than one would be required in exchange for our saintly superior."[10]

Schwindenhammer's next bulletin was dated January 30 at 3:00 P.M. "My dear confreres," it said, "the news is hardly reassuring. Our beloved Father seems to be dying little by little. He can scarcely be understood when he speaks. This morning, at six o'clock, he felt he had taken a turn for the worse and asked that the prayers for the dying be recited. The whole community gathered around and I said them aloud. The good Father told me that he followed them through to the end. He felt a bit better after that, but it is an improvement on which we cannot rely. His resignation, his calm, his spirit of surrender are keeping up admirably. He does not ask to live or die, thereby illustrating perfectly the old adage, 'As a man lives, so shall he die.'

"He is being himself right up to the last moment, simple, without any shadow of singularity, no striking manner of acting or suffering. When he has pain, he says so quite frankly. He's been going through a martyrdom this whole morning. Several times he repeated to me this morning: 'Humanly speaking, this is unbearable.'

---

[9] Briault 426 f.
[10] N. D. 13, 656.

"He is not disfigured; only a little thinner than before. His face is very yellow because of the fluid from the liver. There is always a smile on his lips. His eyes are still quite clear. Now and then he turns them to the crucifix at the foot of his bed."[11]

That evening the Fathers gathered around the bed but Le Vavasseur, fearing the burden of their presence on the patient, asked them to go to their rooms and promised to call them if anything happened. Then, to ease the thirst from which Francis constantly suffered now, he gave him a drink of water. It brought on such a fit of vomiting that it began to look like death might come through strangulation. However, after the community had rushed back into the room, the poor gaunt frame began to breathe easier again. The end was not yet.

Father Schwindenhammer reported it all in his next day's letter to the scholasticate. He also recorded how he and Father Lannurien had been with the sick man the evening before and had his assurance that his suffering was being offered up for all the confreres and especially for Bishop Kobès and Dakar. "Be fervent," he had said, "always fervent. And above all, charity. Charity above all. Charity in Jesus Christ, charity through Jesus Christ, charity in the name of Jesus Christ. Fervor, charity, union in Jesus Christ!"[12]

Then, when the community gathered in his room that evening, Father Le Vavasseur suggested that he give them a final message. It required considerable effort on his part, but he opened his eyes, looked all around, and said very deliberately: "I am seeing you for the last time. I am happy to see you." In an almost inaudible voice he proceeded: "Sacrifice yourselves for Jesus, for Jesus alone . . . God is everything; man is nothing. The spirit of sacrifice . . . and zeal for the glory of God . . . and the salvation of souls."[13] Then of his own accord, he tried to lift his arm and bless the assembled confreres.

February 1 brought with it the slow and painful symptoms of the last agony. On Monday, February 2, the feast of Our Lady's Purification, he lay in a coma all morning. At 3:15 that afternoon, Schwindenhammer finished his daily bulletin right from the bedside of the dying superior. "Our beloved Father was almost completely unconscious. He seemed unable to hear or see anything. He

[11] N. D. 13, 658. [12] N. D. 13, 659. [13] N. D. 13, 660.

went on that way till two o'clock. Then all of a sudden he awoke, opened his eyes, looked around and appeared to recognize things. Someone held a crucifix up before him. He looked and then gazed at it eagerly, earnestly, and tenderly. They pronounced a few ejaculations for him such as 'Jesus, Mary, and Joseph; *In manus tuas, Domine, commendo spiritum meum; monstra te esse matrem';* and so on. He looked as though he understood. Once he turned his eyes toward the crucifix and then raised them to heaven with that indescribable look that used to be characteristic of him in moments of fervent and earnest prayer.

"But when I held up to him an image of Mary with the infant Jesus in her arms, his eyes really glowed with life. His face, drawn by suffering and the approach of death, assumed such an expression of indescribable love and tenderness that it almost seemed to be radiating shafts of light. He appeared to be listening to someone and hearing celestial harmonies that swept him up in ecstasy. . . . I shall say more about that at another time. . . . This letter must be mailed at four o'clock and it is already three forty-five.

"His breathing is slowing up. He is passing away. In five or six minutes it will be over. . . . They are beginning the *Magnificat* in the chapel. He will be dead before they finish it."[14]

Rohrbacher, the church historian, was there when death came. His account of it noted an appropriate circumstance. "Father Libermann's death, precious in the sight of the Lord, took place on February 2, 1852, the Feast of the Presentation of Jesus in the Temple, just when the community, assembled in choir for Vespers of that day, was singing the words, *'Et exaltavit humiles,'* 'He hath exalted the humble.' They were distinctly audible in the dying priest's room. I was a witness to it, for I stood near the bed."[15]

Francis Libermann was dead. The tired head had fallen to one side and the delicate frame lay motionless. Those soft dark eyes that had seen so much trouble, that radiated so much love, were closed forever. The mouth that gave expression to so much wisdom and consolation had now lapsed into silence. Nothing was left of the constant smile but two deep lines that served to emphasize the

[14] N. D. 13, 663 f.

[15] René Rohrbacher, *Histoire universelle de l'Eglise,* 2nd ed., Paris, 1850 ff., 17, 671.

boundless peace of his spiritualized features. Here at last was rest for one who suffered so much pain, here was the solitude with God for which he had longed amid the Umbrian hills, here was the quiet for which his heart had pined on noisy stagecoaches and in bustling offices. No man could disturb it, intrude upon it, or shatter it with the endless cares of life. He lay white and still, like a trim and solitary ship in safe haven after stormy seas, anchored for all eternity.

Visitors came. They approached silently and looked down on the finely-chiseled profile that shone pale and clear in the last rays of the setting sun. Deeply moved, they stood gazing at the remains of one who had lived for God alone, one who had never thought of himself. In this spent body there had burned a fire so great and ardent that generations yet unborn would feel its warmth. From it had issued a light by which thousands crying like an infant in the night would some day find the way.

This lonely pilgrim from Judaism, this wanderer who strayed until he found Christ in a strange seminary cell, had kept faith with the grace of God from the first moment it invaded his shy and timid soul. Forgetful of self, he had sought Jesus alone, yet he found a limitless assignment. Sick, tired, and fearful, he had felt the goad of grace deep in his anxious soul and had gone down the long and bitter way without resisting it.

Even as the shadows lengthened, a circle of light seemed to spread out from the deathbed of this man whose end was but a glorious beginning. God had cast him into the Christendom of his age as one might drop a stone on the placid surface of a pool, and like the sinking stone he sent forth widening circles across the medium he had set in motion. One by one the luminescent rings would radiate across the earth as time went on. One might even see them now in the growing dusk, peopled with figures of the present, past, and future, glowing with forms that traced their origin or drew their inspiration from the soul that penetrated deep in the heart of Christendom only because he had penetrated so deeply into the heart of Christ. They glide through the room in rhythmic procession.

First are his sons of future ages: Frenchmen and Germans, Americans and Dutch, Brazilians and Spaniards, Poles and English, Irish and Canadians, Africans and Belgians, Portuguese and Swiss. As their circle expands, another and another pays its debt of ghostly homage. They come from all levels of civil and religious life. There is the scarlet of cardinals, the purple of archbishops and bishops, the serried ranks of clerics — all crediting their training to the wisdom of this humble man who held fast to the ancient Spiritan tradition and gave them teachers for every grade of learning. There are the professors and scholars for whom Pope Pius XII himself thanked this farsighted planner. There are the long files of legislators, jurists, doctors, industrialists, and teachers whom his sons have educated. There are the liberators of Ireland who owe so much to his schools. There is the archbishop from distant Canada who tells him that Spiritan-trained priests rank with Sulpician products as the best clergy in the world.

They now make way for the noble young figure of a man who comes to smile his fond approval on the late departed. He is Claude Francis Poullart des Places, founder of the Holy Ghost Society and predecessor of him who lies there so peacefully. He sees in this colleague not only the most renowned member of his Congregation, but the boundless force that expanded its influence even beyond the level that his sons had attained in the glorious days of the eighteenth century.

The procession moves on and the circles stretch out in majestic grandeur. Now come the dark-skinned children of a once neglected continent, gratefully bowing to the one who gave them life and hope. After them, the homeless boys who found shelter and a loving heart because he had turned their way. Soldiers and sailors salute him. Prisoners, orphans, the sick and the weak, beggars and lepers all come to do him homage, for they too had a place in his heart and plans. The neglected and abandoned of all lands and of every rank file past the prostrate form: expatriates and oppressed, the nervous and mentally ill, penitents and converts, all press forward to acknowledge their debt to him who is at once their brother, their father, and their patron.

Beyond them, stretching off toward the horizon, throng numberless fervent souls to voice their thanks for his spiritual message of simplicity and loving surrender in God's service whereby the ascent to holiness has been made smoother and easier for them.

Father Libermann is still sending forth those circles of light.

Trains and cars, ocean liners and planes carry an ever growing phalanx of his sons to distant parts of the globe. Wherever they go, schools, colleges, churches, and seminaries rise and flourish. The Congregation of the Holy Ghost has grown worldwide in its scope, its men and resources are turned to a host of varying tasks, but behind each black-robed Spiritan stands the inspiring figure of Francis Libermann, whispering to them and to the world at large: "Be fervent, always fervent. And above all, charity. Charity above all."

BIBLIOGRAPHY

L'Ami de la Religion (*et du Roi*), Paris, 1814–1862. Ecclesiastical news bulletin.

Léon Aubineau, *Les Serviteurs de Dieu,* Paris-Tournai, 1860. V. II–XI. Le R.P. Libermann, août 1855 (pp. 1–30).

H. Alves, A. Brasio, A. Moura, *Um Judeu Salvador da Raça Preta,* Viana do Castelo, 1939, 210 pp.

Henri Bergson, *The Two Sources of Morality and Religion.* Garden City, 1956.

Louis Barazer de Lannurien, C.S.Sp. Unpublished manuscript about the "Fusion" and the aims of the Congregation.

Pierre Blanchard, "La sainteté selon le P. Libermann," *La vie spirituelle,* 1953, pp. 157–186. Translated into English by Fr. Joseph A. Lauritis, C.S.Sp. under the title *Spiritual Guide for Our Times,* Washington, 1955, 50 pp.

"L'abnégation chez le V. P. Libermann," *Le renoncement dans la vie chrétienne selon St. Jean Eudes et ses disciples,* Paris, 1956, pp. 93–110.

Le Vénérable Libermann, Paris, 1960. Two volumes, 573 and 517 pages.

Maurice Briault, C.S.Sp., *Le Vénérable Père F.-M.-P. Libermann,* Paris, 1956, 580 pp.

Bulletin Général (de la Congrégation du St.-Esprit), Paris, 1857 ff.

Adolphe Cabon, C.S.Sp., ed., *Notes et Documents relatifs à la Vie et l'Oeuvre du Vénérable François-Marie-Paul Libermann,* Paris, 1929–1956, 13 vols., 2 appendices and 1 vol. of "compléments."

Le première expédition des missionnaires du St.-Coeur de Marie en Guinée (Paris, 1930).

"La spiritualité du Vén. Libermann," *La vie spiritualle,* Vol. 50, 1937, pp. 42–60.

Mgr. Carméné, *Panégyrique du Vén. P. Libermann,* Martinique, 1876, 20 pp.

Centenaire du Séminaire Pontifical Français de Rome, 1853–1953, Rome, 1953, 62 pp.

E. Conrad, C.S.Sp., *Vie populaire du Vénérable Libermann. Du Judaisme à l'Apostolat des Noirs,* Metz, 1926, 113 pp. Paris-Auteuil, 1931, 127 pp.

Van Jood tot Negerapostel, Dutch translation by Tine Beljaars, Gemert, n.d.

J. Delaplace, C.S.Sp., *Le P. Jacques-Désiré Laval,* Paris, 1932, 396 pp.

Vie du Vénérable P. Libermann, Paris, 1878, 350 pp.

Leben des ehrwürdigen P. Libermann, German translation by I. Müller, Regensburg, 1881, 224 pp.

Vida do Veneravel Padre Francisco Libermann, Portuguese translation by C. de S. Guimaraes, 1892, 540 pp.

L. Dohmen, C.S.Sp., *Der Ehrw. P. Libermann. Ein Apostel der Neger im 19. Jahrhundert,* Speyer am Rhein, 1947, 180 pp.

H. Döring, C.S.Sp., *Vom Juden zum Ordenstifter,* Knechtsteden, 1920, 352 pp.

A. Emonet, C.S.Sp., Manuscript about Father Schwindenhammer. *Panégyrique du Vénérable P. François-Paul-Marie Libermann, Cayenne,* 1876, 16 pp.

Alfonso Eschbach, C.S.Sp., *Vita del Ven. Servo di Dio Francesco-Maria-Paolo Libermann,* 2nd ed. Roma, n.d., 131 pp.

Jean Galopeau, C.S.Sp., "Étude sur le V. Libermann et l'érection des Diocèses coloniaux au XIX siècle," *Revue d'Histoire des Missions,* 1928, pp. 225–271.

Mgr. J. Gay, C.S.Sp., *La doctrine missionnaire du Vén. Père Libermann,* Paris, 1943, 173 pp.

Libermann, Bruges, 1955, 154 pp.

The Spirit of Venerable Libermann, Society of St. Paul, 1954.

P. Goepfert, C.S.Sp., *The Life of the Ven. F. M. P. Libermann,* Dublin, 1880, 558 pp.

G. Goyau, "La doctrine missionnaire du Père Libermann," *Ètudes missionnaires,* April, 1937, pp. 1–20.

L. J. Hampson, C.S.Sp., *Divine Love and Renunciation According to the Writings of the Ven. F. M. P. Libermann,* Doctoral thesis, Freiburg (Switzerland), 1939.

Sister M. Aquinas Healy, R.S.M., "Venerable Francis Libermann, Apostle of the Future," *The Catholic World,* Vol. 195, June, 1962, pp. 169–175.

Helen Walker Homan, *Star of Jacob,* New York, 1953, 329 pp.

Bernard J. Kelly, C.S.Sp., *The Spiritual Teaching of Venerable Francis Libermann,* Dublin, 1955, 201 pp.

Philippe Kieffer, C.S.Sp., "Le Vénérable P. François Libermann," *Les Contemporains,* no. 984, 16 pp.

Henry J. Koren, C.S.Sp., *The Spiritans,* Pittsburgh, 1958, 641 pp.

Knaves or Knights? A History of the Spiritan Missionaries in Acadia and North America, 1732–1839, Pittsburgh, 1962, 220 pp.

G. Lee, C.S.Sp., *The Life of the Venerable Francis Libermann,* St.

Louis, 1911, 321 pp. 2nd ed., London, 1937.
E. Leen, C.S.Sp., *The Voice of a Priest,* London, 1947. Introduction.
Henri Le Floch, *Claude Poullart des Places,* Paris, 2nd ed., 1915, 683 pp.
L'Acte d'Union, Rome, 1915, 52 pp.
Mgr. L. Le Hunsec, C.S.Sp., *Circulaire à l'occasion du centenaire de la Fusion des deux Sociétés du Saint-Ésprit et du Saint-Coeur de Marie,* Paris, 1948.
Leon Leloir, W. F., *Libermann,* Namur, 1939; Gentinnes, 1952, 62 pp.
Mgr. A. Le Roy, C.S.Sp., *Le R.P. Frédéric Le Vavasseur,* Paris, n.d., 264 pp.
L. Liagre, C.S.Sp., *Le Vénérable Père Libermann. L'Homme, la Doctrine,* Paris, 1948, 238 pp.
"Sainte Thérèse de l'Enfant Jésus et le Vénérable Libermann," *Annales de S. Thérèse de Lisieux. Études et Documents Thérèsiens,* Oct., 1936, pp. 121–128; janvier 1937, pp. 22–32.
Francis Libermann, C.S.Sp., *Directoire spirituel ou instructions du Vén. F.M.P. Libermann aux membres de la Congrégation* (ed. J. B. Pascal, C.S.Sp., Paris, 1910, 620 pp.
Écrits spirituels du Vén. Libermann, Paris, 1891, 696 pp.
Onderrichtingen over de heiligheid, Dutch translation of Dr. L. Vogel, C.S.Sp., Rijswijk, 1941, 158 pp.
Over het affective inwendige gebed, Dutch translation of Dr. L. Vogel, C.S.Sp., Rijswijk, 1935, 72 pp.
Onderrichtingen over de meditatie, Dutch translation of Dr. L. Vogel, C.S.Sp., Rijswijk, 1935, 72 pp.
Lettres spirituelles du Vén. Libermann, 3 vols.; 385 selected spiritual letters. 3rd ed., Paris, 1889, 550, 612, 676 pp.
Lettres spirituelles de notre Vénérable Père aux membres de la Congrégation, Paris, 1889, 717 pp. 143 letters.
Geestelijke brieven van de Eerbw. Dienaar Gods F.M.P. Libermann, Dutch translation of Dr. L. Vogel, Vol. I, 368 pp., Vol. II, 366 pp. Gemert, 1938.
Choix de lettres spirituelles adressées à des personnes du monde par le Vén. Libermann. Paris, 1894, 302 pp.
Das Ideal des Priestertums, Briefe des ehrw. P. Libermann. German translation of I. Heilgers. Paderborn, 1893, 200 pp.
Ideales Leben und Streben der christlichen Frauen und Jungfrauen. Briefe des ehrw. P. Libermann, German translation of I. Heilgers. Paderborn, 1894, 303 pp.
The spiritual letters of the Venerable Francis-Mary-Paul Libermann, translated by the Rev. L. Grunenwald, C.S.Sp., Vol. I, Detroit, Michigan, 1901, 109 pp.
The Spiritual Letters of Venerable Francis Libermann, Vol. 1. Letters to Religious Sisters and Aspirants, Pittsburgh, 1962, 260 pp.

Commentaire des douze premiers chapitres du S. Évangile selon S. Jean par le Vén. Libermann, 1st ed., Ngazobil, 1872, 710 pp. 2nd ed., Paris, n.d.

Commentaire de St. Jean. Textes choisis par le R. P. L. Vogel, C.S.Sp. Collection *"Les Grand Mystiques."* Paris, 1958, 317 pp.

Die Gründung der afrikanischen Mission, durch den ehrwürdigen P. Libermann. Instructions for his missionaries selected from his letters by I. Heilgers. Paderborn, 1896, 259 pp.

A. Limbour, C.S.Sp., "Le Père François-Xavier Libermann," *Notices biographiques,* III, 1906–1909, pp. 1–66.

Victor Lithard, C.S.Sp., "Le Vénérable Libermann, auteur spirituel," *Revue d'Ascetique et Mystique,* Vol. 19, 1939, pp. 141–170.

Spiritualité Spiritaine, Paris, 1939, 272 pp.

Edward Loffeld, C.S.Sp., "Een Missie-Generaal en een Missie-plan," *Het Missiewerk,* Vol. 22, 1941, pp. 65–79; 131–141; 184–196. Father Libermann's plans for Africa.

A. Loogman, C.S.Sp., and M. Witte, C.S.Sp., *Een bekeerde Jood en zijn werk,* Amsterdam, 1922, 64 pp.

Mgr. Luquet, *Considérations sur les Missions catholiques et voyage d'un missionnaire dans l'Inde,* Paris, 1853. This work pays considerable attention to the relations between Father Libermann and the "Propaganda."

Mgr. G. Malberti, *Compendio della vita del Ven. Servo di Dio F.M.P. Libermann,* Roma, 1876, 103 pp., 1894, 45 pp.

A. H. Maslow, *Motivation and Personality,* New York, 1954, 411 pp.

Martin, "Le R. P. Libermann et la Congrégation du Saint-Esprit et du Saint-Coeur de Marie," Extrait de la *Revue des Sciences ecclesiastiques,* Amiens, 1873, 47 pp.

Wulstan Mork, O.S.B., "Venerable Libermann and St. Benedict," *American Benedictine Review,* 1957, pp. 133–143.

Ethel Murray, *Venerable Paul Libermann,* London, 1922, 28 pp.

Notes et Documents rélatifs à l'histoire de la Congrégation du St. Ésprit. 1703–1914, Paris, 1917. Records the most important documents regarding the history of the Congregation.

Notices Biographiques, Paris, 1908 ff. 4 vols. Another volume bears the title *Biographies.* Short biographies of deceased Spiritans.

R. Piacentini, *Le Piere Claver de l'Ile Maurice, J. D. Laval.* Issoudun, 1950, 135 pp.

Cardinal J. B. Pitra, O.S.B., *Vie du Vénérable Serviteur de Dieu F.M.P. Libermann,* Paris, 1855, 1872, 1882 (2 ed.), 1913, 608, 676, 634, 575 pp.

Leben des Ehrwürdigen Dieners Gottes Franz-Maria-Paul Libermann, German translation by I. Müller, Stuttgart, 1893, 496 pp.

Van Jood tot Ordestichter, Dutch translation by Tine Beljaars, adaptation by L. Vogel, C.S.Sp., Rijswijk, 1935, 346 pp.

Richael J. O'Carroll, *The Venerable F.M.P. Libermann, Director of Souls,* Doctoral thesis, Friburg (Switzerland), 1939.

Francis Libermann, Dublin, 1953, 128 pp.

J. Th. Rath, C.S.Sp., *Der Sklaven Knecht, J. D. Laval,* Donauwörth, 1949, 180 pp.

Père Rétif, S.J., *Pauvreté Spirituelle et Mission d'après le Pere Libermann,* Paris, 1955, 206 pp.

Réné Rohrbacher, *Histoire universelle de l'Église,* 2nd ed., Paris, 1855 ff.

Jean Jacques Rousseau, *Èmile,* Paris, n.d., 3 vols.

J. Simon, *Le prêtre d'après le vénérable Libermann,* Mulhouse, 1952, 184 pp.

M. L. de Sion, *Triomphe par l'échec; Le Vénérable Libermann,* Paris, 1954, 222 pp.

L. Vogel, C.S.Sp., *Claude-Francois Poullart des Places, eerste Stichter der Congregatie van den H. Geest,* Gemert, 1941, 260 pp.

Dienaar der slaven. Het leven van J. D. Laval, Rhenen, 1952.

"De spiritualiteit van de Eerbw. Pater F.M.P. Libermann," *Ons geestelijk leven,* Vol. 28, 1952, pp. 279–290.

J. Vulquin, C.S.Sp., *L'Ésprit du Vénérable Libermann,* Paris, 1889, 158 pp.

La Direction spirituelle d'après les écrits et les exemples du Vénérable Libermann, 3rd ed., Paris, 1940, 176 pp.

The Way of Peace, n.p., 1944, 32 pp. Libermann and St. Thérèse.

INDEX OF NAMES

INDEX OF SUBJECT MATTER

Because I
was a "little one,"
I pleased
the
Most
High ~~